Early praise for *Seven More Languages in Seven Weeks*

I'm tired of learning new programming languages and thought seven additional somewhat esoteric languages wouldn't be very useful. I couldn't have been more wrong. I loved it. The languages were suitably interesting and compellingly presented, and I now want to experiment with them.

➤ **Brian Sletten**
    President, Bosatsu Consulting, Inc.

Languages are not just new syntax, they are new ways of thinking about problems. What is the best way to think about user interfaces or scientific computing or distributed systems or safety guarantees? As you dive into each of the languages in this book you will get a glimpse of new abstractions and principles that will help you write better programs in any language. Do it!

➤ **Evan Czaplicki**
    Creator of Elm, Prezi

If you think reading a book about programming languages won't change your thinking about programming, I dare you to read the chapter on Idris—unless the idea of reasoning about your C++ (or C# or Java) code more clearly and reducing hundreds or thousands of lines of code down to two is not appealing to you, of course.

➤ **Ted Neward**
    Author, speaker, mentor, Neward and Associates, LLC

Just as an artist's choice of oil, acrylic, or watercolor paint constrains the range of effects they can achieve, the languages we choose constrain the programs we can write. Learning a new language enables you to both conceive new solutions and express them in new ways. Read this book to add seven particularly interesting languages to your repertoire.

➤ **Paul Butcher**
  Author of *Seven Concurrency Models in Seven Weeks*

Seven More Languages in Seven Weeks is a well-paced introduction to a set of fascinating languages that will be new to many. This one goes at just the right tempo and provides enough detail to be useful—but not so much as to douse natural curiosity. Definitely a book I would recommend to others wanting to expand their programming horizons.

➤ **Matthew Wild**
  Author, Prosody IM XMPP server

Seven More Languages in Seven Weeks not only introduces us to a wide spectrum of languages, but also challenges us on how we think about language use and design. Software development is a demanding career and learning new languages will always be essential. That is why the *Seven in Seven* series is one of the most invaluable reads for any serious programmer.

➤ **Daniel Hinojosa**
  Developer, speaker, instructor, author of *Testing in Scala*

Seven More Languages in Seven Weeks

Languages That Are Shaping the Future

Bruce A. Tate
Fred Daoud
Ian Dees
Jack Moffitt

The Pragmatic Bookshelf

Dallas, Texas • Raleigh, North Carolina

Our Pragmatic courses, workshops, and other products can help you and your team create better software and have more fun. For more information, as well as the latest Pragmatic titles, please visit us at *http://pragprog.com*.

The team that produced this book includes:

Jacquelyn Carter (editor)
Potomac Indexing, LLC (indexer)
Liz Welch (copyeditor)
Dave Thomas (typesetter)
Janet Furlow (producer)
Ellie Callahan (support)

For international rights, please contact *rights@pragprog.com*.

Printed in the United States of America.
ISBN-13: 978-1-941222-15-7
Printed on acid-free paper.
Book version: P1.0—November 2014

Contents

Foreword

Back in 2010, I was deeply troubled. The growing list of difficulties in writing concurrent software was nagging at me. The tools I had at hand were clunky, and none of them provided a mental model that helped me reason about the problems I was facing.

I decided it was time for a change.

However, out of the hundreds of programming languages out there, how could I possibly find one that fit my criteria? How could I even filter this huge set into a smaller one that I could explore in more detail? Then I found that someone had decided to tell the exact story I wanted to hear: Bruce Tate had just written *Seven Languages in Seven Weeks*, which explored Ruby, Io, Prolog, Erlang, Scala, Clojure, and Haskell.

I was familiar with many of the languages in *Seven Languages in Seven Weeks* but the book did more than just introduce programming language constructs. It introduced their philosophy, community, and thinking models. To me, the book was telling a story about concurrency, and as I read the book, a very clear picture about immutability, threads, futures, actors, software transactional memory, and more was being painted.

Once I finished the book, I knew exactly which languages and paradigms I wanted to explore next. I bought a heap of books about Erlang, Clojure, and Haskell and I also started writing code right away.

Months later, though, I still hadn't found one language that fit all my criteria. I wanted the robustness and distribution of the Erlang VM, but I also wanted the metaprogramming and polymorphism from Clojure alongside a syntax I was comfortable with. That's when I decided to create the Elixir programming language that runs on the Erlang virtual machine.

Now, four years later, Elixir is one of the languages covered in *Seven More Languages in Seven Weeks*.

The interesting thing is that the first book was not a story about concurrency but that's how I read it. *Seven Languages in Seven Weeks*, as any other excellent book, gives space for the reader to include her own experiences as part of the story, allowing each reader to learn different lessons and, in this particular case, choose other languages to explore next.

This is what makes *Seven More Languages in Seven Weeks* even more ambitious. Many of the languages in the book are relatively new and in active development, which brings a whole new range of ideas and lessons to be learned. It also opens up the possibility for readers to pick their next languages and not only master them but become part of the language development itself.

Seven Languages in Seven Weeks had a deep impact on my programming career, and I am certain reading this book will do the same for yours.

And remember: Reading *Seven More Languages in Seven Weeks* is just the start of a journey.

José Valim
Creator of Elixir

Acknowledgments

We'd like to make a deal with you. If you haven't already programmed your virtual video recorder to skip this page, we'll try to make it interesting and entertaining. The names on this page deserve to be read. Many of them are shaping the way we all think about programming, and still others put in the tireless, thankless work to make this book worth reading.

If each chapter of a *Seven Languages* book is some kind of a metaphor, which movie character should we curse with acknowledgments? Perhaps we'll serve up some form of Bill Murray. Is it Bill Murray in *Groundhog Day*, where each book shows you the same chapter with only slight variations of words but a same dreariness in sentiment and tone? Or maybe we'll plod gracelessly unaware into your thoughts uninvited, like Bill in *What About Bob?*

We've hidden several Bill Murray movie references in this chapter. See how many you can find.

The Languages

The stars of *this* show are the seven programming languages. Each of them has a role to play in exercising the poltergeists that haunt our current dusty mental motels. We'd like to offer a warm thanks to the creators of those languages, and also to the angels who helped accelerate our transition from novices to, well, slightly more knowledgeable novices.

Lua

We'd like to thank Roberto Ierusalimschy for recognizing the importance of a single, unifying abstraction. Lua's tables are versatile enough to build object systems, custom data structures, and even video game levels. The clean implementation underneath makes it a breeze to run Lua anywhere, to embed it into your own projects, and to extend it in new ways.

Special thanks to Matthew Wild for bringing the eyes of a seasoned Lua developer to our prose. Your hard-won experience with the language in the real world helped us stay on course.

Factor

We'd like to thank Slava Pestov for taking the concatenative programming model and giving it a full-featured, practical environment in which to thrive. Discovering this way of thinking about programs has been extremely enlightening. Having a platform on which to build real applications makes the language all that much more valuable.

A special thank-you also goes to John Benediktsson for reviewing the chapter and being one of the most active and helpful people in the Factor community. The combination of your knowledge, responsiveness, and willingness to aid others is truly inspiring.

Elm

Thank you, Evan Czaplicki. You've created a fantasyland for your users. No more square pegs in round holes. Building for browsers finally feels right. Thanks also for helping us in the midst of your travel, even as you scurried between your San Francisco apartment and Budapest hotel. We know permission forms are a pain and don't always happen at the most convenient times.

Elixir

José Valim has had such a profound impact on this book. Your words in the foreword inspired us; your language captivates us. We've all seen inventors who strut around like mafia kingpins, but you've always entered each relationship with humility and respect.

We'd also like to yell a special shout-out to Eric Meadows-Jönsson. Your review of our Elixir chapter went above and beyond. You're the reason our code is at Elixir 1.0 levels. Our readers appreciate it and we appreciate it. We expect great things from you.

Julia

Bruce first heard about Julia at a conference in London. He was starting to pull together the language lineup and the team for this book. Several people mentioned Julia, but we were concerned that it wouldn't have enough ideas that would advance the story we were trying to tell. Boy, were we wrong. Thanks to Jeff Bezanson, Stefan Karpinski, Viral Shah, and Alan Edelman. Your community has grown from a group of disjointed strangers who barely knew Julia to a family that cares about the language and about each other. Such a quick change does not happen accidentally. You were tremendously helpful and responsive throughout the whole process.

miniKanren

Chalk one more language up to CodeMesh and London. Bruce saw David Nolen's demo of Core.Logic a few years before this book came to fruition, and saw more than another Clojure framework. It was a unique and interesting programming model. You can't get smart by writing the same object-oriented programs over and over. Real growth requires exploring the unknown, and sometimes radically different concepts. Thanks to David for your inspiration and your support.

Thanks also to Stuart Halloway, our good friend and one of Clojure's most loyal and passionate stewards. Stuard for short.

Idris

We'd venture to guess that many of these languages will stretch our readers, sometimes unpleasantly. Truth be told, sometimes the languages stretch even this team of authors. As we were writing the early prose and code for the Idris chapter, something was lost in translation and we had a hard time making sense of it all. Thanks to Edwin Brady for walking the razor's edge between the practical and the academic. You've created a language that's audacious in its goals and stunning in its execution. It probably doesn't register with you that some would even question who would even attempt such a language. Well, we know. Ed would.

The Authors

While some of those we wish to thank are collective, some of the thanks are deeply personal.

From Bruce Tate

Every time I write another book, there inevitably comes a time when I'm doing too much, and I morph into a hostile curmudgeon, a scrooge who snipes at the first target that presents itself, even if that target is just announcing that dinner is ready. Writing technical books is not as lucrative as it used to be, even successful books. Those who write do it out of love, and often at a cost to those around them. Maggie, Kayla, and Julia (the person, not the language), you've been that target too often. But you also inspire me and lift me when I'm low.

Terry Cole, you're one of the bravest people I've ever met. Your work with street youth impacts me deep beneath the surface. A part of each book goes to your mission, and when I am dragging, I can just open a picture of one of the kids and I'm ready to write again.

From Fred Daoud

After *Seven Web Frameworks in Seven Weeks*, I didn't think I'd be writing for a while. When Bruce invited me to participate in *Seven More Languages*, I was so honored that I couldn't refuse. I'm very grateful for the opportunity to work with such a great team of authors, and to discover a fantastic lot of languages that challenge the imagination and thrill the programming senses.

On a more personal note, my acknowledgments could not be complete without thanking my wife Nadia for being the most beautiful person I know in the universe (and beyond). The best times in my life are those spent with you, and they provide a much-needed balance against the time I spend hacking on a computer.

From Ian Dees

To my wife Lynn, and to my daughters, Avalon and Robin, thank you for being amazing, creative people.

To my fellow authors Bruce, Fred, and Jack, it's been an honor to be part of this project. Thank you for inviting me to join it. Your work sets a high standard, and living up to it (or trying to!) has made me a far better programmer and writer than I was before.

To my teammates at work, thank you for setting a similarly high bar, and for putting up with the occasional bout of, "You have *got* to see this new feature of Lua/Idris...."

From Jack Moffitt

I have been reliving the same nine months over again. Before *Seven Web Frameworks in Seven Weeks* was even finished, Bruce approached me about helping to write this book. My love for languages and the enjoyment I had working with Bruce, Fred, and Pragmatic Programmers made working on another book an easy decision.

I'd like to thank my wife Kim, my son Jasper, and my daughter Beatrix for supporting me through another book. Kim is my sounding board for ideas and helped with this project as she does with all my projects. My kids kept me from working too hard.

The Book

All of the books in this series require a little more commitment than your typical technical book. Those who write the books are learning many new concepts just one step ahead of our readers. We also need excellent support, often from reviewers who get nothing more than thanks here. Often, reading our early prose must seem like a stroll through Zombieland, and several reviewers went above and beyond by reading a chapter or two twice or more. Our thanks go out to John Benediktsson, Jeff Bezanson, Edwin Brady, Erin Chapman, Evan Czaplicki, Alan Edelman, John Heintz, Daniel Hinojosa, Carsten Jørgensen, Stefan Karpinski, Eric Meadows-Jönsson, Ted Neward, David Nolen, Viral Shah, Brian Sletten, José Valim, Matthew Wild, and Simon Wood. We literally could not have written this book without you.

We know we're going to miss someone, so if your name is not where it should be, please accept our sincerest apology. We appreciate your effort.

Beta readers, you had this story when it was a tiny glowing ember, and nursed it to a raging fire. We depend on you and your comments and enthusiasm more than you can know.

We'd also like to thank the production team. We know you're all mentioned on the copyright page but we would like to mention you here as well: Jackie Carter, the editor; Liz Welch, the copy editor; Seth Maislin, the indexer; and Janet Furlow, the production manager. The whole industry knows that Prag books are special, and you're the team that helps us maintain such high-quality standards over time. Thanks once again.

Finally, we'd like to thank Dave and Andy for believing in this concept, not once but twice. You've built a special place to work and a great place for authors to feel respected and appreciated. We write because we love it, and we love it because you make this a special place to be.

To all of you, we send our love and respect.

Thank you.

Introduction

by Bruce Tate

In a warm room in 2012 London, I was nervous. I'd given this same talk to crowded rooms around the world. Sure, I was confident that the crowd would laugh at my usual jokes, and even applaud almost on demand, but this time, there was a catch. Four creators of the seven languages in my book were in the audience right in front of me. I was worried about having enough credibility to talk about these beautiful creations in this setting. In the end, I may have stumbled a time or two, but the talk went fine. Joe Armstrong, the creator of Erlang and a dear friend now, even complimented me on the talk, and he invited me to come keynote the Erlang Users Community in Stockholm six months later.

The most poignant moment for me, though, was a listener's question. She asked, "Can you really learn seven languages in seven weeks?" We both knew the answer. As with spoken languages, it takes months or even years of immersion to really learn a programming language. So why should we even try?

Each new language exposes you to a vocabulary, but not one of words. This new vocabulary is composed of the ideas that you use to shape your world. Though the precise *syntax* will almost certainly not commute from your sandbox into your production solutions, you'll see that many of the *idioms* do. When you work through Elixir macros, you'll learn to express your code in templates, and this metaprogramming can radically improve any programmer. When you work through Factor, you'll learn to naturally compose functions in powerful and interesting ways that might not have seemed natural before. And after a few weeks with miniKanren, expressing programs as individual steps may no longer seem as effective as expressing a few simple rules.

Think of a painter who has learned to express depth after trying a hand at sculpture, or a young business executive who learns new spreadsheet techniques after taking a new math or programming class. Ideas are the currency of our trade. Each idiom that you master *increases your worth.*

Each *Seven in Seven* book tries to tell a story, making informed choices that will teach you the idioms we think you most need to know. Our job as authors is to find the right set of languages that expose you to the most important idioms you're likely to see. To do that, we need to have a strong understanding of where our industry is heading.

The Lay of the Land

From a hardware perspective, we believe that multicore programming, quality, and complexity are driving a strong push toward functional languages. Mobile devices are also exploding, though mobile technologies remain behind other kinds of programming.

We also believe that software complexity is shaping functional programming as we speak. Crosscutting concerns and code quality strongly favor languages with metaprogramming features. Better typing models, like the one in Haskell, are making a strong comeback so that the compiler can catch more bugs *before* code reaches production.

Against that backdrop, it's time to crack open seven more languages. You'll notice at least three big differences between this book and the first as you read. First, I've gone from one author to four. Next, the author team allows greater depth per language, so the overall book is longer and ramps up each language more quickly. Finally, most of these languages are new, rather than spreading out languages over four different decades as I did in the first book.

Meet the Team and Languages

We'd normally introduce the author team elsewhere, but since these language experts are actually your guides, I'd like you to meet them and know the languages they will show you.

Bruce Tate (Elixir, Elm)

I am Bruce Tate, a mountain biker, kayaker, and father of two from Austin, Texas. Currently, as CTO of icanmakeitbetter.com, I run a small team of programmers in Ruby, but will move into Elixir development soon. You probably know me as the author of the first book in the *Seven in Seven* series, *Seven Languages in Seven Weeks [Tat10].*

Elixir

I chose Elixir because it is a unique combination of a pure functional language on the Erlang virtual machine with a rich Ruby-like syntax and Lisp-style macros. Syntax matters to me, maybe more than anything else. Representing ideas to English speakers requires a rich and powerful syntax.

Elm

I chose Elm because it represents a radical departure from the callback-centric style of development in browsers today. Simplifying code in the browser is actually one of the most active language frontiers. Elm is a language dedicated to reactive programming, a style that uses data flows and functions to propagate change. Representing user interactions as signals that map onto functions simplifies the most complex of JavaScript applications significantly by removing callbacks.

Fred Daoud (Factor)

Fred is a passionate software developer from Montreal, Canada. He loves learning new languages, frameworks, and programming techniques, going from OO to FP and intrigued by the reactive model. Fred is the coauthor of *Seven Web Frameworks in Seven Weeks [MD14]*.

Factor

Fred chose Factor because this concatenative, stack-based programming model radically changes the way programmers think. It's not just a mental exercise, either; Factor comes with a full-featured library, UI framework, and web framework. Building one Factor application will change the way you use your native language.

Ian Dees (Lua, Idris)

By day, Ian Dees slings code, tests, and puns at a Portland-area test equipment manufacturer. By night, he converts espresso into programming books, including *Cucumber Recipes*. Ian tweets as @undees.

Lua

Ian chose Lua because it is a fast, flexible language that is ideal for adding scripting to an existing project. He fell in love with the embeddable prototype language while building a production system with it.

Idris

Ian was captivated by the potential of dependent types in languages like Agda and Idris when he saw a presentation on applying the lessons of these languages to C++ or Java. Since then, he's always wanted to explore these concepts in greater detail.

Jack Moffit (Julia, miniKanren)

As a developer and manager at the Mozilla Foundation, Jack is regularly exposed to new languages and technologies. He's been writing for five years on a variety of topics, including most recently coauthoring *Seven Web Frameworks in Seven Weeks* [MD14].

miniKanren

miniKanren is not really a language in its own right. Instead, it's a domain-specific language for logic programming. When combined with a functional programming language with macros like Clojure, the result is a striking new programming model. Often, logic programmers find it difficult to tie their logic programs to the outside world. Embedding a logic DSL in a general purpose language solves this problem. You'll find that this combination opens up a whole new programming paradigm, and that's why Jack chose it.

Julia

Jack chose Julia because it's an interesting and radical departure from the work he's been doing with Clojure and Erlang. Julia is focused on computing statistics and multidimensional math. It's designed from the inside out with concurrency and distribution in mind. R is the dominant technical computing language today, but performance is sometimes an Achilles heel. Early Julia users have commented on substantial performance improvements in Julia based on its language features.

Who Should Read This Book

Like the other books in this series, *Seven More Languages in Seven Weeks* is a little different from your typical technology book. We're going to try to cover much more breadth, and we're going to push you, and we think you'll be pleased with the result. Still, it's not for everyone.

Don't Buy This Book...

...until you've read this section and can live with the challenge. Mostly, understand that our goal is to make you as self-sufficient as possible, and ramp up much more quickly than typical one-technology technical books do. There's a cost. You will have to do more of the work.

We're Not Your Install Guide or Support Channel

Those who have read a *Seven in Seven* book know that we will not focus our attention on getting you started, and we won't try to attempt to support seven languages across seven platforms each. We can't. We have chosen to avoid languages with paid support. You can tap the programming community of each of these languages for help. In most cases, they will be quite willing to help.

You also will not get a rich installation guide for each language, and you might find that the output for a particular exercise looks slightly different on your system. If you are a reader who likes every character to match, and want your hand held throughout the process, sorry. We just can't help you. In fact, we think that the process of building and supporting your own installation will help you learn your chosen language much more quickly.

Instead, we'll offer you a deal. If you will work a little harder to support your own installation, we'll take you deeper. Our goal is to get to the point that you'll solve a nontrivial problem in *each language*. It's a demanding goal, but we think we've accomplished it.

We Will Speak in Four Voices

I never expected to write another *Seven Languages* book because the first one was so demanding and because the original list of languages was so compelling. I never thought that I'd find seven languages to match the original list, and if I did, I was sure I did not want to commit another year or two to the effort. I told myself that changing voices across authors in a *Seven Languages* book would not work.

You see, even though it was made of different languages, the original book told a story of where our industry was at the time. The languages moved from object oriented toward more declarative and more functional languages, ending in the purely functional Haskell. The collection works precisely because it is not seven disjointed essays. Surely, a team of authors would distract from the broader story and the unity of the whole.

Then, Eric Redmond and Jim R. Wilson attacked *Seven Databases in Seven Weeks [RW12]* and blew me away. They wrote a book that told a story of where the database industry is going, and they told it well. Having two authors made it easier to keep up with the rapidly changing versions.

Here's the catch. They wrote primarily in first person plural. Learning languages is a little different from learning to use a database engine.

Each exploration is a deeply personal experience. I believe that if we can let you into the head of the person who wrote each chapter, if you can more deeply share their experience, your own learning experience will be that much richer and more powerful. For that reason, each author will write about their languages in the first person. When you see those "I" and "mine" statements instead of "we" and "our," you'll know why. We're trying to give you a more personal experience. We think you'll appreciate the difference.

We Won't Be Dry

Some want terse. We're not that.

You'll notice that we compare each language to a movie character. We do this because based on our experience, we need to help readers with the transition from one language to the next. We find that these metaphors serve our purposes better than a stodgy history lesson. We know that this style will put some of you off. That's OK. We believe that writing in this way keeps most of our readers engaged and opens learning channels. For the rest, we believe our story is compelling enough that most readers will slog through our metaphors.

Buy This Book...

...if you can live with these ground rules. We think you're in for a treat. This mix of languages will captivate and delight you. The mix of authors will take you into places that a single-author team can't. When all is said and done, our goal is for you to think this book makes you a better programmer and improves your code in whatever language you might choose.

A Final Charge

Language study becomes much more relevant when you can use more than one language. Things certainly seem to be heading that way. It's becoming cool to be a language geek again. This book will show you a mix of static and dynamic typing and five different programming models.

One of the most gratifying things about the first *Seven in Seven* book was the explosion of discussions on blogs and podcasts. As you explore this book, we encourage you to ask your own questions, and talk about them where others can see the discussions. Tap the wisdom of the crowd.

Online Resources

The apps and examples shown in this book can be found at the Pragmatic Programmers website for this book.[1] You'll also find the community forum and the errata-submission form, where you can report problems with the text or make suggestions for future versions.

---

1. http://pragprog.com/book/7lang

CHAPTER 1

Lua

by Ian Dees

In 2004, we were hacking our way through a tangled jungle of hardware test code. The proprietary scripting engine at its core had looked like a golden idol when it was still on its pedestal: gleaming, powerful, and ready to make us wealthy. But once we had it in our satchel, we saw that the whole setup was a trap.

The plugin API was an unstoppable boulder that threatened to squash our own code. Constrained schedules didn't leave us enough room to duck out of the way. Each system crash felt like a dart to the spleen.

Then, like Indiana Jones, Lua swashbuckled its way into our project, toting a metaphorical bullwhip to solve our problems with cultured wit and fearless performance. With Lua on our side, everything changed:

- Since Lua's function inputs and outputs are flexible, our test modules no longer needed to know anything about the scripting runtime.
- With rich syntax and proper semantics, our code became easier to read and understand.
- Because of Lua's famously clean code, we all but eliminated crashes in the engine.

The project kept trucking along for several years, with Lua serving admirably at its core. I'll always remember how this quick, portable little language outdid the competition, and did so with style.

Intrigued? Let's get started.

Day 1: The Call to Adventure

When we first built our system, we found writing configuration files burden-some. The file formats we could use to describe test inputs and outputs just weren't that expressive.

Take comma-separated values (CSV), for instance. Say you wanted to describe characters and vehicles for a video game. Your CSV configuration file might start like this:

```
name,    treasure1, treasure2, treasure3, treasure4, treasure5
knight, -1000,     +200,        --,          --,         --
```

Now, say you wanted to add a square vehicle to the in-game world, and make it so you can't accidentally change the width without also changing the height:

```
name,       width,      height
mine cart, $cube_size, $cube_size
```

Here's the problem: CSV doesn't support collections or constraints. You'd have to work around these limitations by adding extra columns you seldom use, or by rolling (and supporting!) your own dialect.

Now, let's see what the same configuration might look like in Lua:

```lua
Monster{
   name     = "knight",
   treasure = {-1000, 200}
}

local cube_size = 20

Vehicle{
   name     = "mine cart",
   width    = cube_size,
   height   = cube_size
}
```

Beautiful. In one sweeping move, we've solved both CSV's awkward collection syntax and its inability to handle constraints—by switching to a language that was designed precisely to implement these features.

You can even bring your monsters to life right in your level design.

```lua
Monster{
   name = "cobra",
   speed = function() return 10 * damage_to_player() end
}
```

In this case, we've added some custom behavior to one particular adversary, right alongside the rest of its attributes.

The Week Ahead

On Day 1, we're going to install Lua and find our way around. You'll learn the basic data types and write a few simple Lua programs.

The second day, we'll dive into the key idea that makes Lua so expressive: tables. These are a sort of array-meets-dictionary object that you can use to implement everything from smart configuration files to a homemade object system. We'll also look at Lua's powerful concurrency features.

To cap off our adventure, on Day 3 we'll use Lua for its intended purpose: an expressive description language used together with fast, low-level C code. Specifically, we're going to write a music player that takes descriptions of notes and chords, then plays them live on your computer.

First things first, though. Today, we'll learn a little about Lua as a language. Then, we'll write some simple Lua programs with numbers, strings, Booleans, functions, and conditionals. These constructs will likely feel familiar to you, but Lua presents them in a particularly approachable way.

Lua at a Glance

Lua is a *table-based* programming language, built on a single powerful abstraction that you can use to implement your own programming style—procedural, object-oriented, event-driven, and so on.

Lua's tables lend themselves really well to the *prototype* style of object-oriented programming. In this style, classes and instances aren't separate concepts. You don't create a set of blueprints (classes) and then spin up a bunch of individual objects based on those blueprints.

Instead, in a prototype system, you create a single instance that looks like the objects you need in your program. Then, you clone this one instance a bunch of times and customize each clone. These systems are just as powerful as traditional class-based systems but have a simpler feel.

Installing Lua

By design, Lua is extremely portable. Its authors stick to a strict subset of ANSI C known to work across compilers and platforms. They were so successful in their dedication that Lua was one of only two scripting languages I could get to compile for a particularly limited embedded platform. (The other language was REXX, if you're curious.)[1]

One of the most fun ways to install Lua is simply to compile it yourself from the source.[2] If you're in a hurry, you can download a prebuilt binary for one of nearly a dozen platforms.[3]

Interactive Development

Like many of its fellow scripting languages, Lua supports an interactive read–eval–print loop (REPL). To start it, just type lua at the command line:

```
$ lua
Lua 5.2.3  Copyright (C) 1994-2013 Lua.org, PUC-Rio
>
```

Notice we're using Lua 5.2.3, the latest version as of this writing. Much of this code will work fine in older versions, but we tested most extensively with 5.2.

We'll stay in the REPL for much of this chapter. The bits after the leading > or >> are for you to type in.

Go ahead and type a value into the REPL, such as the year one of my favorite adventure movies was made:

```
> 1989
stdin:1: unexpected symbol near '1989'
```

Interesting. Lua doesn't print the value by default. We can deal with that easily enough. You could print() or return the value explicitly, or just add an =, like this:

```
> print(1989)
1989
> return 1989
1989
> =1989
1989
```

If you wanted to get out of the REPL, you'd just type Ctrl-D. But stick around, so we can kick the tires a bit first.

---

1. http://en.wikipedia.org/wiki/Rexx
2. http://lua-users.org/wiki/BuildingLua
3. http://lua-users.org/wiki/LuaBinaries

First Glimpse

Lua has a friendly, approachable syntax. There's no need to fuss over semi-colons or where the whitespace goes. In fact, whitespace doesn't matter much in Lua at all. Both of the following statements have the same output:

```
> print "No time for love"
No time for love
> print
>> "No time for love"
No time for love
```

You don't even need to place line breaks between statements:

```
> print "No time" print "for love"
No time
for love
```

Lua's types are similarly easy to use.

Building Blocks

Like most scripting languages, Lua is *dynamically typed*, meaning that while variables in a program don't have types, runtime values do. Lua has the usual basic types you'd expect: numbers, Booleans, and strings:

```
> =3.14
3.14
> =true
true
> ="The dog's name was 'Indiana!'"
The dog's name was 'Indiana!'
```

Wondering about integers? Nope, Lua doesn't have them. In a typical Lua installation, 64-bit floating-point numbers are the only choice, just like JavaScript. (One minor exception: For embedded platforms with no floating-point numbers, you can rebuild Lua from source to use integers instead.)

Strings can be enclosed either in single or double quotes. Backslashes allow you to escape special or unprintable characters:

```
> ='Separated\tby\t\ttabs'
Separated       by              tabs
```

You concatenate strings with the .. operator:

```
> ='fortune' .. ' and ' .. 'glory'
fortune and glory
```

You take the length of a string with #:

```
> =#'professor'
9
```

nil is its own type in Lua, representing "not found" or "does not exist." (It's also useful for deleting items from collections, as you'll see on Day 2.)

```
> =some_variable_that_does_not_exist
nil
```

Now that you've seen the fundamental building blocks of Lua data, let's put them together into expressions.

Expressions

Arithmetic in Lua looks like math in just about any language. As you'd expect, multiplication and division take precedence over addition and subtraction. You can group operations with parentheses.

```
> =6 + 5 * 4 - 3 / 2
24.5
> =6 + (5 * 4) - (3 / 2)
24.5
> =(6 + 5) * (4 - 3) / 2
5.5
```

Lua has built-in operators for exponentiation (^) and modulo arithmetic (%):

```
> =1899 % 100
99
> = 2 ^ 3
8
```

Instead of Boolean operators, Lua uses the and, or, and not keywords. Conveniently, logical expressions *short-circuit*, meaning that Lua evaluates both halves of an expression only if it needs to.

```
> =not ((true or false) and false)
true
> =true or spill_antidote()
true
```

(No antidotes were spilled in the running of this code.)

You can compare any values for equality and inequality with == and ~=, respectively. The relative comparisons <, <=, >, and >= are usable only with strings and numbers:

```
> ='cobras' < 'rats'
true
```

```
> =#'cobras' < #'rats'
false
> =42 < '43'
stdin:1: attempt to compare number with string
...
> =true < false
stdin:1: attempt to compare two boolean values
```

We have got a handle on data types and expressions. Let's breathe some life into them with a few functions.

Functions

Lua function definitions look like those in any common scripting language:

```
>  function triple(num)
>>      return 3 * num
>> end
>
> =triple(2)
6
```

Strictly speaking, the function name isn't necessary; you could just as easily type the following:

```
> =(function(num) return 3 * num end)(2)
6
```

In Lua, functions are *first-class values*; they can be treated just like any other value in Lua. In particular, they can be assigned to variables, passed as parameters into other functions, and stored in data structures.

For example, you could easily write a function call_twice() that takes a second function f() and returns a third function ff that calls f twice:

```
>
> function call_twice(f)
>>      ff = function(num)
>>          return f(f(num))
>>      end
>>      return ff
>> end
>
> function triple(n)
>>      return n * 3
>> end
>
> times_nine = call_twice(triple)
>
> =times_nine(5)
45
```

The ability to treat code as data is crucial for Lua's power and compactness. We'll see more examples of these techniques later on.

Flexible Arguments

What happens when you try to call a function with too few arguments? Some languages shut you down with an error message. Others, like Haskell, return a new function. Lua simply assigns a value of nil to all the unused parameters:

```
> function print_characters(friend, foe)
>>      print('*Friend and foe*')
>>      print(friend)
>>      print(foe)
>> end
> print_characters('Marcus', 'Belloq')
*Friend and foe*
Marcus
Belloq
> print_characters('Marcus')
*Friend and foe*
Marcus
nil
```

Any extra parameters are just ignored:

```
> print_characters('Marcus', 'Belloq', 'unused')
*Friend and foe*
Marcus
Belloq
```

You can also explicitly create *variadic functions*, that is, functions with an arbitrary number of inputs. You do so by making the last parameter in the function declaration an ellipsis (...):

```
> function print_characters(friend, ...)
>>      print('*Friend*')
>>      print(friend)
>>
>>      print('*Foes*')
>>      foes = {...}
>>      print(foes[1])
>>      print(foes[2])
>> end
>
> print_characters('Marcus', 'Belloq')
*Friend*
Marcus
*Foes*
Belloq
nil
```

Tail Calls

One other nice programmer convenience for functions in Lua is *tail call optimization*. This comes into play when you have a recursive function whose recursive call is the very last thing it does:

```
function reverse(s, t)
    if #s < 1 then return t end
    first = string.sub(s, 1, 1)
    rest  = string.sub(s, 2, -1)
    return reverse(rest, first .. t)
end

large = string.rep('hello ', 5000)
print(reverse(large, ''))
```

Many scripting language implementations would choke on that call; for instance, a JavaScript version fails with a stack error in the current release version of Google Chrome. Lua, however, correctly optimizes the recursive call into a simple goto and completes the calculation.

```
> print_characters('Marcus', 'Belloq', 'Donovan')
*Friend*
Marcus
*Foes*
Belloq
Donovan
```

We assign the entire list of arguments to the foes table, which we're treating like a simple array here. That's one of the unique features of Lua's tables that we'll see on Day 2.

Multiple Return Values

By the same token, you can also return multiple values from a function and either use them or ignore them:

```
> function weapons()
>>     return 'bullwhip', 'revolver'
>> end
>
> w1 = weapons()
> print(w1)
bullwhip
>
> w1, w2 = weapons()
> print(w1)
bullwhip
> print(w2)
revolver
>
```

```
> w1, w2, w3 = weapons()
> print(w1)
bullwhip
> print(w2)
revolver
> print(w3)
nil
```

The rules are the same as for parameters: unused values are ignored, and unused variables are nil.

Keyword Arguments

Lua doesn't have a special syntax for keyword arguments like those in Python or Ruby.[4] But you can get the same effect by passing a table as a function argument:

```
> function popcorn_prices(table)
>>      print('A medium popcorn costs ' .. table.medium)
>> end
>
> popcorn_prices{small=5.00,
>>              medium=7.00,
>>              jumbo=15.00}
A medium popcorn costs 7
```

In this example, the table is the set of size names and prices between the curly braces (with no surrounding parentheses—Lua lets us leave them out in this case). The function reads a specific value from the table with a dotted notation: table.medium.

You can build quite a lot with just functions; a whole programming language, even! But for convenience's sake, let's look at some control structures.

Control Flow

Lua's built-in control flow constructs are the if statement, two flavors of for loop, and while loops.

The if statement may have an else clause and zero or more elseifs. Unlike some scripting languages, Lua's if doesn't return a value; you'll need to store results in a variable or print them:

```
> film = 'Skull'
>
> if film == 'Raiders' then
>>     print('Good')
```

---

4.   https://docs.python.org/release/1.5.1p1/tut/keywordArgs.html

```
>> elseif film == 'Temple' then
>>     print('Meh')
>> elseif film == 'Crusade' then
>>     print('Great')
>> else
>>     print('Huh?')
>> end
Huh?
```

for loops work over a series of numbers (with an optional step argument):

```
>  for i = 1, 5 do
>>     print(i)
>> end
1
2
3
4
5
>  for i = 1, 5, 2 do
>>     print(i)
>> end
1
3
5
```

You can also use for to loop over items in a collection, but we won't get to that until we talk about tables later on.

The final built-in control construct in Lua is the while loop (and its cousin, the repeat loop, which you'll learn more about during the exercises):

```
>  while math.random(100) < 50 do
>>     print('Tails; flipping again')
>> end
Tails; flipping again
Tails; flipping again
```

Lua doesn't limit you to just the "big three" control structures of if, for, and while. If you combine them with the ability to pass functions around like data, you can build whatever control structures your program needs. In the exercises for Day 1, you'll do just that.

Variables

We've seen variables already in some of the examples today, but until now we've glossed over how they work. Let's take a closer look.

One quirk of Lua is that variables are global by default:

```
>   function hypotenuse(a, b)
>>      a2 = a * a
>>      b2 = b * b
>>      return math.sqrt(a2 + b2)
>> end
>
> =hypotenuse(3, 4)
5
> =a2
9 -- WHOOPS!
```

You'd probably prefer that our temporary a2 variable not leak outside the function. Fortunately, all we have to do is preface our local variable definitions with the local keyword:

```
>   function hypotenuse(a, b)
>>      local a2 = a * a
>>      local b2 = b * b
>>      return math.sqrt(a2 + b2)
>> end
```

I was initially surprised that local isn't the default in Lua. But it turns out that there are good reasons for this.[5] If we really want to forbid creating globals accidentally, Lua's tables offer a way; we'll do something very close to this on Day 2.

Leaving Behind the REPL

So far, we've been typing all these expressions into the REPL. This is the best way to learn Lua, and it makes it easy to build up a program while you're typing it.

However, in a minute I'm going to invite you to do some exercises. You may want to work on these in a text editor and then run them from the command line. To do so, just save your program with a .lua extension and then run it with the same lua command you used to launch the REPL, like so:

```
lua my_program.lua
```

While it's not as interactive as the REPL, saving to a file makes it easier to correct typos when you're striking out on your own.

---

5.   http://lua-users.org/wiki/LocalByDefault

What We Learned in Day 1

Today, you got to know the basics of Lua syntax. You saw how easy it is to define functions, including fancy higher-order functions that take other functions as input. You now know enough Lua to write a few simple programs, and in a moment you will.

At this point, you're probably thinking Lua is an easy-to-use scripting language, but with nothing particular to make it stand out in a crowd. That was certainly my first reaction when I encountered the language.

Then I ran into Lua's killer feature that makes its expressiveness possible: tables. On Day 2, you'll see what's so special about them.

Your Turn

Find...

- The Lua wiki, which supplements the built-in docs with community-maintained explanations and examples
- The online version of *Programming in Lua, First Edition* (the newer paid editions are good too, but this one is both helpful and free)
- The latest version of the Lua reference manual
- The difference between a while loop and a repeat loop

Do (Easy):

- Write a function called ends_in_3(num) that returns true if the final digit of num is 3, and false otherwise.
- Now, write a similar function called is_prime(num) to test if a number is prime (that is, it's divisible only by itself and 1).
- Create a program to print the first n prime numbers that end in 3.

Do (Medium):

- What if Lua didn't have a for loop? Using if and while, write a function for_loop(a, b, f) that calls f() on each integer from a to b (inclusive).

Do (Hard):

- Write a function reduce(max, init, f) that calls a function f() over the integers from 1 to max like so:

```
function add(previous, next)
    return previous + next
end
```

```
reduce(5, 0, add) -- add the numbers from 1 to 5

-- We want reduce() to call add() 5 times with each intermediate
-- result, and return the final value of 15:
--
add( 0, 1) --> returns 1; feed this into the next call
add( 1, 2) --> returns 3
add( 3, 3) --> returns 6
add( 6, 4) --> returns 10
add(10, 5) --> returns 15
```

- Implement factorial() in terms of reduce().

Day 2: Tables All the Way Down

Today, we're going to look at two concepts that define the Lua experience: *tables* and *coroutines*. As with many prototype languages, tables define your *data*. Coroutines define your *control flow*. Both are simple but tremendously powerful, underpinning everything from Lua's object system to your own domain-specific languages.

Let's begin with tables.

One of the first things new programming language tutorials do is inundate you with a laundry list of data structures: arrays, tuples, vectors, lists, dictionaries, and so on. Each of these has its own API, syntax, quirks, and performance characteristics.

These collections are all useful, but when I'm first trying out a language, I'm usually wondering about much more basic things:

1. Where do I keep things when I need to access them by name?
2. Where do I store values in a particular order?

Lua answers both of these questions with one single data structure: the table.

Tables As Dictionaries

Like Python's dictionaries or Ruby's hashes, Lua's tables are collections of keys (names) with associated values. You create a table with curly braces, an expression known in Lua as a *table constructor*:

```
> book = {
>>    title  = "Grail Diary",
>>    author = "Henry Jones",
>>    pages  = 100
>> }
```

To get data back out of the table, you just write the table name, a dot, and the key you want to read:

```
> =book.title
Grail Diary
```

Using the same dot notation, you can add or modify items:

```
> book.stars  = 5                -- new item
> book.author = "Henry Jones Sr." -- modified item
```

What about keys with spaces or decimal points in them? Or keys you calculate at runtime? For these cases, you put the key in square brackets:

```
> key = "title"
> =book[key]
Grail Diary
```

You can actually use any data type as a table key with this syntax: Booleans, functions, and even other tables. Most of the time, though, you'll encounter string and number keys.

To remove an item from a table, just set its key to the special value nil:

```
> book.pages = nil
```

Lua doesn't ship with a function to print the contents of a table. Fortunately, we can define a simple one that will work for these first few examples. With the REPL still running, switch to your editor and save the following code in a file called util.lua:

```
lua/day2/util.lua
function print_table(t)
   for k, v in pairs(t) do
      print(k .. ": " .. v)
   end
end
```

pairs() is a built-in Lua function. More specifically, it's an *iterator*, which is a function designed to plug seamlessly into a for loop. For the gory details on how to build one, see the relevant chapter in the online Lua book.[6] The gist is that pairs() returns a new function, which the for loop calls over and over until it returns nil.

Our print_tables function won't correctly handle nested tables or indeed much of anything beyond the basics. But it'll do for now. You can bring it into the REPL by using the dofile() function:

---

6.   http://www.lua.org/pil/7.1.html

```
> dofile('util.lua')
```

As an alternative, you can launch Lua with your library preloaded by using the -l option like so:

```
$ lua -l util
```

dofile() is a blunt instrument that just slurps up the file you give it. It doesn't check to see if the code is already loaded, and it doesn't let you customize where Lua looks for files. Later, we'll use Lua's module system, which does both of these and more.

Here's the output of print_tables() on the book table we defined earlier:

```
> print_table(book)
author: Henry Jones
title: Grail Diary
pages: 100
```

So far, the table seems like an ordinary dictionary type. But keys and values aren't the only trick up its sleeve.

A Dictionary in Array's Clothing

Sometimes, you need to store data in a specific order. Other languages give you lists or arrays for this purpose, with a separate syntax and API from dictionaries.

In Lua, there's no need for a second abstraction. Lua views arrays as just a special case of key-value storage, where the keys are sequential numbers. You use the same syntax to create an array as you did before; just leave out the keys:

```
> medals = {
>>     "gold",
>>     "silver",
>>     "bronze"
>> }
```

You read and write array contents using a familiar square-bracket notation:

```
> =medals[1]
gold
> medals[4] = "lead"
```

Notice that, like mathematicians and civilians, Lua counts array indices starting at 1.

At this point, you're probably wondering, "How can Lua arrays possibly be efficient?" In most languages, dictionaries are slower than arrays; hashing a string takes a lot longer than just incrementing a pointer.

Fortunately, the Lua runtime provides a special fast track for arrays.[7] As long as you're adding values consecutively and using numeric keys, Lua will store and access the data efficiently.

Arrays and dictionaries aren't mutually exclusive in Lua. You can mix both styles in the same table, and Lua will figure out how to store everything efficiently. Some programmers adopt the convention of separating the array and dictionary parts with a semicolon:

```
> ice_cream_scoops = {
>>    "vanilla",
>>    "chocolate";
>>
>>    sprinkles = true
>> }
>
> =ice_cream_scoops[1]
vanilla
> =ice_cream_scoops.sprinkles
true
```

Storing items by name or number is a nice parlor trick, but what if you need something like custom lookup logic? For that, we turn to Lua's *metatables*.

Metatables

In all the tables we've seen so far, you pass in a key, and Lua retrieves a value for you. This lookup logic is built into Lua.

Sometimes, this default behavior isn't what your program needs. Say, for example, you want to supply a default value other than nil for unrecognized keys. Or perhaps you need to log all reads/writes to a particular table. You can implement both of these behaviors using a data structure known as a metatable.

The name *metatable*—the "table behind the table"—sounds a bit abstract, but if you've used JavaScript's prototypes or Python's special double-underscore method names, you'll find Lua's approach familiar.[8,9] Just think of it as "custom behavior" for now.

---

7.   http://www.lua.org/pil/27.1.html
8.   https://developer.mozilla.org/en-US/docs/Web/JavaScript/Guide/Details_of_the_Object_Model
9.   https://docs.python.org/2.5/ref/specialnames.html

Every table in Lua has a corresponding metatable, containing functions for reading/writing keys, iterating contents, and overloading operators. Most tables have their metatable set to nil, which punts table operations to Lua:

```
> greek_numbers = {
>> ena  = "one",
>> dyo  = "two",
>> tria = "three"
>> }
>
> =getmetatable(greek_numbers)
nil
```

But you can easily override Lua's default behavior. The way Lua prints tables to strings is about as useful as a bullwhip against a loaded M1917.

For instance, the way Lua prints tables to standard output is a little terse:

```
> =greek_numbers
table: 0x7fec0ad002b0
```

It'd be nice if we could actually see the keys and values, without needing to call a separate function. Fortunately, we can.

All we have to do is create a metatable, and store a function inside it under the name of _tostring. Lua will call this function whenever someone tries to display our table. We can use a slight variation on the print_table() function we wrote earlier, where we return the contents as a string instead of printing them to the console.

Add the following code to your util.lua:

lua/day2/util.lua
```
function table_to_string(t)
   local result = {}

   for k, v in pairs(t) do
      result[#result + 1] = k .. ": " .. v
   end

   return table.concat(result, "\n")
end
```

This new function just stores each key-value pair in a list, then concatenates them into a string at the end. With larger tables, this approach is faster than building a single string item by item.

Now, reload util.lua in the REPL:

```
> dofile('util.lua')
```

Finally, we can connect our custom output logic:

```
>  mt = {
>>      __tostring = table_to_string
>> }
>
> setmetatable(greek_numbers, mt)
>
> =greek_numbers
ena: one
tria: three
dyo: two
```

We've changed the default behavior for printing tables to strings. Now, when we call print(), Lua will look for _tostring in the metatable and find this function. The end result is a much more descriptive output.

Now that we've dipped our toes in with an easy function, let's look at a more complicated case.

Reading and Writing

By design, Lua's tables are pretty forgiving. If you try to read a key that's not in the table, nothing bad happens; you just get nil back. Say you wanted to create a stricter table, where reading a nonexistent key, or overwriting an existing key, caused a runtime error.

This task takes just a few easy steps in Lua:

1. Write a pair of functions to implement the custom read/write behavior you want to see.
2. Store these functions in a table under the names __index and __newindex.
3. Set this table as your data's metatable.

Let's look at step 3 first. Place the following code into strict.lua:

lua/day2/strict.lua
```
local mt = {
    __index    = strict_read,
    __newindex = strict_write
}

treasure = {}
setmetatable(treasure, mt)
```

The strict_read() function will read the underlying data from a private table that we'll never access directly. Add the following code to the *top* of the file:

lua/day2/strict.lua
```lua
local _private = {}

function strict_read(table, key)
   if _private[key] then
      return _private[key]
   else
      error("Invalid key: " .. key)
   end
end
```

Lua will pass the table and key we're reading into our lookup function; all we have to do is return the underlying data, if it exists.

The strict_write() function is similar; it needs to check the private table to see if the key's already there. This definition goes right after the one for strict_read():

lua/day2/strict.lua
```lua
function strict_write(table, key, value)
   if _private[key] then
      error("Duplicate key: " .. key)
   else
      _private[key] = value
   end
end
```

Load your strict.lua file into the REPL using dofile() or the -l option. Then, try stashing some treasure in your treasure chest:

```
> treasure.gold = 50
>
> =treasure.gold
50
>
> =treasure.silver
strict.lua:8: Invalid key: silver
...
>
> treasure.gold = 100
strict.lua:16: Duplicate key: gold
...
```

So far, we've used metatables for custom lookup logic, and custom output formats. You can also use them to overload arithmetic, logical, and comparison operators. The process is exactly the same: you store functions in a table with special key names like __add or __sub, then call setmetatable() to bind the custom behavior to your data.

In the next section, you'll see just how powerful metatables can be: we're going to build our own object-oriented system on top of Lua's primitives.

Roll Your Own OO

Lua comes with its own syntax for object-oriented programming. But I'm going to show you how easy it is to roll your own OO scheme using the powerful abstractions built into the language. Afterward, we'll see what a short step it is from our homegrown solution to a typical Lua one.

The kernel of an object-oriented program is the idea of autonomous objects sending one another messages. You can implement this idea in Lua with what you've already seen, using plain ol' tables and functions.

Say you're building a game and want your player to face a boss-level baddie during the final stage. The game engine responds to an attack on the villain by sending the take_hit() message.

Functions in Lua are just ordinary data values that can be stored and passed around. So, you can make take_hit() into a function and store it inside the bad guy's table right alongside the state:

```lua
dietrich = {
    name      = "Dietrich",
    health    = 100,

    take_hit = function(self)
        self.health = self.health - 10
    end
}

dietrich.take_hit(dietrich)
print(dietrich.health)        --> 90
```

Presumably, the game has more than one villain. If many of them are going to be sharing an implementation of take_hit(), we need to know whose health we're docking. That's the purpose of the self parameter passed into the function. (We'll see a way to hide that in a moment.)

Notice that there's no distinct Villain class that we're instantiating (yet)—just a table with some data inside it. If we want to make another villain, we're going to have to initialize the fields ourselves, or copy them from another villain.

```lua
clone = {
    name      = dietrich.name,
    health    = dietrich.health,
    take_hit = dietrich.take_hit
}
```

Assuming we made the clone of our opponent before damaging the original, we can see that they are indeed two distinct objects:

```
print(clone.health) --> 100
```

All that manual copying of fields is going to get tiresome. Let's fix that next.

Prototypes

To set up the fields automatically each time we create a new villain, we'll write a function. To keep things modular, we'll store this and all villain-related functions in a Villain table. Here's a quick first pass, which we'll soon see has some problems:

```
Villain = {
   health = 100,

   new = function(self, name)
      local obj = {
         name   = name,
         health = self.health,
      }

      return obj
   end,

   take_hit = function(self)
      self.health = self.health - 10
   end
}

dietrich = Villain.new(Villain, "Dietrich")
```

We now have a function that will spin up villains reliably for us. We don't really need hundreds of copies of the same take_hit() function floating around, so we've moved it into the common Villain table. But now, we can't use dietrich the way we used to:

```
Villain.take_hit(dietrich)  --> ok
dietrich.take_hit(dietrich) --> error: attempt to call field
                            --> 'take_hit' (a nil value)
```

dietrich no longer has a field called take_hit(). This behavior lives in the Villain object now. It'd be nice to use a prototype-based approach like JavaScript, where the object system looks in our prototype Villain object if it can't find what it's looking for in dietrich.

As we saw in *Metatables*, on page 17, we can implement any lookup behavior we like using Lua's powerful metatables. Here's the revised body of the new function:

```
new = function(self, name)
   local obj = {
      name   = name,
      health = self.health,
   }

➤    setmetatable(obj, self)
➤    self.__index = self

   return obj
end,
```

Those two extra lines delegate field lookup to the Villain prototype. You've probably noticed one key difference from how we used metatables earlier. Our previous metatables used special functions for custom behavior. Here, we're using a table instead. This is Lua-speak for "use this table's fields as backup."

Now, take_hit() works the way we expect:

```
dietrich = Villain.new(Villain, "Dietrich")
dietrich.take_hit(dietrich) --> ok
```

So far, we've just made copies of a single Villain object. How do we create different kinds of villains?

Inheritance

One nice thing about prototype-based object systems is that you don't need a special mechanism for inheritance. You just clone objects the way you've been doing.

If, for instance, you want to start churning out supervillains who have more effective armor, all you have to do is create a single SuperVillain prototype and start cloning it:

```
SuperVillain = Villain.new(Villain)

function SuperVillain.take_hit(self)
   -- Haha, armor!
   self.health = self.health - 5
end

toht = SuperVillain.new(SuperVillain, "Toht")
toht.take_hit(toht)
print(toht.health) --> 95
```

This is starting to look like a fully featured object system. Passing each object around twice is getting tiresome, though.

Syntactic Sugar

The final step to take us from the ground up to Lua's object model is a bit of syntactic sugar. When you call table:method() instead of table.method(self), you can leave out the self parameter—Lua passes it in implicitly for you.

```lua
Villain = { health = 100 }

function Villain:new(name)
    -- ...same implementation as before...
end

function Villain:take_hit()
    -- ...same implementation as before...
end

SuperVillain = Villain:new()

function SuperVillain:take_hit()
    -- ...same implementation as before...
end
```

Now, our homegrown object system looks a lot like what we'd see in any other language:

```lua
dietrich = Villain:new("Dietrich")
dietrich:take_hit()
print(dietrich.health) --> 90

toht = SuperVillain:new("Toht")
toht:take_hit()
print(toht.health)      --> 95
```

So far today, we've started with a simple, flexible data structure and used it to build sophisticated constructs in just a few lines of code. Next, we're going to do the same thing for control flow.

Coroutines

Everything we've asked Lua to do has fit in a sequence of one-at-a-time tasks. You may be wondering about how Lua handles multithreading.

It doesn't.

Yes, you read that right. Lua does not come with a threading API. Instead, it ships with a simpler, easier-to-understand primitive for multitasking: the coroutine.

Coroutines have been around for a few decades. Like threads, they allow your program to have multiple tasks in progress. Unlike threads, coroutines aren't preemptive. You have to add code to your program to point out explicitly when the current task can safely be paused so that another task can run.

Why should we use them, then, if they require juggling by the programmer? Because they're conceptually simpler, and they eliminate a whole class of concurrency problems. When you look at a piece of code, you know exactly when it can or can't be interrupted.

Coroutines vs. Threads

If coroutines are so great, why doesn't every language use them? Like every programming language feature, coroutines involve trade-offs. What we gain in simplicity and correctness, we lose in multicore processing.

A single Lua process with many coroutines can only use one of your system's cores at a time. However, it's easy to spin up multiple Lua interpreters within a single process, and run these across multiple cores.[a]

Another thing to watch out for with coroutines is that they do not play well with blocking I/O calls. If your coroutine-based program uses the network, you'll want to use the nonblocking select() function and friends.[b]

---

a.   http://www.inf.puc-rio.br/~roberto/docs/ry08-05.pdf
b.   http://www.lua.org/pil/9.4.html

Single Tasks: Generators

Let's start with a simple example. We're going to create a coroutine and assign a task to it. The coroutine starts in the paused state, so right away we'll resume() it to get it to start working. Inside the coroutine, we'll add code to yield() after each piece of work is done.

First, let's define a function that has a long task to perform—an infinitely long one, in fact.

```
> function fibonacci()
>>    local m = 1
>>    local n = 1
>>
>>    while true do
>>      coroutine.yield(m)
>>      m, n = n, m + n
>>    end
>> end
```

This function never returns; instead, each time it computes a new Fibonacci number, it yields to the caller. What's the difference between yielding and returning? When we yield, we can come back to the same spot in our program later.

To start this coroutine, we create it with the coroutine.create() function, then call it using coroutine.resume():

```
> generator = coroutine.create(fibonacci)
> succeeded, value = coroutine.resume(generator)
> =value
1
```

At that moment, the program jumps inside fibonacci() and runs until it hits the yield(). Then, execution jumps back to the caller, right after the call to resume(). resume() returns a status flag, plus anything that was passed into yield().

Each time we call resume(), we pick up right where we left off the last time we yield()ed:

```
> succeeded, value = coroutine.resume(generator)
> =value
1
> succeeded, value = coroutine.resume(generator)
> =value
2
```

This approach is handy for any task that you want to break into chunks to keep your program responsive during a long computation or network operation.

Multitasking

Coroutines are simple, but they're powerful enough to implement thread-like behavior. Operating system schedulers are tens of thousands of lines long, but you're going to write one in a couple dozen![10]

What we want is to be able to define a couple of top-level functions that are going to appear to run concurrently:

```
function punch()
   for i = 1, 5 do
      print('punch ' .. i)
      scheduler.wait(1.0)
   end
end
```

---

10. http://code.openhub.net/project?pid=bQ7OKaOjylw&prevcid=1&did=kernel%2Fsched

```
function block()
    for i = 1, 3 do
        print('block ' .. i)
➤       scheduler.wait(2.0)
    end
end
```

...and then schedule them to run like so:

```
scheduler.schedule(0.0, coroutine.create(punch))
scheduler.schedule(0.0, coroutine.create(block))

scheduler.run()
```

None of this thread-like API exists; we're going to have to build it. The basic idea is to keep a list of everything we need to do in the future, sorted by when we need to do it.

Check out the syntax we're using to call our scheduling functions. This is Lua's module system, which (like everything else) is built on top of tables. We'll use this system to define our API.

Place the following code in scheduler.lua:

lua/day2/scheduler.lua
```
local pending = {}

local function schedule(time, action)
➤   pending[#pending + 1] = {
        time   = time,
        action = action
    }

    sort_by_time(pending)
end
```

Each time we want an action to happen in the future, we throw it into the pending array, which we keep ordered by timestamp (number of seconds since the program started).

The hash symbol in #pending, by the way, is the length operator. You used it on Day 1 to get the length of a string. Here, you can see that it works on arrays as well. The highlighted line is a common Lua idiom for appending to an array.

One other thing to note here: to avoid name collisions, we're making schedule and all other functions in this file local. Later on, we'll specifically expose just the ones we want callers to see.

The sort_by_time() routine just leans on Lua's built-in table.sort() function, which takes an optional comparison function to compare the two entries in the array. Put this code at the top of scheduler.lua:

```
lua/day2/scheduler.lua
local function sort_by_time(array)
   table.sort(array, function(e1, e2)
                        return e1.time < e2.time
                     end)
end
```

Remember that our coroutines are supposed to be lightweight. They need to get in, do their work, and either return or yield quickly. So our wait() function shouldn't actually wait. Instead, it should yield back to the scheduler:

```
local function wait(seconds)
   coroutine.yield(seconds)
end
```

The main run() loop just needs to busy-wait until it's time to run the nearest task in the future, then resume that task. If the task calls wait(), the number of seconds will get yielded back to us. We use that information to schedule a future resumption of that task:

```
local function run()
   while #pending > 0 do
      while os.clock() < pending[1].time do end -- busy-wait

      local item = remove_first(pending)
      local _, seconds = coroutine.resume(item.action)

      if seconds then
         later = os.clock() + seconds
         schedule(later, item.action)
      end
   end
end
```

When the work is complete, the coroutine won't yield anything to us. The call to resume() will return nil, and we won't schedule that task anymore.

The only function left to implement is remove_first(), which will delete and return the first item from the array. This is all stock Lua table manipulation:

```
local function remove_first(array)
   result       = array[1]
   array[1]     = array[#array]
   array[#array] = nil
   return result
end
```

Let's wrap this API up in a nice Lua module. This is just a plain ol' table with the functions and names we want to make available to callers. The following code goes at the end of scheduler.lua:

```
return {
    schedule = schedule,
    run = run,
    wait = wait
}
```

And now to run our program! Create a new file called punch.lua with the following line at the top of it:

lua/day2/punch.lua
```
scheduler = require 'scheduler'
```

We use require() instead of dofile() to load our module. These are similar functions, but require() does more for you:

- Checks to see if you've already loaded the module
- Searches multiple (configurable) library paths
- Safely namespaces the code in a local variable

Next, add the punch() and block() functions we saw at the beginning of this section, plus the setup calls to schedule() and run(). When you run lua punch.lua, you should see five punches flying by, with blocks happening about half as frequently. Looks like we're better at offense than defense.

An Interview with Roberto Ierusalimschy, creator of Lua

Us: Why did you write Lua?

Roberto: Back in 1993, I was working as a consultant for Tecgraf, a partnership between my university (PUC-Rio) and Petrobras (the Brazilian Oil Company). There were two programs with somewhat similar problems for end-user configuration. People there had developed some little languages for their specific needs, but soon they realized that they needed more power from their languages, such as full arithmetic expressions, variables, conditionals, and even some abstractions (functions). However, they did not want to entangle their entire program with this configuration language. At that time, the only language with that profile was Tcl, but its syntax was too confusing for our users, who were mainly non-professional programmers (such as geologists and mechanical engineers). So, we started Lua for the very specific goal of providing a good language for programs that needed a good configuration language.

Us: What do you like the most about Lua?

Roberto: Lua is a language with a very clear and small set of goals. It does not try to be everything for everybody. I am the first to recommend other languages when that is the case. Language design involves many trade-offs, and different languages solve those trade-offs in different ways, which are good or bad for different uses and users. A good programmer should know how to choose the best tool for each problem.

Us: *What kinds of problems does it solve the best?*

Roberto: *I think Lua is best suited for what it was created, real scripting. Nowadays, most people use "scripting language" as almost a synonym for dynamic language. But scripting has a more specific meaning, of a language to "orchestrate," or to "glue," software that is frequently written in a different language. (Thinking about the script of a game like the script of a movie gives a good idea of what I mean by "scripting.") Lua has always been developed with this kind of use in mind.*

Us: *What is a feature that you would like to change, if you could start over?*

Roberto: *That is a tricky question to answer ;) The new vararg mechanism, which was implemented only in version 5.1 of the language (in 2006), is something that I do not like much. Frequently I think the old mechanism was better, but I do not think we can roll back to it. The pattern matching functions are another area where I would like to use something based on PEGs, but I cannot see a roadmap from the current system for a new one.*

Us: *What's the most surprising place you've ever seen Lua used in production?*

Roberto: *Maybe games. Now games are the main niche of the language, but it was not like that in the beginning. We hardly thought about games in the first years of the language. When Grim Fandango came out, that was a big surprise for us. It is also a little surprising to see Lua embedded in so many devices, such as keyboards, printers, routers, cameras, and the like.*

What We Learned in Day 2

What a day! Take a second to pat yourself on the back. You've implemented an object-oriented programming system and a thread-like concurrency API. And you've done so with compact, modular, easy-to-read code.

What made this day possible was Lua's composable primitives: tables and coroutines. We saw how tables do dual duty as arrays and dictionaries, and how Lua provides hooks for us to extend their behavior.

Next, we looked at coroutines, Lua's approach to concurrency. Even though coroutines expose a tiny API, we can use them to build sophisticated and powerful multitasking programs.

Tomorrow, we're going to teach Lua to interact with C++ code and generate some music. Remember that scheduler we wrote today? We're going to need it to manage all the different voices that are contributing to our song.

Your Turn

Find...

- The LuaRocks system for installing Lua modules onto your system
- The open source LOOP library that implements a more sophisticated scheduler than the one we've written here
- The list of all metatable functions that Lua recognizes (in addition to the _tostring, _index, and _newindex functions we used)
- The name of the table where Lua keeps its global variables

Do (Easy):

- Write a function called concatenate(a1, a2) that takes two arrays and returns a new array with all the elements of a1 followed by all the elements of a2.
- Our strict table implementation in *Reading and Writing*, on page 19 doesn't provide a way to delete items from the table. If we try the usual approach, treasure.gold = nil, we get a duplicate key error. Modify strict_write() to allow deleting keys (by setting their values to nil).

Do (Medium):

- Change the global metatable you discovered in the Find section earlier so that any time you try to add two arrays using the plus sign (e.g., a1 + a2), Lua concatenates them together using your concatenate() function.
- Using Lua's built-in OO syntax, write a class called Queue that implements a first-in, first-out (FIFO) queue as follows:

    - q = Queue.new() returns a new object.
    - q:add(item) adds item past the last one currently in the queue.
    - q:remove() removes and returns the first item in the queue, or nil if the queue is empty.

Do (Hard):

- Using coroutines, write a fault-tolerant function retry(count, body) that works as follows:
    - Call the body() function.
    - If body() yields a string with coroutine.yield(), consider this an error message and restart body() from its beginning.
    - Don't retry more than count times; if you exceed count, print an error message and return.
    - If body() returns without yielding a string, consider this a success.

Example usage:

```
retry(
    5,

    function()
        if math.random() > 0.2 then
            coroutine.yield('Something bad happened')
        end

        print('Succeeded')
    end
)
```

Most of the time, the inner function will fail; retry() should keep trying until it's achieved success or tried five times.

Hint: You may need to create more than one coroutine.

Day 3: Lua and the World

You've started down the path to adventure, treading lightly at first through Lua's gates. You've found the simplicity and power in its data structures and concurrency routines. Now, it's time to apply that knowledge and use Lua to build a real project.

Today, we're going to make music with Lua. Lua doesn't come with a sound library, but there are plenty around that are written in other languages. We'll use one of Lua's strongest features, its C interface, to control an open source music library.

A few stalwart adventurers have blazed this trail before us. They've used Lua's expressiveness for their program's logic, C for the performance-critical code, and the techniques in this chapter to glue the two together. For instance, Adobe Lightroom,[11] World of Warcraft,[12] and Angry Birds[13] all use Lua either internally or as a customer-facing extensibility language.

Making Music

There are lots of ways to make music with a computer. Today, we'll generate Musical Instrument Digital Interface (MIDI) notes using a C++ library.[14] This means we'll start the day with just enough C++ to show off Lua's awesome C

---

11. http://www.adobe.com/devnet/photoshoplightroom.html
12. http://www.wowwiki.com/Lua
13. http://stackoverflow.com/a/4430719
14. http://www.midi.org

integration. We'll quickly step back into the world of Lua, where we can wrap everything in an expressive API.

In Good Company

We'll be in good company in choosing MIDI for making music with software. Topher Cyll used a similar technique to generate drum beats in *Practical Ruby Projects [Cyl07]*. Giles Bowkett has built on Topher's work and written algorithms in Ruby and Coffee-Script that write new songs.[a]

Here, we're going to focus on the more modest goal of playing songs that already exist, and providing the easiest Lua API we can.

---

a.   http://singrobots.com

Outfitting for Adventure

Before you set out on today's adventure, you'll need some supplies. Specifically, you'll need to have the following programs installed and ready to go:

- A C++ compiler for your platform
- The CMake tool for building C++ projects[15]
- The Lua C headers and libraries (these should have come with your Lua distribution)
- The RtMidi sound library[16]
- A MIDI synthesizer app, so you can hear your music

The installation instructions vary greatly from platform to platform. Here's a quick summary of the steps you need for Windows, Mac, and Linux. If you get stuck, drop us a line in the forums.[17]

Windows

1. Install Visual Studio Express 2013 for Windows Desktop.[18]
2. Download the source code to RtMidi, open the .sln file in Visual Studio, and build the library.
3. Download and install the Windows version of CMake.
4. Install the VirtualMIDISynth MIDI player.[19]

---

15. http://www.cmake.org
16. http://www.music.mcgill.ca/~gary/rtmidi
17. http://forums.pragprog.com
18. http://www.visualstudio.com/en-us/products/visual-studio-express-vs.aspx
19. http://coolsoft.altervista.org/virtualmidisynth

Mac

1. Make sure you have a C++ compiler on your system, such as the Xcode command-line tools.[20]
2. Install the Homebrew package manager.[21]
3. Add the C sound project package sources:

```
brew tap kunstmusik/csound
```

4. Install Lua, CMake, and RtMidi:

```
brew install lua cmake rtmidi
```

5. Download and install the SimpleSynth MIDI player.[22]

Linux

Here's how to get rolling on Ubuntu Linux; you'll need to tweak these instructions for your distribution.

1. Using the Synaptic package manager, add the universe repository to make more packages available.[23]
2. Install the compilers, Lua, CMake, and RtMidi:

```
sudo apt-get install build-essential lua5.2 lua5.2-dev cmake rtmidi
```

3. Install and configure a MIDI synthesizer for Linux.[24] MIDI on Linux is a bit more of a Wild West situation, but one approach is to use a synthesizer called ZynAddSubFX together with a helper program called padsp:[25,26]

```
sudo apt-get install zynaddsubfx pulseaudio-utils
```

Creating the Project

Our goal is to produce a command-line program, play, that will play whichever song we give to it. Songs will be in a Lua-based music notation we're going to invent. The system will consist of three parts:

1. A short C++ routine to create a new Lua interpreter and run a script supplied by the musician (that's you!)

---

20. https://developer.apple.com/downloads/index.action
21. http://brew.sh
22. http://notahat.com/simplesynth
23. https://help.ubuntu.com/community/Repositories/Ubuntu
24. http://tedfelix.com/linux/linux-midi.html
25. http://zynaddsubfx.sourceforge.net
26. https://wiki.ubuntu.com/PulseAudio

2. A Lua function that sends messages to MIDI devices; written in C++, but playable from Lua

3. A library of Lua helper routines to provide an easy syntax for writing music

A Tiny Interpreter

Let's start with the Lua interpreter. Create a file in your project directory called play.cpp with the following contents:

```
lua/day3/a/play.cpp
extern "C"
{
#include "lua.h"
#include "lauxlib.h"
#include "lualib.h"
}
```

This will make the main Lua runtime and its auxiliary libraries available to your C++ program. The extern "C" wrapper tells the compiler and linker that the external Lua code is C, rather than C++.

Now, add a main() function, the place where command-line C programs begin their lives:

```
lua/day3/a/play.cpp
int main(int argc, const char* argv[])
{
    lua_State* L = luaL_newstate();
    luaL_openlibs(L);

    luaL_dostring(L, "print('Hello world!')");

    lua_close(L);
    return 0;
}
```

Here, we use luaL_newstate() to create a new Lua interpreter. The default interpreter is designed to be lightweight, so bringing in Lua's standard libraries requires a call to a second function, luaL_openlibs().

Once our interpreter is loaded and ready, we send it some Lua code with the luaL_dostring() function. Eventually, this Lua code will contain a song. For now, we'll just print some text to the console.

At the end of the program, we tear down our interpreter with lua_close().

Building the Project

Now we're ready to build. This takes two steps:

1. Create a project file using CMake
2. Compile the C program with make or Visual Studio

CMake just needs a quick description of your project to get started. Place the following text in a file called CMakeLists.txt:

lua/day3/a/CMakeLists.txt
```
cmake_minimum_required (VERSION 2.8)
project (play)
add_executable (play play.cpp)
target_link_libraries (play lua)
```

If your Lua headers are somewhere other than the system-wide default location, you may need to add an include_directories() line; for example:

lua/day3/a/CMakeLists.txt
```
include_directories(/usr/local/include)
```

Now, tell CMake to create your project file by typing the following command into the terminal from your project directory:

```
$ cmake .
```

On Mac and Linux, this will generate a Makefile, which you can use to build the project by typing the make command. On Windows, CMake will create a .sln file you can load into Visual Studio and build. Go ahead and do that step now.

Once you've built the project, you should have a program called play.exe or play in your project directory. If you're on Windows, run your program like so:

```
C:\day3> play.exe
Hello world!
```

On Mac and Linux, type the following command:

```
$ ./play
Hello world!
```

Did you get the console message? Excellent! Now, let's create some sound.

Adding Audio

First, we need to bring in the RtMidi library. Add the following code to the top of your C++ program, just after the closing brace of the extern "C" block:

```
lua/day3/b/play.cpp
#include "RtMidi.h"
static RtMidiOut midi;
```

The RtMidiOut object is our interface to the MIDI generator. Here, we're just stashing it in a global variable. Normally we'd use Lua's sophisticated *registry* to store this kind of data, but that'd be overkill for our purposes.[27]

Now, update your main() function to connect to your MIDI synthesizer:

```
lua/day3/b/play.cpp
int main(int argc, const char* argv[])
{
➤    if (argc < 1) { return -1; }
➤
➤    unsigned int ports = midi.getPortCount();
➤    if (ports < 1) { return -1; }
➤    midi.openPort(0);

     lua_State* L = luaL_newstate();
     luaL_openlibs(L);

➤    lua_pushcfunction(L, midi_send);
➤    lua_setglobal(L, "midi_send");
➤
➤    luaL_dofile(L, argv[1]);

     lua_close(L);
     return 0;
}
```

The highlighted lines show the new additions. First, we use the RtMidi API to look for a running synthesizer (and exit the program if we fail to find one). Next, we open the Lua interpreter like we did before. Then, we register a C++ function that will do the grunt work of playing the notes. Finally, we run our Lua code and close the interpreter.

How do we connect C or C++ code to Lua? Lua uses a simple stack model to interoperate with C. We push our function's memory address onto the stack, then call the built-in lua_setglobal() function to store our function in a Lua variable.

You'll notice that we've also changed luaL_dostring() to luaL_doFile(). This loads the Lua code from an external file (we get the filename from the user via the command line; for example, play song.lua). This way, we don't have to keep recompiling our C++ program every time we make a tweak to our Lua code.

---

27. http://www.lua.org/pil/27.3.1.html

Let There Be Sound

And now for the music! To play a note, we need to send two MIDI messages to the synthesizer: a Note On message and a Note Off message. The standard assigns a number to each of these messages, and specifies that they each take two parameters: a note and a velocity.[28]

That means our midi_send() Lua function will take three arguments: the message number, plus the two numeric parameters. When Lua encounters a call like the following one:

```
midi_send(144, 60, 96)
```

...it will push the values 144, 60, and 96 onto the stack, then jump into our C++ function. We'll need to retrieve these parameters by their position on the stack. The top of the stack is at index -1 in Lua; this would be the last value pushed, or 96.

Because Lua is dynamically typed, these values could be anything: numbers, strings, tables, functions, and so on. We're in complete control of what goes in the .lua script, though. We're not going to pass in anything other than numbers, and so that's the only case we'll handle here. Add the following code to your C++ program, just above your main() function:

```
lua/day3/b/play.cpp
int midi_send(lua_State* L)
{
    double status = lua_tonumber(L, -3);
    double data1  = lua_tonumber(L, -2);
    double data2  = lua_tonumber(L, -1);

    // ...rest of C++ function here...

    return 0;
}
```

If our function needed to hand any data back to Lua, we'd push one or more items back onto the stack and return a positive number. Here, we return zero to indicate no data.

Updating the Project File

All that's left is to convert these three numbers into the format RtMidi needs, and send them to the synthesizer. Add the following code to your midi_send() function, just before the return:

---

28. http://www.midi.org/techspecs/midimessages.php

```
lua/day3/b/play.cpp
std::vector<unsigned char> message(3);
message[0] = static_cast<unsigned char>(status);
message[1] = static_cast<unsigned char>(data1);
message[2] = static_cast<unsigned char>(data2);

midi.sendMessage(&message);
```

We now need to link our project to both Lua and RtMidi. Change the target_link_libraries() line of your CMakeLists.txt file to the following:

```
lua/day3/b/CMakeLists.txt
target_link_libraries (play lua RtMidi)
```

Go ahead and rebuild your project. While that's cooking, let's write a short Lua test program to play a single note, middle C, for one second. The following code goes into one_note_song.lua:

```
lua/day3/b/one_note_song.lua
NOTE_DOWN = 0x90
NOTE_UP   = 0x80
VELOCITY  = 0x7f

function play(note)
    midi_send(NOTE_DOWN, note, VELOCITY)
    while os.clock() < 1 do end
    midi_send(NOTE_UP, note, VELOCITY)
end

play(60)
```

Give it a try! Start your MIDI synth, then run your play program:

```
./play one_note_song.lua
```

You should hear a piano note play middle C for one second.

From Notes to Songs

A one-note song is fine if you're Tenacious D.[29] But let's shoot for something a little more ambitious.

First, it'd be nice to write songs in something easier to remember than MIDI note numbers—something closer to musical notation. Let's grab the sheet music to an easily recognizable song, such as *Happy Birthday to You!*, or perhaps the public-domain soundalike *Good Morning to All* (which predates any copyright claims on the former by over 40 years).[30]

---

29. http://en.wikipedia.org/wiki/Tenacious_D
30. http://imslp.org/wiki/File:PMLP98386-Hill-GoodMorningtoAll1893.pdf

Since this book isn't called *Seven Musical Notations in Seven Weeks*, I'll gloss over translating the sheet music, and get straight to the names of the notes in this song. If you'd like to learn more about musical notation, the ReadSheet-Music project has a good tutorial.[31]

The first few notes of the song are D, E, D, G, F#, and they're all the same duration (quarter notes), except F# (which is a half note, lasting twice as long). The song is played in the Middle C octave, which is octave number 4 in scientific pitch notation.[32]

We could represent these notes in Lua in a number of different ways. For now, let's choose a simple string notation: note letter (e.g., Fs for "F sharp"), followed by octave number (e.g., 4), followed by value (e.g., h for "half note").

Place the following song in good_morning_to_all.lua:

```
lua/day3/b/good_morning_to_all.lua
notes = {
    'D4q',
    'E4q',
    'D4q',
    'G4q',
    'Fs4h'
}
```

We need to be able to parse these strings into MIDI note numbers and durations. Since we'll want to reuse this parsing routine from song to song, let's put it in a new file, notation.lua:

```
lua/day3/b/notation.lua
local function parse_note(s)
   local letter, octave, value =
      string.match(s, "([A-Gs]+)(%d+)(%a+)")

   if not (letter and octave and value) then
      return nil
   end

   return {
      note     = note(letter, octave),
      duration = duration(value)
   }
end
```

First, we use Lua's string.match() function to make sure the input follows the pattern we expect. If it does, we then call out to a couple of helper functions

31. http://readsheetmusic.info/readingmusic.shtml

32. http://en.wikipedia.org/wiki/Scientific_pitch_notation

to calculate the MIDI note number and the duration in seconds. Finally, we return a table with the keys note and duration.

The first helper function, note(), is straightforward multiplication and addition. The following definition goes at the top of notation.lua:

```
lua/day3/b/notation.lua
local function note(letter, octave)
   local notes = {
      C  = 0,     Cs = 1,     D  = 2,     Ds = 3,     E  = 4,
      F  = 5,     Fs = 6,     G  = 7,     Gs = 8,     A  = 9,
      As = 10,    B  = 11
   }

   local notes_per_octave = 12

   return (octave + 1) * notes_per_octave + notes[letter]
end
```

To translate from a note value (for example, q for "quarter note") to a number of seconds, we need to know the tempo of the song. We'll pick a default tempo of 100 beats per minute, and let individual songs override that if they need to. Put this definition just after note():

```
lua/day3/b/notation.lua
local tempo = 100

local function duration(value)
   local quarter    = 60 / tempo
   local durations = {
      h  = 2.0,
      q  = 1.0,
      ed = 0.75,
      e  = 0.5,
      s  = 0.25,
   }

   return durations[value] * quarter
end
```

The ed entry in the table, incidentally, is a dotted eighth note, lasting one and a half times as long as a regular eighth note. We'll need that for another song later on.

Looping through this table to play these notes is easy enough. Back in good_morning_to_all.lua, add the following function:

```
lua/day3/b/good_morning_to_all.lua
scheduler = require 'scheduler'
notation  = require 'notation'
```

```
function play_song()
  for i = 1, #notes do
    local symbol = notation.parse_note(notes[i])
➤   notation.play(symbol.note, symbol.duration)
  end
end
```

Since we're specifying both a note number and a duration now, we'll need a new definition of play(). We need to send the Note On message, wait for the right duration, and then send Note Off.

How can we wait without blocking the entire program? Wait, didn't we encounter a situation like this before on Day 2? Go grab that awesome scheduler you wrote in *Multitasking*, on page 26, and drop a copy into this project. Then, add the following code to notation.lua:

lua/day3/b/notation.lua
```
local scheduler = require 'scheduler'

local NOTE_DOWN = 0x90
local NOTE_UP   = 0x80
local VELOCITY  = 0x7f

local function play(note, duration)
  midi_send(NOTE_DOWN, note, VELOCITY)
  scheduler.wait(duration)
  midi_send(NOTE_UP, note, VELOCITY)
end
```

Since we're making a Lua module, we'll need to export our public functions at the end of the file:

lua/day3/b/notation.lua
```
return {
  parse_note = parse_note,
  play = play
}
```

Just to recap, notation.lua now contains the following items in order:

1. Our private helper functions, note() and duration()
2. The public parse_note() function
3. The public play() function with a few local variables
4. The return statement describing our Lua module

Using the scheduler does add one extra step to the song. We'll have to kick off the event loop at the end of good_morning_to_all.lua:

```
lua/day3/b/good_morning_to_all.lua
scheduler.schedule(0.0, coroutine.create(play_song))
scheduler.run()
```

Ready to give your song a listen?

```
./play good_morning_to_all.lua
```

Now that we've programmed an easy song, let's sink our teeth into something a little more substantial.

Voices

Our little homegrown Lua musical notation is coming along nicely. There are just a couple of things that are going to get tiresome as we encode longer songs:

- The lack of an API for multiple voices
- The need to enclose all the notes in quote marks

What we'd really like to do is write something like the following:

```
song.part{
    D3q, A2q,  B2q, Fs2q
}

song.part{
    D5q, Cs5q, B4q, A4q
}

song.go()
```

...and have both of these parts play at the same time. Thanks to our scheduler, we can handle the simultaneous playing. Add the following code to notation.lua, before the final return:

```
lua/day3/b/notation.lua
local function part(t)
   local function play_part()
      for i = 1, #t do
         play(t[i].note, t[i].duration)
      end
   end

   scheduler.schedule(0.0, coroutine.create(play_part))
end
```

This function takes an array of notes, t, creates a new function play_part() that plays these particular notes in order, and then schedules this part to be played as soon as the top-level song calls run().

That just leaves the question of how to get rid of the quote marks. Without quotes, the names of our notes become global variable lookups. Lua stores its global variables in a table called _G. All we have to do is use the metatable techniques from Day 2 to do the note lookup on the fly:

lua/day3/b/notation.lua
```lua
local mt = {
    __index = function(t, s)
        local result = parse_note(s)
        return result or rawget(t, s)
    end
}

setmetatable(_G, mt)
```

This function will be called for any global variable lookup, not just the ones in our songs. So if there's a typo in our program somewhere, it will hit this same lookup function. That's why we fall back on looking up the value in _G. The rawget() call, incidentally, bypasses our custom lookup function—so we won't get in an infinite loop if we're looking for an undefined name.

All that's left are a couple of utility functions. We need to let the musician set the song tempo, and we should provide a wrapper around scheduler.run(), so that the final song doesn't need to load the scheduler module explicitly:

lua/day3/b/notation.lua
```lua
local function set_tempo(bpm)
    tempo = bpm
end

local function go()
    scheduler.run()
end
```

Don't forget to update your module's return statement to add the new public functions:

lua/day3/b/notation.lua
```lua
return {
    parse_note = parse_note,
    play = play,
    part = part,
    set_tempo = set_tempo,
    go = go
}
```

Now, we have all we need to take on a more complex song.

Canon in D

You can find lots of public-domain musical scores at the Petrucci Project.[33] I've chosen Pachelbel's Canon in D.[34]

Here's a small part of the canon:

```
lua/day3/b/canon.lua
song = require 'notation'

song.set_tempo(50)

song.part{
    D3s,  Fs3s, A3s,  D4s,
    A2s,  Cs3s, E3s,  A3s,
    B2s,  D3s,  Fs3s, B3s,
    Fs2s, A2s,  Cs3s, Fs3s,

    G2s,  B2s,  D3s,  G3s,
    D2s,  Fs2s, A2s,  D3s,
    G2s,  B2s,  D3s,  G3s,
    A2s,  Cs3s, E3s,  A3s,
}

song.part{
    Fs4ed,             Fs5s,
    Fs5s, G5s, Fs5s, E5s,
    D5ed,              D5s,
    D5s,  E5s, D5s,  Cs5s,

    B4q,
    D5q,
    D5s,  C5s, B4s,  C5s,
    A4q
}

song.go()
```

If you type this all in and run ./play canon.lua, you'll be treated to one of my favorite pieces of music—with multiple parts playing at the same time, no less!

---

33. http://imslp.org/wiki/Main_Page
34. http://imslp.org/wiki/File:WIMA.7c2a-PachelbelCanon.pdf

What We Learned in Day 3

On the final step of our journey through Lua, we learned Lua's clean C API. By pushing and popping arguments and return values off Lua's stack, we can easily exchange data between the Lua and C worlds.

We put this newfound knowledge together with the metatable and coroutine skills we learned on Day 2, as we wrote a simple MIDI player in C++ and Lua. This is exactly the sort of thing people use Lua for: wrapping low-level libraries into an easy-to-use interface. And this is how I got out of that jungle of code I mentioned at the beginning of Day 1.

Your Turn

Find...

- How the luaL_dofile() function signals an error in the script
- How to retrieve Lua error information from the stack in C
- The *busted* unit test framework

Do (Easy):

- Find the music for your favorite adventure movie's theme song, and translate it to Lua. Play it with the music player you wrote.
- The way it stands, we have to put require 'notation' at the beginning of every song and song.go() at the end. Modify play.cpp to do this for you so that songs can just contain the tempo and parts.

Do (Medium):

- We've always played notes at one constant volume. Design a notation for louder or quieter notes, and modify your music player to support it.
- If there's an error in the Lua script, the whole C++ program just exits without a word. Modify play.cpp to report any error information returned from the Lua interpreter.

Do (Hard):

- The current implementation of play.cpp opens one global MIDI output port. Change it to allow the user to pass a port into midi_send() so that you can control more than one device from the same script.

Wrapping Up Lua

A lot of programmers see the surface of Lua's clean syntax and assume it's just another everyday scripting language. I certainly had that feeling at first glance. But I hope that as you've taken a deeper look at its tables and coroutines, you've enjoyed their beauty and simplicity.

Strengths

Recall Lua's original goal: to be an approachable, portable language for stitching together software components. These are all properties of a good configuration language—small wonder, then, that this sweet spot is where Lua shines.

Lua's source code is easy to read, runs quickly, and works on a huge variety of platforms. A newer implementation of the language, LuaJIT, takes these advantages even further with faster performance and a friendlier C interface.[35]

Finally, Lua is easy to drop into your project. With just a couple of header files and libraries, you can spin up a Lua interpreter and make your program scriptable. You can even sandbox the embedded interpreter, limiting its access to (for instance) the network and filesystem—a vital safeguard if you're running scripts written by end users.[36]

Weaknesses

The great thing about Lua is that you can build everything yourself. The downside is that you often *have* to build everything yourself. Lua stays agnostic on object frameworks, control flow, and so on—which means that there's rarely one official, batteries-included implementation of these things.

While Lua is faster than its contemporaries, it does fall behind in a few performance categories. It requires a bit of creativity to do string handling efficiently.[37] Developers also need to do a little heavy lifting in Lua to take advantage of multicore systems.

Finally, Lua has a few Pascal-like quirks that rub some people the wrong way. In particular, the 1-based array indexing and do/end notation are surprising for people new to the language.

---

35. http://luajit.org/luajit.html
36. http://www.luafaq.org/#T1.32
37. http://lua-users.org/lists/lua-l/2005-10/msg00137.html

Final Thoughts

Lua's prototype-based object approach proves that you don't need classes to build a great object system. If you're interested in other prototype systems, check out Self, Io, and of course JavaScript.[38,39,40]

I'll never forget how Lua taught me the key lesson that code is just data. Just like any other kind of data, you can spin up new functions on the fly, store them, and pass them around your program. This mindset made me a better programmer, no matter which language I'm writing in.

Congratulations on making it through this adventure. I hope you had a good time, and wish you well as you head off to Factor.

---

38. http://selflanguage.org
39. http://iolanguage.org
40. https://developer.mozilla.org/en-US/docs/Web/JavaScript

CHAPTER 2

Factor

by Fred Daoud

One of my favorite programming techniques is function composition. Start with the input, pass it through a series of functions, with the output of one function being the input to the next function, and use the output of the last function as the final result. Each function is small and focused. You solve problems by creating and connecting blocks of code.

Function composition is the essence of Factor. Be aware that Factor is unlike any other language you've tried, and its paradigm might alter your mind. It will seem unorthodox, like Mr. Miyagi's famous training regime for the Karate Kid. Just paint the fence, Reader-san, and give your mind a little time to acclimate. I promise it's worth it.

Here's a quick glimpse of Factor. Whereas in JavaScript you might have:

```
var x = f(42);
var y = g(x);
return h(y);
```

or even:

```
return h(g(f(42)));
```

in Factor, you write:

```
42 f g h
```

No variable names, and no parentheses, dots, or any other punctuation to indicate function composition. It's implied that the result of calling one function (called a *word* in Factor) is made available to the next word. This is handled automatically by Factor using the *stack*, which is simply a container that holds values. Words take their input from the stack and push their result onto the stack, which is then operated on by the next word.

Also notice that the words f g h are called in the same order as we read them, left to right.

In the JavaScript version, f is a function, and the parentheses in f(42) indicate to *apply* f to the value 42. This makes JavaScript an *applicative* language. Most other languages, such as Java, Ruby, Python, Clojure, Scala, Haskell, and Erlang, are applicative.

Factor is a *concatenative* language because instead of applying functions (or words), you concatenate them, simply writing them one after the other. Function composition is the default way of dealing with an expression such as f g h. Other concatenative languages include Forth, Joy, PostScript, Cat, Om, Retro, and Kitten. If you are familiar with Forth or Joy, you'll notice some similarities in Factor.

Instead of writing

```
wrapWordsAsList(capitalize(strip(text)))
```

you can write

```
text strip capitalize wrapWordsAsList
```

It's a beautiful expression of programmer intent. Let's discover more about Factor.

Day 1: Stack On, Stack Off

Over the next three days, we'll learn more about Factor and explore what makes its programming model unique. Day 1 will be spent experimenting with code in Factor's interactive environment. We'll get a feel for how Factor code works and we'll get used to using the stack to communicate input and output values.

On Day 2, we'll learn how to expand beyond the confines of the interactive sandbox and organize Factor code into source files. We'll run standalone programs and write unit tests. Day 3 will conclude our Factor adventure with a deeper exploration of the concatenative programming style. We'll solve two sample problems using pipelines of functions, which is one area where Factor really shines. We'll end the journey by looking at where to go for more documentation and examples.

Let's get started by getting Factor up and running.

Installing Factor

The easiest way to install Factor is to download a binary page from Factor's home page.[1] Then, follow the instructions to launch the Factor UI for your operating system.[2]

Using the Listener

Most recent programming languages come with an interactive console where you can type snippets of code and see the results on the command line. Factor has that, but it also has a much richer graphical version. The Factor UI, called the Listener, is an interactive graphical environment where you can not only experiment with Factor code, but also trigger autocomplete as you type, browse documentation, jump to source code within your favorite code editor, and more.[3]

Figure 1, *The Factor Listener*, on page 52 shows an example of the Listener window. In the screenshot, you can see how the Listener shows the state of the stack and how clear empties the stack. You can trigger autocomplete by typing the first few letters of a word and pressing `Tab`, which pops up a list of possible completions.

While in the Listener, you can type in Factor code and see the results. After every line of code that you write, the Listener shows you the values that are currently on the stack. You can navigate among your previous and next lines of code with `Ctrl+P` and `Ctrl+N`.

Getting Stacked

Now, breathe in, breathe out, Reader-san. It's time to say hello to Factor. Type the following code in the Listener. The IN: scratchpad prompt indicates that you are currently in the scratchpad vocabulary. Don't worry about vocabularies right now; we'll discuss them later.

```
IN: scratchpad "Hello, world" print
Hello, world
```

This prints *Hello, world* as you would expect. What might not be so obvious, however, is that print is not a message passed to the "Hello, world" string. Rather, "Hello, world" is pushed onto the stack and the print word takes a value from the stack and prints it. You can see how this happens step by step in the Listener.

---

1. http://factorcode.org/
2. http://concatenative.org/wiki/view/Factor/Running%20Factor
3. http://docs.factorcode.org/content/article-ui-tools.html

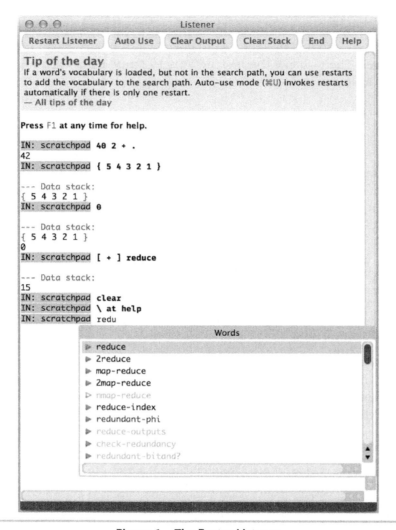

Figure 1—The Factor Listener

Enter the clear command to clear the stack, then just type "Hello, world" and press Enter:

```
IN: scratchpad clear
IN: scratchpad "Hello, world"

--- Data stack:
"Hello, world"
```

You now have "Hello, world" on the stack. You can even push another string onto the stack:

```
IN: scratchpad "Hello, Factor"

--- Data stack:
"Hello, world"
"Hello, Factor"
```

Now you have two values on the stack. Try entering the print word:

```
IN: scratchpad print
Hello, Factor

--- Data stack:
"Hello, world"
```

As you can see, print took the last value from the stack, "Hello, Factor", and printed it out. That leaves the previous value, "Hello, world", on the stack. Next, try typing length:

```
IN: scratchpad length

--- Data stack:
12
```

The length word took "Hello, world" from the stack and pushed the length of the string back onto the stack. Every word in Factor takes zero or more values from the stack and pushes zero or more values onto the stack. The next word then works with the resulting stack, and so on. When running a Factor program, the net effect of all the words assembled together should be consistent, with each word having at least as many values on the stack as they expect to pull out, and pushing out as many values as they claim to. When the stack contains more values than a word needs to use, the extra values simply remain on the stack.

One more tidbit of information before we move on: a comment in Factor code starts with ! followed by a space, and discards all input until the end of the line:

```
! This is a comment
"Hello, world" print ! this prints "Hello, world"
```

Let's continue with some simple math.

Factor Math

The words +, -, *, and / take two values from the stack and push the result back. The . word takes a value from the stack and pretty-prints it. Ending a line of code with . in the Listener is a convenient way of seeing results without accumulating values on the stack. Give it a try:

```
IN: scratchpad 40 2 + .
42
IN: scratchpad 40 2 - .
38
IN: scratchpad 20 9 * 5.0 / 32 + .
68.0
```

You can see that math in Factor uses the postfix notation. Here, you see the difference between calculating 20 + (5 * 4) and (20 + 5) * 4:

```
IN: scratchpad 5 4 * 20 + .
40
IN: scratchpad 20 5 + 4 * .
100
```

Words are called in the order that they appear, so it's just a matter of arranging the expression in the right order. You don't have to worry about operator precedence ambiguity.

Data Types

Factor uses standard data types such as strings, numbers, Booleans, and sequences. Let's have a closer look.

Booleans

Factor represents Boolean values with t and f. Let's see them in the Listener by trying out some Boolean tests with = and >:

```
IN: scratchpad 4 2 = .
f
IN: scratchpad 4 2 > .
t
IN: scratchpad "same" "same" = .
t
IN: scratchpad "same" length "diff" length = .
t
```

In Boolean contexts, any value other than f is considered as true, including zero, empty strings, and empty sequences.

Sequences

So far, we've been working with single values. Factor supports sequences of values as well, such as lists and maps.

You can create a list of values by delimiting them with { and }, with a space between each value, such as { 4 3 2 1 }. Don't forget the space after the { and before the }. As in Lisp, there are no comma separators, and no more errors due to a forgotten trailing comma.

Maps are key-value pairs, so you define them as such: a list of lists where each nested list contains two values, the key and the value. For example:

```
{ { "one" 1 } { "two" 2 } { "three" 3 } { "four" 4 } }
```

To look up a value from a map, provide the map and the key to the word of, or the key and the map to the at word:

```
IN: scratchpad { { "one" 1 } { "two" 2 } { "three" 3 } } "one" of .
1
IN: scratchpad "two" { { "one" 1 } { "two" 2 } { "three" 3 } } at .
2
```

Things are getting interesting. Let's look at quotations next.

Quotations

Words can be placed on the stack to be used by other words. Often known as anonymous functions in other languages, words that are used as values are called *quotations*. Quotation literals are delimited by square brackets:

```
[ 42 + ]
```

This defines a quotation that, when executed, adds 42 to the value that resides on top of the stack. You can then use call to execute the quotation. Try it out:

```
IN: scratchpad 20

--- Data stack:
20

IN: scratchpad [ 42 + ]

--- Data stack:
20
[ 42 + ]

IN: scratchpad call

--- Data stack:
62
```

Quotations are more interesting when used with conditionals.

Conditionals

Reminiscent of Io from the original *Seven Languages in Seven Weeks [Tat10]*, conditionals in Factor take quotations as arguments. The if word takes a value and two quotations and calls the first quotation if the value is anything but f (false). In the latter case, the second quotation is called:

> ## Don't Forget the Spaces!
>
> Factor uses less punctuation than most programming languages, but whitespace is
> significant. Each token in a line of Factor code is separated by one or more spaces—
> that can take some getting used to because you need spaces in places where they
> are not required in other languages.
>
> For example, { and } indicate the beginning and end of a sequence. Don't forget the
> surrounding spaces! If you write {1 2 3 4}, without a space after { and before }, Factor
> sees {1 and 4} as invalid tokens. Similarly, you need a space after the [and before
> the] when writing a quotation.
>
> In other cases, it's important *not* to use spaces. The math.ranges vocabulary has a [1,b]
> word that creates a range sequence from 1 to the value that's on the stack. [1,b] is
> just the name of the word; the []'s are not special syntax, the 1 is not a value, and
> the b is not a variable. You can't write 10 [5,b] and expect a range from 5 to 10. Instead,
> you'd write 5 10 [a,b], because [a,b] is the word to get a range using two values from
> the stack.

```
IN: scratchpad 10 0 > [ "pos" ] [ "neg" ] if .
"pos"
IN: scratchpad  -5 0 > [ "pos" ] [ "neg" ] if .
"neg"
IN: scratchpad  "cool" [ "yes" ] [ "no" ] if .
"yes"
```

As we have seen thus far, the arguments to a word belong before the word,
since they get placed on the stack for the word to consume. Looking at the
previous code, we can see how that can take some getting used to for the
venerable if. After seeing so much code in the form of

```
if <condition> <true branch> <false branch>
```

it can take a bit of brain rewiring to decipher

```
<condition> <true branch> <false branch> if
```

If all you need is to pick one of two values depending on a condition, it's more
concise to use ?, which accepts values instead of quotations:

```
IN: scratchpad 10 0 > "pos" "neg" ? .
"pos"

IN: scratchpad -5 0 > "pos" "neg" ? .
"neg"
```

Two siblings of if are when and unless. These are conditionals with no else clause:

```
IN: scratchpad 10 0 > [ "pos" . ] when
"pos"
```

```
IN: scratchpad -5 0 > [ "neg" . ] unless
"neg"
```

Let's press on to rearranging the values that are on the stack.

Stack Shuffling

Sometimes the values on the stack are not quite as you need them. They might be in reverse order, or you might want a value to remain on the stack after you have used it. *Shuffle words* reorder, duplicate, or eliminate values on the stack. Shuffle words include dup, drop, nip, swap, over, rot, and pick, and are best illustrated with examples. Observe what happens to the values on the stack after calling the stack shuffling word. Also note that the Listener prints the data stack in reverse order. The value that you see at the bottom of the output is actually the top of the stack. This might seem surprising, but it is meant to conveniently keep the objects that are going to be operated on closer to the input fields in the Listener.

```
IN: scratchpad 1 dup ! duplicates a value
--- Data stack:
1
1
IN: scratchpad clear

IN: scratchpad 1 2 drop ! drops the top value
--- Data stack:
1
IN: scratchpad clear

IN: scratchpad 1 2 nip ! drops the second value
--- Data stack:
2
IN: scratchpad clear

IN: scratchpad 1 2 swap ! swaps two values
--- Data stack:
2
1
IN: scratchpad clear

IN: scratchpad 1 2 over ! duplicates the second value over to the top
--- Data stack:
1
2
1
IN: scratchpad clear

IN: scratchpad 1 2 3 rot ! rotates three values
```

```
--- Data stack:
2
3
1
```

Wax on, wax off. Sometimes Mr. Miyagi's car needed wax, and sometimes Daniel-san needed to wax the car just to learn how to do it. So it is with the Factor stack. You sometimes need to shuffle the stack. Most of the time, however, you'll be using higher-order words—*combinators*—for an elegant solution to the problem of excessive stack shuffling.

Higher-Order Words with Combinators

Earlier, we used quotations to push snippets of code on to the stack. Combinators are related—they use quotations to operate on values from the stack.

In Quebec, Canada, we have a Goods and Services Tax (GST) of 5%, and a Provincial Sales Tax (PST) of 9.975%. (Don't ask.) Let's say we wanted to calculate the GST and PST for a base price. First, we want to multiply the base price by 0.05, but we need to dup the base price so that we keep it on the stack. Otherwise, we won't have the base price available for multiplying by 0.09975 to calculate the PST.

IN: scratchpad **44.50 dup 0.05 ***

```
--- Data stack:
44.5
2.225
```

We now have the base price and the GST on the stack. We need to swap the values so that we can multiply the base price by 0.09975 to calculate the PST:

IN: scratchpad **swap 0.09975 ***

```
--- Data stack:
2.225
4.438875
```

We have calculated the GST and PST, but we needed to do a bit of stack shuffling to get the desired result. Our line of code to calculate the taxes on a base price of 44.50 is:

IN: scratchpad **44.50 dup 0.05 * swap 0.09975 ***

```
--- Data stack:
2.225
4.438875
```

You can imagine how stack shuffling can quickly get out of hand and hurt your head as you try to keep track of what's on the stack.

Fortunately, Factor has several combinators that reduce or eliminate stack shuffling and make your code clearer. In the previous example, all we really wanted to do was to apply two operations on a value and get the two results. The word bi does exactly that. It takes a value and two quotations and applies each quotation to the value. Our tax calculation code becomes:

```
IN: scratchpad 44.50 [ 0.05 * ] [ 0.09975 * ] bi

--- Data stack:
2.225
4.438875
```

Much better. Factor has several words for applying quotations to values. Whereas bi applies two quotations to one value, bi@ applies one quotation to two values. We could use it to calculate the GST to two base prices:

```
IN: scratchpad 44.50 22.50 [ 0.05 * ] bi@

--- Data stack:
2.225
1.125
```

The other variant of bi is bi*, which takes two values and two quotations, applying the first quotation to the first value and the second quotation to the second value:

```
IN: scratchpad 44.50 22.50 [ 0.05 * ] [ 0.09975 * ] bi*

--- Data stack:
2.225
2.244375
```

Factor has several combinators for applying quotations to values:

- dip applies a quotation to the second value on the stack, keeping the first value intact.

- keep applies a quotation to a value and puts the value back on top of the stack.

- tri, tri@, and tri* correspond to their bi equivalents, with three values and three quotations.

Combinators are fundamental in Factor. It's worth looking them over in the Factor documentation.[4]

Well, that was a good first day spent taming the Factor stack. Let's recap and do a few exercises.

What We Learned in Day 1

We spent our first day discovering Factor's intriguing programming style. We discussed how Factor uses a stack to hold values from one word to the next. We learned about data types, math operators, sequences, and quotations. Finally, we concluded the day by talking about conditionals, stack-shuffling words, and the all-important combinators, which give Factor many crafty ways of manipulating the stack.

Your Turn

Use the Listener for today's exercises. After finding some key Factor reference points, fire up the Listener and use the exercises to get the hang of putting parameters before function calls, using the stack, and composing words by chaining them together. Time for some code karate training, Reader-san.

Find...

- The Factor GitHub repository, from which you can explore the source code.

- Factor's mailing list.

- The Factor Handbook, from which you can browse documentation for everything that comes with Factor.

- How to open the documentation for a specific word directly from the Listener. Use this to find the documentation for sq.

- How to run the command-line version of the Listener.

Do (Easy):

- Using only * and +, how would you calculate $3^2 + 4^2$ with Factor?

- Enter USE: math.functions in the Listener. Now, with sq and sqrt, calculate the square root of $3^2 + 4^2$.

- If you had the numbers 1 2 on the stack, what code could you use to end up with 1 1 2 on the stack?

---

4. http://docs.factorcode.org/content/article-combinators.html

- Enter USE: ascii in the Listener. Put your name on the stack, and write a line of code that puts "Hello, " in front of your name and converts the whole string to uppercase. Use the append word to concatenate two strings and >upper to convert to uppercase. Did you have to do any stack shuffling to get the desired result?

Do (Medium):

- The reduce word takes a sequence, an initial value, and a quotation and returns the result of applying the quotation to the initial value and the first element of the sequence, then the result of applying the quotation to the result and the next element of the sequence, and so on. Using reduce, write a line of code that returns the sum of the numbers 1, 4, 17, 9, 11. Try it out on your own first, but if you are truly stuck, look back carefully over the pages you've just read. There is a hint hiding somewhere.

- Now calculate the sum of the numbers 1 to 100 in a similar fashion. Do not manually write the sequence of numbers. Instead, enter USE: math.ranges in the Listener, and use the [1,b] word to produce the sequence.

- The map word takes a sequence and a quotation, and returns a sequence of results of applying the quotation to each value. Using map and the words that you have learned so far, write a line of code that returns the squares of the numbers 1 to 10.

Do (Hard):

- Write a line of code that, given a number between 1 and 99, returns the two digits in the number. That is, given 42 <your code>, you should get 4 and 2 on the stack. Use the words /i, mod, and bi to accomplish the task.

- Repeat the previous exercise for any number of digits. Use a different strategy, though: first convert the number to a string, then iterate over each character, converting each character back to a string and then to a number. Enter USE: math.parser in the Listener and use number>string, string>number, 1string, and each.

Day 2: Painting the Fence

Today, we will move our exploration of Factor from the Listener to source files. We'll learn how to define words, organize them into modules called *vocabularies*, run them as standalone programs, and test them with unit tests.

Defining Words

We've been using Factor words that are defined in the library. Let's see how we can define our own words. A word definition starts with a colon, a space, and the name of the word. Then comes the *stack effect*, the code for the word, and finally a space and a semicolon. For example:

```
: add-42 ( x -- y ) 42 + ;
```

That defines a word which adds 42 to the number that's on the stack. The (x -- y) part is the stack effect: the number of values that the word takes from the stack and pushes back onto the stack, on the left and right side of the --, respectively. You can see examples of stack effects by typing a word in the Listener and looking at the declaration appear at the bottom of the window. Try typing +, you should see the following show up:

```
IN: math MATH: + ( x y -- z )
```

The stack effect of + shows that it takes two values from the stack and pushes one value back. Words are allowed to take no value from the stack or push no value back. For example, try looking at the stack effect for print and read1.

When you look at the stack effect for a word, notice that the symbols such as x and y are not variable names; they are not used in the code for the word. Instead, they are just symbols, indicating the number of values. Although the names are arbitrary, there are some naming conventions for the stack effect, such as str, obj, seq, elt, and so on, to make the definition more descriptive.

Here is a word that takes a sequence of numbers and returns their sum:

```
: sum ( seq -- n ) 0 [ + ] reduce ;
```

I'll say it again: don't forget the spaces! You need spaces after the colon, around the parentheses, around the double-dash, and before the semicolon. Forgetting those spaces is an easy mistake to make when coming to Factor from another programming language.

Returning Multiple Values

We've seen words that use multiple values from the stack, but what about returning more than one value? In most languages, this cannot be done without artificially returning multiple values by stuffing them into a single collection. The caller must then unpack the collection to get the multiple values back.

Not so in Factor:

```
IN: scratchpad : first-two ( seq -- a b ) [ first ] [ second ] bi ;
IN: scratchpad { 34 32 64 19 } first-two

--- Data stack:
34
32
```

Simply by declaring multiple names on the right-hand side of -- in the word's stack effect, we can write words that return multiple, individual values.

Getting Help

Before moving on to vocabularies, I'll mention another useful bit of information about Factor words. Within the Listener, you can quickly get to the documentation for a word. Type a backslash, a space, followed by the word and finally help:

```
IN: scratchpad \ at help
```

This opens the help browser for the at word, as shown in Figure 2, *The Factor help browser*, on page 64.

Other commands you can use in the Listener to get help are about and apropos. For example:

- "sequences" about : documentation for the sequences vocabulary
- "json" apropos : show vocabularies, words, and articles that contain json

The online help is a tremendous resource for discovering the words within the Factor libraries. Now that we can also define our own words, let's see how we organize them into vocabularies.

Working with Vocabularies

Words are organized into vocabularies. Think packages, modules, or namespaces. When you typed a word such as print in the Listener, the following appeared at the bottom of the window:

```
IN: io : print ( str -- )
```

The vocabulary in which the word is defined appears after IN:. So print belongs to the io vocabulary.

For convenience, the Listener automatically loads a number of vocabularies. You can get a list of the 50 or so vocabularies that are initially loaded in the Listener by typing interactive-vocabs get [print] each.

Figure 2—The Factor help browser

If you type a word that belongs to a vocabulary that the Listener does not load by default, you'll get an error message. For example:

```
IN: scratchpad 4.2 present
No word named "present" found in current vocabulary search path
```

You can load a vocabulary with USE: as follows:

```
IN: scratchpad USE: present
IN: scratchpad 4.2 present

--- Data stack:
"4.2"
```

After loading the present vocabulary, we were able to use the present word. To load multiple vocabularies, either repeat USE: for each vocabulary, or write USING: followed by the list of vocabularies to load and ending with a semicolon:

```
USE: io
USE: math.functions

USING: io math.functions ;
```

Those two ways of loading vocabularies are equivalent.

Within a vocabulary, you can define a *symbol* with SYMBOL: and use it to stash a value with set. You can later retrieve the value with get. For example:

```
IN: scratchpad SYMBOL: tax-rate
IN: scratchpad 0.05 tax-rate set
IN: scratchpad tax-rate get

--- Data stack:
0.05
```

You can also use on, off, and toggle for a symbol that holds a Boolean value:

```
IN: scratchpad SYMBOL: flag
IN: scratchpad flag on
IN: scratchpad flag get .
t
IN: scratchpad flag off
IN: scratchpad flag get .
f
IN: scratchpad flag toggle
IN: scratchpad flag get .
t
```

For an integer value, use inc and dec:

```
IN: scratchpad SYMBOL: counter
IN: scratchpad counter inc
IN: scratchpad counter get .
1
IN: scratchpad counter dec
IN: scratchpad counter get .
0
```

Symbols are a convenient way to store values and communicate them between vocabularies.

Let's march on to creating vocabularies in source files and using them in standalone programs.

Running Standalone Programs

We'll now create a simple vocabulary and use it in a standalone program. Start from an empty factor directory and create an examples subdirectory. Within examples, create two more subdirectories: greeter and hello. Finally, create

a greeter.factor and a hello.factor file within those subdirectories so that you end
up with the following structure:

```
factor
`-- examples
    |-- greeter
    |   `-- greeter.factor
    `-- hello
        `-- hello.factor
```

We'll start by creating the greeter vocabulary. Add the following to greeter.factor.

factor/examples/greeter/greeter.factor
```
IN: examples.greeter

: greeting ( name -- greeting ) "Hello, " swap append ;
```

IN: declares this as the examples.greeter vocabulary. Note the file path under
factor, which is examples/greeter. That needs to match the vocabulary name.

Next, we've defined a greeting word that takes a name and returns a greeting.
Let's use this in another vocabulary, examples.hello, which we will then run as
a standalone program. Create the hello.factor file as follows:

factor/examples/hello/hello.factor
```
USE: examples.greeter
IN: examples.hello

: hello-world ( -- ) "world" greeting print ;

MAIN: hello-world
```

We've declared that we want to use our examples.greeter vocabulary and that
we are defining the examples.hello vocabulary. Then, we created a word that
uses the greeting word to print out a greeting. Finally, we used MAIN: to indicate
what word to call when running this file as a standalone program. Note that
the stack effect of the word called by MAIN: must be (--).

Now try running the program from the command line by typing factor factor/exam-
ples/hello/hello.factor:

```
$ factor factor/examples/hello/hello.factor
factor/examples/hello/hello.factor

7: USE: examples.greeter
                   ^
Vocabulary does not exist
name "examples.greeter"
(U) Quotation: [ c-to-factor -> ]
...(rest of output omitted for brevity)...
```

Beware of the Conflicting factor Utility

If you are using a Linux/Unix-based system and factor does not work as expected, it may be because of a conflict with the built-in utility for printing prime factors.[a] To resolve the conflict, set your PATH environment variable so that the path to the factor executable for the Factor language is ahead of the path to the built-in factor utility.

---

a.   http://linux.die.net/man/1/factor

Factor did not find our examples.greeter vocabulary. We need to indicate the root paths from which Factor will search for vocabularies. You can do this by creating a .factor-roots file in your home directory and indicating the full paths to the root directories where you have your Factor source files, one path per line. For example, here is my .factor-roots file:

```
/home/freddy/svn/prag/7lang/Book/code/factor
```

You also have another option. You can use an environment variable named FACTOR_ROOTS and set to the list of paths, separated by : if you're on Linux or Mac, or separated by ; if you're on Windows.

After setting up your Factor roots configuration, try running factor factor/examples/hello/hello.factor again:

```
factor/examples/hello/hello.factor

7: USE: examples.greeter
                 ^
/home/freddy/svn/prag/7lang/Book/code/factor/examples/greeter/greeter.factor

6: : greeting ( name -- greeting ) "Hello, " swap append ;
                                                   ^
No word named "swap" found in current vocabulary search path
(U) Quotation: [ c-to-factor -> ]
...(rest of output omitted for brevity)...
```

What? Using swap worked fine in the Listener, but here it crashes and burns. That's because standalone code does not automatically include vocabularies the way that the Listener does. We need to load the kernel vocabulary to use swap, and we also need sequences to use append. Here is the full greeter.factor file:

factor/examples/greeter/greeter.factor
```
USING: kernel sequences ;
IN: examples.greeter

: greeting ( name -- greeting ) "Hello, " swap append ;
```

Similarly, we need to load the io vocabulary to use print in hello.factor:

```
factor/examples/hello/hello.factor
USE: io
USE: examples.greeter
IN: examples.hello

: hello-world ( -- ) "world" greeting print ;

MAIN: hello-world
```

Paint the fence. Up, down. In standalone programs, we need to be explicit in loading all the vocabularies that we wish to use. Now, running factor hello.factor gives us the expected result of printing "Hello, world".

Writing Unit Tests

Exploring code in the Listener is nice. However, when you close the Listener, your code is gone. So we saw how to write and run Factor code in source files. Verifying that the code gives the correct results, though, is a manual process. Let's learn how to automate the process with unit tests.

Unit tests not only confirm that your code is working, but they are also a great way to experiment with a language. You run your tests to verify that the results match what you expect while you are learning the language. You also get to keep all of your code in source files, and run all your tests again at any time to make sure everything still works. Now that we know how to run code standalone, let's write some unit tests.

The Factor library includes a tools.test vocabulary with a unit-test word. To run a test, you call unit-test with two values on the stack: a sequence of values that represents the stack that you expect, and a quotation that contains the code that you want to test. If running the code produces values on the stack that match up with the expected sequence, the test passes. For example, here is a simple unit test for our greeting word:

```
factor/examples/greeter/greeter-tests.factor
USING: examples.greeter tools.test ;
IN: examples.greeter.tests

{ "Hello, Test" } [ "Test" greeting ] unit-test
```

Try running the code from the command line just like a standalone program:

```
$ factor factor/examples/greeter/greeter-tests.factor
Unit Test: { { "Hello, Test" } [ "Test" greeting ] }
```

When running unit tests, errors are shown when the actual result does not match the expected output. When running this test:

```
factor/examples/test/failing-unit-test.factor
USING: examples.greeter tools.test ;
IN: examples.failing-unit-test

{ "Hello World" } [ "world" greeting ] unit-test
```

we get:

```
$ factor factor/examples/test/failing-unit-test.factor
Unit Test: { { "Hello World" } [ "world" greeting ] }
=== Expected:
"Hello World"
=== Got:
"Hello, world"
(U) Quotation: [ c-to-factor -> ]
...(rest of output omitted for brevity)...
```

The output shows the expected and actual outputs for the unit test that failed.

Remember that each test consists of a sequence containing the values that we expect to be on the stack, followed by a quotation of the code we are trying out, and ending with the unit-test word.

Next, let's see how we can write unit tests that match up with the vocabularies that we create, and how to run a whole suite of tests with a single command.

Running a Test Suite

Remember how we defined an examples.greeter vocabulary in the examples/greeter/greeter.factor file. To write corresponding tests for our vocabulary, we used the examples/greeter/greeter-tests.factor file. Following this convention makes it easy to run all unit tests defined in examples.* vocabularies with a test suite, as follows:

```
factor/examples/test-suite/test-suite.factor
USING: tools.test io io.streams.null kernel namespaces sequences ;
```

❶ USE: examples.greeter

```
IN: examples.test-suite
```

```
: test-all-examples ( -- )
```
❷ `    [ "examples" test ] with-null-writer`
❸ `    test-failures get empty?`
❹ `    [ "All tests passed." print ] [ :test-failures ] if ;`

```
MAIN: test-all-examples
```

Let's break that down.

❶ After importing the vocabularies that we need with USING:, we import the vocabulary that we are testing, examples.greeter with USE:. We could have included examples.greeter on the USING: line, but importing it separately makes our intent clearer and makes it cleaner to add more examples.* vocabularies to test, one per line.

❷ Simply calling "examples" test runs all tests for all loaded vocabularies that start with examples. However, the output shows the code for all the unit tests, whether passing or failing, making it somewhat difficult to see the tests results at a glance. By using with-null-writer, we are suppressing that output.

❸ After running the tests, the test-failures symbol contains a list of failures. We retrieve the list with get, and verify whether it contains any values with empty?.

❹ Depending on whether the list of failures is empty, we either print the "All tests passed" message to the output, or call the :test-failures word, which prints out the test failures.

Now, we can run our unit tests:

```
$ factor factor/examples/test-suite/test-suite.factor
All tests passed.
```

When we create another vocabulary, we can simply add a USE: line to test-suite.factor to include its unit tests in the test suite.

Excellent. This is a good stopping point for today. Now, let's hear from Slava Pestov, creator of Factor. He has some interesting thoughts on his journey.

An Interview with Slava Pestov, Creator of Factor

Us: *Why did you write Factor?*

Slava: *Factor was originally a scripting language for a 2D game I built with a friend in college, back in 2003. We never got very far with the game itself, but it was enough to flesh out the basics of the language and have something to apply them to.*

The scripts I wanted to write here would consist of lists of strings, and not code. I didn't realize it at the time, but I wanted something with homoiconic syntax. There were a few other scripting languages for Java at the time, such as Groovy, and even a Common Lisp implementation (ABCL), which had fancier syntax for these things. I decided to write my own language, though, because I wanted something really simple, and also just because it would be fun.

I picked postfix syntax on a whim. At the time, I had heard of Forth but didn't know much about it. Then I came across Joy, a language by Manfred von Thun which incorporated elements of Forth and Lisp by replacing Forth's control structures with higher order functions that took code blocks as parameters. A code block in Joy is just a list literal. It was very elegant, and I managed to implement something similar in a few hundred lines of Java code.

Factor was more like Joy than Forth in the early days. In particular, the lexical syntax was fixed, with no "parsing words." It wasn't until I started working on the native implementation of Factor that I took the time to properly learn Forth. At this point I had another epiphany and realized that most of the actual parser can be scrapped, and syntax elements such as "[" and "]" can become ordinary words (functions) in the language.

Eventually I cleaned the code up and split it off from the game engine and released Factor to the concatenative mailing list.

Us: *Why did you decide to move Factor away from the JVM?*

Slava: *I wanted to experiment with an image-based runtime and a self-hosting parser written in Factor, which was not really possible on the JVM. Also, once again with the learning experience aspect, I wanted to learn enough to implement the minimal possible VM instead of relying on something else.*

While working on the Java implementation I had already figured out that over time, I can replace primitives with Factor definitions making use of lower-level primitives, and simplify the design that way. Before starting work on the C implementation, I tried to really limit the scope of what would be written in C. I wrote a simple C interpreter that read an image file containing a heap dump. At the same time, I wrote a Factor parser in Factor which would read source code and output it in the form of this image file. I ran this parser in the Java implementation, and used it to generate image files for testing the C implementation. It was a while before the C implementation could itself run the parser. I was learning C at the same time, and even a simple copying garbage collector is quite tricky the first time you do it!

Once the C implementation was good enough to bootstrap itself, I stopped working on the Java port. The initial version of the C VM was only something like 7,000 lines of C, with the rest in Factor. There was something very satisfying about being able to do so much with so little "real" code. Compilation to native x86 code came very soon after. Writing a JIT in C is actually really simple. You allocate some memory with the right protection bits, write some machine code there, and cast it to a function pointer. Optimizations are the hard part...

Us: *What do you like the most about Factor?*

Slava: *I enjoyed working in an interactive development environment. From the start the goal of Factor was to enable quick experimentation with fast turnaround for testing changes, so I took care to structure the system so that almost any type of change to the source code could be reflected in the running program without* *having to restart. Smalltalk and Lisp environments were a big inspiration for me in this regard.*

There is something very hypnotizing about concatenative syntax. Once you learn to think in it without mentally translating back and forth, certain refactorings that can be hard to envision in an applicative language become simple sequences of copy/paste operations. I beseech every programmer to read the Joy papers, even if you have no interest in using a concatenative language, just to learn about the combinators that abstract over many common recursion and iteration patterns in a novel way.

With Factor, often when you first write some code it looks very haphazard and messy. Then you think about it really hard, whip it into shape, come up with some new abstractions, and maybe even also apply them to a previously written library or two. It can feel like a lot of work but in the end what you're producing feels more like a general set of tools, rather than a single piece of code. To a large extent, concatenative languages were uncharted territory. By encouraging contributors to submit code to the main repository, Factor really pushed the bar in terms of what could be done with concatenative languages, by facilitating the development of new idioms and abstractions.

Finally, the best parts of working on Factor were the simple joy of learning about language design, compilers, and operating systems, and collaborating with all of the extremely talented contributors.

What We Learned in Day 2

Today was about taking our Factor code to the next level, from the experimental ground of the Listener to a more durable form, source files. We saw how to run the code as a standalone program. We spent the rest of the day learning how to write unit tests and running a complete test suite from the command line.

Your Turn

You can always use the Listener for feeling your way around with Factor code, but ultimately the goal in today's exercises is to write code in source files.

Find...

- A third way of adding directories to the list of vocabulary roots. Remember that the two ways we discussed were the .factor-roots file and the FACTOR_ROOTS environment variable.

- The tool that Factor provides to deploy a program as a truly standalone application, meaning that the executable can be run without Factor being installed on the target machine.

Do (Easy):

- Create an examples.strings vocabulary and write a word named palindrome? that takes a string from the stack and returns t or f according to whether or not the word is a palindrome (a word that is spelled the same frontward and backward, such as *racecar*).

- In the appropriate vocabulary for associating tests with the examples.strings vocabulary, write two unit tests for palindrome?, one that expects t and one that expects f.

- Add the examples.strings to the test suite so that its tests are included when running test-suite.factor.

Do (Medium):

- Create an examples.sequences vocabulary and write a find-first word that takes a sequence of elements and a predicate, and returns the first element for which the predicate returns true. Write a corresponding unit test that confirms its behavior. What happens if none of the elements satisfy the predicate?

- In an examples.numberguess vocabulary, write a standalone program that picks a random number from 1 to 100 and asks the user to guess, printing out "Higher", "Lower", or "Winner" accordingly.

Do (Hard):

- Enhance the test-suite.factor program so that it prints out how many tests have run, and in case of failures, how many tests failed.

- Make test-suite.factor interactive by turning it into a command-line program that asks the user which vocabularies to test via the console, then runs the tests and outputs the results.

Day 3: Balancing on a Boat

On our third and final day of Factor, we will focus on data structures called *tuples*, and use them to create a flexible cart checkout application. We'll see more of Factor's sweet spot—function composition in the concatenative style—both in the checkout example and in a revisitation of the classic "FizzBuzz" programming quiz. We'll wrap up the chapter with a few places to look to continue your exploration of Factor.

Tuples

Factor has an object system, and tuples are classes of objects for storing values into named slots. To define a class, use TUPLE: followed by the class name and the names of the slots:

```
factor/examples/tuples/tuples.factor
USE: kernel

IN: examples.tuples

➤ TUPLE: cart-item name price quantity ;
```

This defines a cart-item class with a name, a price, and a quantity. The cart-item word represents the class, and an instance of the class can be created by passing the class word to new:

```
factor/examples/tuples/tuples-tests.factor
cart-item new
```

That creates a cart-item instance with empty slots. We can read and write values to slots using words that Factor automatically generates for us when we create a tuple with the TUPLE: declaration. These words are named slotname>>, >>slot-name, and change-slotname for every slot name in the tuple. For example, we can read and write the price slot as follows:

- price>> reads the value from the price slot.
- >>price sets a value to the price slot.
- change-price changes the value of the price slot using a quotation.

All three words operate on an instance of the cart-item class. Here are the first two in action:

```
factor/examples/tuples/tuples-tests.factor
cart-item new 4.95 >>price
cart-item new 4.95 >>price price>>
```

The first line creates an instance of cart-item and sets its price to 4.95, leaving the populated cart-item instance on the stack. On the second line, we have the same code but we then call price>> on the instance. That would put 4.95 onto the stack.

The change-price word is useful for setting a new value based on the previous value. Without change-price, discounting the price of a cart-item by 50% is tedious:

```
factor/examples/tuples/tuples-tests.factor
cart-item new 25.00 >>price
➤ dup price>> 0.5 * >>price
```

We have to make a copy of the cart-item, get the price out, multiply by 0.5, and set the result back into the cart-item instance.

Using the change-price word makes this easier. A quotation contains the code that changes the price:

```
factor/examples/tuples/tuples-tests.factor
cart-item new 25.00 >>price
[ 0.5 * ] change-price
```

Nice! That is much simpler and clearly expresses our intent.

The convenience doesn't end there. Factor also has a few helpers for constructing instances of tuples.

Tuple Constructors

To create an instance of a class by specifying values for slots in the same order as they appear in the TUPLE: declaration, we use the, um, suffocatingly named *boa constructor*. The word boa stands for *By Order of Arguments* and is used like this:

```
factor/examples/tuples/tuples-tests.factor
"Seven Languages Book" 25.00 1 cart-item boa
```

That creates a fully populated cart-item instance.

While boa requires values for all slots to be on the stack, you can still define a word that passes some values to boa and lets the caller specify the remaining values. This is a convenient way of defining a constructor with default values for some of the slots:

```
factor/examples/tuples/tuples.factor
: <dollar-cart-item> ( name -- cart-item ) 1.00 1 cart-item boa ;
```

We defined a <dollar-cart-item> word that takes a name and creates a cart-item instance with a price of 1.00 and a quantity of 1. Creating a cart-item with those defaults becomes:

```
factor/examples/tuples/tuples-tests.factor
"Paint brush" <dollar-cart-item>
```

Note that the <>'s in the word name are not special syntax. They are just a convention for constructor words.

Another syntax for creating tuples is T{ }. You indicate the tuple class, followed by key-value pairs for the slots. For example:

```
factor/examples/tuples/tuples.factor
: <one-cart-item> ( -- cart-item ) T{ cart-item { quantity 1 } } ;
```

Calling <one-cart-item> returns a cart-item with its quantity set to 1 and its other slots left empty. The other way to use T{ } is to specify f (false) after the tuple class, to indicate that we are not using key-value pairs, and instead specify slot values in order:

factor/examples/tuples/tuples-tests.factor
```
T{ cart-item f "orange" 0.59 }
```

That gives us a cart-item with name set to "orange" and a price of 0.59, with the quantity left empty. Unlike boa, using the T{ } syntax this way does not require specifying values for all slots.

Now that we can define and instantiate tuples, let's use them to create words that process a cart for checkout.

Processing a Cart for Checkout

We'll begin with a tuple to represent a checkout:

factor/examples/checkout/checkout.factor
```
TUPLE: checkout item-count base-price taxes shipping total-price ;
```

We've included the item count, base price, taxes, cost of shipping, and total price for the checkout.

Our first task is to define a word that takes a cart—a sequence of cart-items—and returns a checkout containing the item count and base price. We'll start with some words for processing a cart to calculate the item count and base price:

factor/examples/checkout/checkout.factor
```
❶ : sum ( seq -- n ) 0 [ + ] reduce ;
❷ : cart-item-count ( cart -- count ) [ quantity>> ] map sum ;
❸ : cart-item-price ( cart-item -- price ) [ price>> ] [ quantity>> ] bi * ;
❹ : cart-base-price ( cart -- price ) [ cart-item-price ] map sum ;
```

❶ The sum word returns the sum of a sequence of values. You may remember 0 [+] reduce from one of the Day 1 exercises.

❷ To calculate the item count for a cart, we can simply map quantity>> over each cart-item to extract a sequence of quantities, and then call sum on that to get the item count.

❸ The price of a single item in the cart is its price multiplied by its quantity. We are using bi, which applies two quotations to a single value, to extract both the price and the quantity from the cart item before multiplying them together.

❹ Mapping cart-item-price over the sequence of cart items, we extract the sequence of prices and sum them up to calculate the base price for the cart.

Next, we'll create a checkout instance from a cart:

factor/examples/checkout/checkout.factor
```
❶ : <base-checkout> ( item-count base-price -- checkout )
    f f f checkout boa ;

❷ : <checkout> ( cart -- checkout )
    [ cart-item-count ] [ cart-base-price ] bi <base-checkout> ;
```

❶ We've defined a word to create a base checkout instance with the item-count and base-price. We're using boa, so we need to specify values for the other slots: taxes, shipping, and total-price. We're filling those slots with f to indicate an empty value.

❷ Using the words that we've defined so far, we can elegantly define a word to accept a cart and return a checkout with the item count and base price. We use bi to call both cart-item-count and cart-base-price, and pass both values on to <base-checkout>.

We now have a basis for calculating the taxes, shipping, and total price.

Assembling Words into Pipelines

Function composition really shines in Factor. Let's assemble a pipeline of words to calculate the additional costs and total price on our base checkout instance.

We'll use the Quebec, Canada tax rates that we used in an earlier example: the GST is 5% and the PST is 9.9975%.

factor/examples/checkout/checkout.factor
```
CONSTANT: gst-rate 0.05
CONSTANT: pst-rate 0.09975

: gst-pst ( price -- taxes ) [ gst-rate * ] [ pst-rate * ] bi + ;

: taxes ( checkout taxes-calc -- taxes )
    [ dup base-price>> ] dip
    call >>taxes ; inline
```

We've written a gst-pst word that calculates the total taxes on a base price by adding the GST and PST, using the constants defined for their respective rates. Then, we have a taxes word to calculate the taxes on a checkout instance. The kicker for the taxes word is that it accepts a tax calculation *as a parameter.*

Whatever you want to call it—a higher-order word, an example of the strategy pattern—either way, it is very cool.

Another nice benefit of the stack is that when you're chaining words together, a word can use a value returned by another word further up the chain, even if there are other words in between. The words in between do not need to carry along the value to make it available to the next word.

First, the taxes word extracts the base-price from the checkout instance, taking care of making a copy with dup so that we still have the checkout on the stack after getting the value out. The code is in a quotation and called with dip so that it operates on the checkout even though we have taxes-calc at the top of the stack.

Once that's done, we're left with checkout, base-price, and taxes-calc. With call, we invoke taxes-calc, which uses base-price to calculate the taxes. We then call >>taxes to store the result back into the checkout.

Finally, notice that the word definition has inline after the semicolon. The Factor optimizing compiler copies definitions of inline words when compiling calls to them, but what we really need to know is that words such as taxes that use quotations as parameters—that is, combinators—must have inline after the semicolon.

All right. Now that we have defined how to calculate the taxes, let's do the same for shipping. The code will look familiar by now:

factor/examples/checkout/checkout.factor
```
CONSTANT: base-shipping 1.49
CONSTANT: per-item-shipping 1.00

: per-item ( checkout -- shipping ) per-item-shipping * base-shipping + ;

: shipping ( checkout shipping-calc -- shipping )
    [ dup item-count>> ] dip
    call >>shipping ; inline
```

Similarly to how we calculated the taxes, we determine the shipping costs using a base charge and a charge per item.

We now have everything we need to calculate the total price of a checkout instance:

factor/examples/checkout/checkout.factor
```
: total ( checkout -- total-price ) dup
    [ base-price>> ] [ taxes>> ] [ shipping>> ] tri + + >>total-price ;
```

We simply call the three words for getting the base price, taxes, and shipping; add them up; and store the result into the checkout instance's total-price slot.

Notice how easy it is to assemble words into pipelines. The implied function composition and automatic use of the stack means that our code reads beautifully. There is very little noise because we don't need any punctuation to assemble words or variable names to transport values from one word to the next.

We've also made taxes and shipping flexible enough that they accept the calculations as parameters, making it a cinch to use different pricing schemes. Here's an example using gst-pst for the taxes and per-item for shipping:

factor/examples/checkout/checkout.factor
```
: sample-checkout ( checkout -- checkout )
    [ gst-pst ] taxes [ per-item ] shipping total ;
```

Very nice. We've assembled the words into a pipeline and the code clearly expresses our intent: use the GST-PST for the taxes, the per-item pricing for shipping, and finally calculate the total.

Let's write a unit test to make sure that it works:

factor/examples/checkout/checkout-tests.factor
```
: <sample-cart> ( -- cart )
    "7lang2" 24.99 2 <cart-item> "noderw" 10.99 1 <cart-item> 2array ;

{ T{ checkout f 3 60.97 9.13 4.49 74.59 } }
[ <sample-cart> <checkout> sample-checkout ]
unit-test
```

When we run the test, we get:

```
$ factor factor/examples/checkout/checkout-tests.factor

=== Expected:
T{ checkout f 3 60.97 9.130000000000001 4.49 74.59 }
=== Got:
T{ checkout f 3 60.97 9.130257500000001 4.49 74.59025750000001...
[Traceback]
```

Hmm. The test didn't pass because of floating-point rounding issues. We can see that the values are close, but we would need to adjust the rounding in order for the values to match and for the test to pass. That will be one of your challenges at the end of the day.

Revisiting Fizz Buzz

Mr. Miyagi asked Daniel-san to wax his car, sand his floors, and paint his house. Daniel wondered what any of that had to do with learning karate.

By the time he was done, Daniel-san had learned a lot more than he realized.

When I first came across the Fizz Buzz quiz, it was not during a job interview.[5] It was used to demonstrate different ways of solving a problem. The goal with Fizz Buzz is simply to loop through the numbers 1 to 100, printing out the number except when:

- the number is a multiple of 3, print "Fizz"
- the number is a multiple of 5, print "Buzz"
- the number is a multiple of 15, print "FizzBuzz"

My initial reaction was that the proposed alternatives were overkill compared to a simple if else. It may have been the case just for solving Fizz Buzz, but that wasn't the point. The idea was to learn powerful solutions for breaking down large, complex problems into smaller, more manageable pieces. Fizz Buzz was used for demonstration purposes.

A Traditional, JavaScript Solution

factor/examples/fizzbuzz/fizzbuzz.js

```javascript
var fizzbuzz = function(t) {
  var results = [];

  for (var i = 1; i <= t; i++) {
    if (i % 15 == 0) {
      results.push("FizzBuzz");
    }
    else if (i % 3 == 0) {
      results.push("Fizz");
    }
    else if (i % 5 == 0) {
      results.push("Buzz");
    }
    else {
      results.push(String(i));
    }
  }
  return results;
};

console.log(fizzbuzz(100)); // prints ["1", "2", "Fizz", "4", "Buzz", ...]
```

---

5. http://imranontech.com/2007/01/24/using-fizzbuzz-to-find-developers-who-grok-coding/

The only detail to watch for is checking for multiples of 15 first. If we check for multiples of 3, 5, and 15 in order, the branch for multiples of 15 would never be reached since those numbers are also multiples of 3 and 5.

In Factor, we can write code that does the same as the pseudocode earlier. Nothing is conventional about Mr. Miyagi, though, so the code looks different:

factor/examples/fizzbuzz/fizzbuzz.factor
```
dup 15 mod 0 =
[ drop "FizzBuzz" ]
[
  ! ...
]
if
```

That is the outer if branch checking for a multiple of 15. We need to dup the value beforehand so that it is still available for other branches, because the value gets consumed when we call 15 mod. If the value is a multiple of 15, we drop it and return "FizzBuzz". Otherwise, nested similar if branches for multiples of 3 and multiples of 5 will be called, with a final else calling present to return the value itself as a string.

Putting it all together, we have the following:

factor/examples/fizzbuzz/fizzbuzz.factor
```
USING: kernel io combinators.short-circuit math math.functions math.ranges
    present sequences ;

IN: examples.fizzbuzz

  : fizzbuzz-traditional ( n -- seq )
❶     [1,b] [
        dup 15 mod 0 =
        [ drop "FizzBuzz" ]
        [
❷         dup 3 mod 0 =
          [ drop "Fizz" ]
          [
❸           dup 5 mod 0 =
            [ drop "Buzz" ]
❹           [ present ]
            if
          ]
          if
        ]
        if
❺     ] map ;
```

❶ ❺ [1,b] produces a range of values and map executes the code for each value.

❷ ❸ Just like we checked for multiples of 15, these branches check for multiples of 3 or 5, returning "Fizz" or "Buzz".

❹ If the value is not a multiple, we use present to return the value itself as a string.

Let's write a unit test to verify that it works:

factor/examples/fizzbuzz/fizzbuzz-tests.factor
```
USING: examples.fizzbuzz tools.test ;

IN: examples.fizzbuzz.tests

CONSTANT: fizzbuzz-30 {
    { "1" "2" "Fizz" "4" "Buzz" "Fizz" "7" "8" "Fizz" "Buzz" "11" "Fizz" "13" "14"
    "FizzBuzz" "16" "17" "Fizz" "19" "Buzz" "Fizz" "22" "23" "Fizz" "Buzz" "26"
    "Fizz" "28" "29" "FizzBuzz" }
}

fizzbuzz-30 [ 30 fizzbuzz-traditional ] unit-test
```

Try adding examples.fizzbuzz to the test-suite.factor program and running it to confirm that the code works as expected.

That's simple enough, but the code is trapped in a tangled mess of if/else clauses. We can do better by breaking up the problem into individual words and composing a solution by assembling the words into a pipeline.

A Functional Pipeline Solution

Let's look at the code first and then break it down:

factor/examples/fizzbuzz/fizzbuzz.factor
```
❶ : mult? ( x/str n -- ? ) over number? [ mod 0 = ] [ 2drop f ] if ;

❷ : when-mult ( x/str n str -- x/str ) pick [ mult? ] 2dip ? ;

❸ : fizz     ( x/str -- x/str )  3 "Fizz"     when-mult ;
  : buzz     ( x/str -- x/str )  5 "Buzz"     when-mult ;
  : fizzbuzz ( x/str -- x/str ) 15 "FizzBuzz" when-mult ;

❹ : fizzbuzz-pipeline ( x -- str ) fizzbuzz fizz buzz present ;

❺ : fizzbuzz-with-pipeline ( n -- seq ) [1,b] [ fizzbuzz-pipeline ] map ;
```

❶ The mult? word determines if x is a multiple of n, first checking whether x is a number. This is because x might be a string when we chain together the FizzBuzz components and one of them decided to return a string. We're using x/str to indicate that x could be a string. If x is not a number, we just drop both values and return false.

❷ when-mult returns str if x/str is a multiple of n, returning x/str otherwise. After calling pick, we have x/str n str x/str on the stack. Using 2dip, we call [mult?] on x/str n. From that, we get t/f str x/str with t/f representing whether the number is a multiple. Finally, we use ? to return str or x/str according to the value of t/f.

❸ That was somewhat bumpy, but from here on out it's a smooth ride. We can neatly express the intent of fizz, buzz, and fizzbuzz in terms of the multiple to look for and the string to return when the value is a multiple.

❹ The pipeline is even more elegant. It's just a combination of what we are looking for, in order of priority: fizzbuzz, fizz, buzz, and lastly present to return the value as a string when none of the multiples match.

❺ The top-level word takes a value n and returns the FizzBuzz sequence from 1 to n, using [1,b] to create the range and map to map fizzbuzz-pipeline over the range and return the results.

We solved the FizzBuzz quiz with a pipeline of words, neatly lined up and divinely devoid of extraneous syntax. That is the beauty of Factor.

Let's finish the day with a bit of *where to go from here* if you'd like to dive even deeper into Factor.

Comes With Everything You See Here

Factor comes with batteries included. Factor is to stack-based, concatenative programming what Clojure is to Lisp: a practical, modern, full-featured implementation of a classic and powerful programming model.

You can quickly get a list of the Factor vocabularies that are loaded within the Listener. But hold on to your hat—there are over 900 of them.

```
IN: scratchpad vocabs [ . ] each
"accessors"
"alien"
"alien.accessors"
...
"alien.remote-control"
"alien.strings"
"alien.syntax"
"arrays"
"ascii"
...(rest of output omitted for brevity)...
```

The Factor repository contains many more vocabularies:

```
IN: scratchpad all-vocab-names length .
2501
```

Still in the Listener, you can click the Help button to open the documentation browser. From there, you can access a wealth of information on the Factor language, development tools, libraries, and more. If you click on *Factor handbook*, you'll get more interesting links to discover. From the *Vocabulary index*, you can see that Factor has vocabularies for many practical purposes. To name just a few:

- db—Relational database abstraction layer
- furnace—Web framework
- game—Game vocabulary
- html—HTML utilities
- json—JSON reader and writer
- smtp—Sending mail via SMTP
- ui—Graphical user interface framework
- zeromq—Bindings to 0MQ

There are plenty more, so when you set out to write an application, make sure to check out the libraries for utilities that you can use.

Editor Integration

The Listener supports integration with several code editors. You can quickly jump to the source code of a word in your favorite editor by loading the corresponding vocabulary and then calling edit to open the editor at the definition of the word:

```
IN: scratchpad USE: editors.gvim
IN: scratchpad \ at edit
```

That opens the gvim editor to the source code for the at word. Other editors are supported, including:

- Emacs
- Gedit
- jEdit
- MacVim
- Notepad++
- Sublime
- TextMate
- Xcode

Type "editors" about in the Listener and scroll down to the *Children* section to see a full list of supported editors.

Demos

Factor also comes with a rich set of sample applications. You can run them from the Listener with:

```
IN: scratchpad "demos" run
```

This displays a menu of sample applications that you can run. Here are just a few examples:

- 24-game
- balloon-bomber
- hello-ui
- maze
- numbers-game
- space-invaders
- sudoku
- tetris

You'll find the source code for all the demos in the extra directory where you installed Factor.

With so much documentation and a rich set of examples, there is plenty to go on to develop practical applications in Factor.

What We Learned in Day 3

Day 3 was about experiencing the Zen of Factor. We saw two examples of solving problems by processing data with a concatenation of words. Factor is very good at this programming style because function composition is the default behavior and the implicit use of the stack eliminates the need for variables. To finish off, we looked at a few more areas to explore within the Factor environment.

Your Turn

Find...

- One more word, aside from the three that we have seen today, that Factor automatically generates for each slot name of a tuple
- How to create a subclass of a tuple
- Whether or not a tuple can extend more than one parent tuple

Do (Easy):

- Define a constructor for cart-item that accepts a price and returns a cart-item with a default name and quantity.
- Write a word that discounts the price of a cart-item by a percentage that is given as a parameter.

Do (Medium):

- Write words that define different tax rates and a new shipping scheme.
- Assemble the tax rates and shipping scheme into a new checkout-processing pipeline.
- Write a unit test to verify that your new tax rates and shipping scheme work correctly.

Do (Hard):

- Make changes to the code so that prices are adjusted in a way that eliminates rounding errors and makes the unit tests pass.
- Enhance the number guessing game that you wrote on Day 2 so that it uses a graphical user interface instead of the command-line console.

Wrapping Up Factor

A concatenative language such as Factor may seem backward at first, but the left-to-right flow of actions reads in the same sequence as we read words on a page. When you edit a line of code with a series of functions and want to process the result with one more function call, you add the word at the end of the line instead of wrapping everything in parentheses and adding the function call at the beginning, as you would do in many other languages.

Strengths

Factor is beautifully devoid of extra syntax and punctuation. Function composition is natural. Instead of naming variables to pass from one function to the next, the stack is used implicitly. Defining a function that returns more than one result is possible—and we really do mean multiple, separate values, not a sequence of values wrapped in a single list.

Beyond the interesting programming model, Factor is also very practical in that in comes with a full-featured library to build real-world applications. Whether building command-line utilities, graphical user interfaces, or web applications, Factor provides support through its many vocabularies.

Everything returns a value with its type. Elm is strongly typed, and both the syntax and tools reflect this value. Let's poke around the edges of the type system:

```
> [1, "2"]
[1 of 1] Compiling Repl                ( repl-temp-000.elm )
Type error on line 5:
A number must be an Int or Float.
...

> 4 + "4"
[1 of 1] Compiling Repl                ( repl-temp-000.elm )
...

    Expected Type: number
      Actual Type: String
> "4" ++ "4"
"44" : String
> 4 ++ 4
[1 of 1] Compiling Repl                ( repl-temp-000.elm )
...
      Expected Type: appendable
...
> [1, 2] ++ [3, 4]
[1,2,3,4] : [number]
```

So Elm is strongly typed and enforces those constraints within lists and across operators. Like the type systems in Haskell and ML, Elm's type system is strong enough to represent complex data types but flexible enough to infer and coerce those types.

Contrast these type errors to JavaScript's behavior, where {} + [] = 0 and {} + {} = NaN. More than just an oddity, bugs like this lead to unpredictable and unstable code. At compile time, we'll need to think a little harder about our types, but our programs will be much more reliable at runtime.

Elm types have a hierarchy, called *type classes*. Presently, you can't build your own instances, but the language does include its own hierarchy of types. For example, both lists and strings are appendable data types so we can use them with the ++ operator.

```
> a = [1, 2, 3]
[1,2,3] : [number]
```

This type system is *type inferred*, meaning you don't have to declare the type of every argument and every variable. The type system is also polymorphic, meaning you can treat types that inherit from the same type class the same.

You will see that Elm takes full advantage of its ML and Haskell heritage to build on some of the best type systems in the world.

```
> a[1] = 2
[1 of 1] Compiling Repl                    ( repl-temp-000.elm )
Syntax Error: There can only be one definition of 'a'.
```

Elm is a single-assignment language, and very strictly so. That's why Elm has no edit-in-place semantics for arrays, though in the REPL, you can redefine whole primitive values for convenience.

Conditionals

Elm provides some control structures, though you won't rely on as many of them quite as often as you would in other languages. Here are a few simple control structures, starting with a simple if.

```
> x = 0
0 : number

> if x < 0 then "too small" else "ok"
"ok" : String
```

That statement will give you the basic one-line if. The multiline if works like a case in Ruby or a switch in Java:

```
> x = 5
5 : number
> if | x < 0 -> "too small" \
|     | x > 0 -> "too big" \
|     | otherwise -> "just right"
"too big" : String
```

The character \ helps when you're running in the REPL. It means continue the statement on the next line. When you're using *pattern matching*, use case. Pattern matching allows us to match the structure of some type. Here, we're matching on the structure of a list:

```
> list = [1, 2, 3]
[1,2,3] : [number]
> case list of \
|    head::tail -> tail \
|    [] -> []
[2,3] : [number]
```

This statement returns the tail of a list, if it exists. Lists with at least one element match the head::tail clause, returning the tail. Empty lists match []. Now that you've seen some basic types, let's build some types of our own.

Building Algebraic Data Types

The beauty and power of a type system becomes much stronger as you build your own complex data types. Take, for example, a chess piece. We need to worry about both color and piece. Use data to define a data type, like this:

```
> data Color = Black | White
> data Piece = Pawn | Knight | Bishop | Rook | Queen | King
> data ChessPiece = CP Color Piece
> piece = CP Black Queen
CP Black Queen : ChessPiece
```

Nice. A *type constructor* allows us to build new instances of a type. Our ChessPiece type consists of the characters CP, our type constructor, followed by a Color and a Piece. Now, we can use case and pattern matching to take the piece apart, like this:

```
> color = case piece of \
|   CP White _ -> White \
|   CP Black _ -> Black
Black : Color
```

That felt like a little too much work, but we'll deal with an alternative shortly. Building a type that works like List is a little trickier. You need to know that Cons constructs a list, given an element and another list, like this:

```
data List = Nil | Cons Int List
```

This definition is recursive! Cons, which is used at compile time to define types, means construct, with head and tail arguments. We define a type of List as either:

- The type Nil, or
- A list constructed with a head of type Int and a tail of type List

That data type is interesting, but we can do better. We can define an abstract list, one that can hold any data type, like this:

```
data List a = Empty | Cons a (List a)
```

In this case, a is some as yet undefined abstract data type. If you're familiar with Java or JavaScript, think of a as a parametric type parameter, such as T in List<T>, with more flexibility and power. This definition defines a List of a as either:

- Empty, or
- A list constructed with a head of something of type a, and a tail of lists having items of that same a

If you want to know how a list is evaluated in Elm, look at the data type. You can represent the type for list [1, 2] as Cons 1 (Cons 2 Empty).

Now when I tell you that you can combine the head of a list with the tail, it makes sense. Cons works on types at compile time. The runtime counterpart of the Cons operator that works on data is ::, and it works just as you'd expect:

```
> 1 :: 2 :: 3 :: []
[1,2,3] : [number]
```

Elm builds the list, right on cue, and then tells us that we're working with a list of numbers. Brilliant. We'll dive a little more into types as we move forward. For now, let's press on. Our chess piece was a little awkward, even if it is reminiscent of Haskell. We can do better. Let's express a chess piece with another data type, the record.

Using Records

We built types for color and piece, and that felt pretty natural. Now, if you have a beard longer than two inches, have a personalized license plate with any form of the word "monad," or think that I/O is for wimps, you probably like using abstract data types for everything. Carry on. For the rest of us, there's an easier way.

Recall that our chess example got a little more complicated when we wanted to extract the color. What we really need is a way to access named fields. That thing is a record, and it's a natural companion to JavaScript's objects. Let's say we want to represent a chess piece with Color and Piece fields:

```
> blackQueen = {color=Black, piece=Queen}
{ color = Black, piece = Queen } : {color : Color, piece : Piece}
> blackQueen.color
Black : Color
> blackQueen.piece
Queen : Piece
```

The . notation is just sugar. .color is actually a function:

```
> .color blackQueen
Black : Color
```

Now, we can freely access the components of our structured type. As with many functional languages, records are immutable, but we can create a new one with updated fields, or even changed fields, like this:

```
> whiteQueen = { blackQueen | color <- White }
{ color = White, piece = Queen } : {piece : Piece, color : Color}
> position = { column = "d", row = 1 }
```

```
{ column = "d", row = 1 } : {column : String, row : number}
> homeWhiteQueen = { whiteQueen | position = position }
{ color = White, piece = Queen, position = { column = "d", row = 1 } }
 : {piece : Piece, color : Color, position : {column : String, row : number}}
> colorAndPosition = { homeWhiteQueen - piece }
{ color = White, position = { column = "d", row = 1 } }
 : {b | position : {column : String, row : number}}
> colorAndPosition.color
White : b
```

Nice. We created three new records, all of different types, by transforming our original record. We'll come back to records after you've learned the greatest building block in Elm, the function.

Working with Functions

As with any functional language, the foundation of Elm is the function. Defining one is trivial. Let's see some primitive functions:

```
> add x y = x + y
<function> : number -> number -> number
> double x = x * 2
<function> : number -> number
> anonymousInc = \x -> x + 1
<function> : number -> number
> double (add 1 2)
6 : number
> map anonymousInc [1, 2, 3]
[2,3,4] : [number]
```

The syntax for creating functions is dead simple and intuitive. add is a named function with two arguments, x and y. Anonymous functions express parameters as \x, and the function body follows the characters ->.

As you'll see with Elixir, Elm lets you compose functions with the pipe operator, like this:

```
> 5 |> anonymousInc |> double
12 : number
```

We take 5, and pass it as the first argument to anonymousInc, to get 6. Then, we pass that as the first argument to double. We can also make that expression run right to left:

```
> double <| anonymousInc <| 5
12 : number
```

Evan Czaplicki, creator of Elm, says he got this feature from F#, which in turn got the idea from Unix pipes, so this idea has been around a while, but it's a good one!

As with any functional language, there are plenty of functions that will let you work with functions in all kinds of ways:

```
> map double [1..3]
[2,4,6] : [number]
> filter (\x -> x < 3) [1..20]
[1,2] : [comparable]
```

[1..3] is a range. You can explore more of List functions with the list library.[4]

When you're composing a solution with Elm, you might be tempted to code each case as a separate function body as you would in Haskell, Erlang, or Elixir, but no luck:

```
> factorial 1 = 1
<function> : number -> number'
> factorial x = x * factorial (x - 1)
<function> : number -> number
> factorial 5
RangeError: Maximum call stack size exceeded
```

It looks like the second call replaced the first. Instead, you need to use the same function body and break the problem up using case or if, like this:

```
> factorial x = \
|   if | x == 0 -> 1 \
|      | otherwise -> x * factorial (x - 1)
<function> : number -> number
> factorial 5
120 : number
```

Simple enough. factorial 0 is 1; otherwise, factorial x is x * factorial (x-1). You would handle list recursion the same way:

```
> count list = \
|   case list of \
|     [] -> 0 \
|     head::tail -> 1 + count tail
<function> : [a] -> number
> count [4, 5, 6]
3 : number
```

The count of an empty list is zero. The count of any other list is 1 plus the count of the tail. Let's see how to attack similar problems with pattern matching.

---

4. http://library.elm-lang.org/catalog/evancz-Elm/0.10.1/List

Pattern Matching

You can use pattern matching to simplify some function definitions:

```
> first (head::tail) = head
<function> : [a] -> a
> first [1, 2, 3]
1 : number
```

Be careful, though. You will need to cover every case in your functions, or you could have some error conditions like this:

```
> first []
Error: Runtime error in module Repl (on line 23, column 22 to 26):

 Non-exhaustive pattern match in case-expression.
 Make sure your patterns cover every case!
```

Since head::tail doesn't match [], Elm doesn't know what to do with this expression. Using a nonexhaustive pattern match is one of the few ways you can crash an ML-family language and it's totally avoidable.

Functions and Types

We quickly glossed over the types of functions. It turns out that Elm is a curried language:

```
> add x y = x + y
<function> : number -> number -> number
```

Notice the data type of the function. You might have expected a function that takes two arguments of type number and returns a type of number. Here's how currying works. Elm can *partially apply* add, meaning it can fill in one of the two numbers, like this:

```
> inc = (add 1)
<function> : number -> number
```

We just created a new *partially applied* function called inc. That new function applies one of the arguments for add. We filled out x, but not y, so Elm is basically doing this:

```
addX y = 1 + y
```

Currying means changing multi-argument functions to a chain of functions that each take a single argument. Now, we can handle the currying ourselves. Remember, curried functions can take no more than one argument at a time:

```
> add x y = x + y
<function> : number -> number -> number
> add 2 1
3 : number
> (add 2) 1
3 : number
```

That's slick. We defined add again, for reference. Then we added 2 and 1, without currying. Then we curried the function ourselves, creating a function that adds two to the first argument, and passed that function a 1.

Whew.

Fortunately, you won't usually need to do the currying because Elm will do it for you, but you can use partially applied functions to create some cool algorithms. Let's go back to add.

Elm infers that you're going to be doing arithmetic with numbers. Elm uses the type class number because that's the type class the + operator supports. You aren't limited to integers, though:

```
> add 1 2
3 : number
> add 1.0 2
3 : Float
> add 1.0 2.3
3.3 : Float
```

So Elm is polymorphic. It figures out the most general type that will work, based on your use of operators. In fact, you can see the same behavior with the ++ operator:

```
> concat x y = x ++ y
<function> : appendable -> appendable -> appendable
```

Elm assumes the function uses two appendable elements, like this:

```
> concat ["a", "b"] ["c", "d"]
["a","b","c","d"] : [String]
> concat "ab" "cd"
"abcd" : String
```

That's polymorphism. As you might expect, you can use polymorphism with points, too. Let's say I have a point and want to compute the distance to the x-axis. That's easy to do:

```
> somePoint = {x=5, y=4}
{ x = 5, y = 4 } : {x : number, y : number}
> xDist point = abs point.x
<function> : {a | x : number} -> number
```

```
> xDist somePoint
5 : number
```

Elm's type inference infers that x and y are numbers within a record. Now, I can pass it any point:

```
> twoD = {x=5, y=4}
{ x = 5, y = 4 } : {x : number, y : number'}
> threeD = {x=5, y=4, z=3}
{ x = 5, y = 4, z = 3 } : {x : number, y : number', z : number''}
> xDist twoD
5 : number
> xDist threeD
5 : number
```

Alternatively, I could use pattern matching, but you'll have to trust me as this would not work in the REPL:

```
xDist {x} = abs x
<function> : {a | x : number} -> number
```

We're using matching to pick off the x field, and the rest of the example works the same way. The point is that records are fully polymorphic too. Elm doesn't care that the records we use are the same type. It only needs the record to have an x field. You're seeing the power of a type system that will do its best to catch real problems but that will get out of the way when there isn't one.

That's probably enough for Day 1. Let's wrap up what we've done so far.

What We Learned in Day 1

We've taken a quick pass through Elm. We found a functional language that has many of the attributes of functional languages in the ML family, tweaked to work on the web. We spent extra time exploring basic pattern matching and working with various aspects of functions. We looked at several ways of composing functions and even looked at how function currying and partial application works.

Your Turn

Elm is a younger language than most of the others in this book. Most of the documentation you'll find is pretty consolidated on the Elm language page, or links off that page. I expect that to change quickly.

Find...

- How do you compile an Elm program?
- Where would you go for Elm support?

Do (Easy):

- Write a function to find the product of a list of numbers.
- Write a function to return all of the x fields from a list of point records.
- Use records to describe a person containing name, age, and address. You should also express the address as a record.
- Is it easier to use abstract data types or records to solve the previous problem? Why?

Do (Medium):

- Write a function called multiply.
- Use currying to express 6 * 8.
- Make a list of person records. Write a function to find all of the people in your list older than 16.

Do (Hard):

- Write the same function, but allow records where the age field might be nothing. How does Elm support nil values?

That's it for Day 1. Tomorrow, we're going to leave the REPL and dive into web applications. We'll explore the basic concept of functional reactive programming. Most of the ideas we'll see involve using signals, which express changing values over time as functions. You'll also see how to combine signals with functions. Then, we'll learn to display text and images.

Day 2: Taming Callbacks

In Day 2, we're going to build the skills necessary to attack the most sophisticated of user interface problems: building a game. We're going to learn to handle user input and output, the most difficult concepts for functional languages. We'll also learn to display images. You'll find that Elm is a natural language for doing so.

As a wanna-be browser language, Elm has a big disadvantage. It's not JavaScript. You'll need to rely on another layer in the browser to compile Elm to JavaScript. But Elm also has a huge advantage.

It's not JavaScript.

If you want to herd sheep like a sheep dog, you don't necessarily have to be a dog. You just have to herd sheep.

Before we get rolling, let's spend some time with Evan Czaplicki, creator of Elm. He'll help us understand the motivations behind the language.

Us: Why did you create Elm?

Czaplicki: I was extremely frustrated by HTML and CSS. Basic things like centering, or even worse vertical centering, were shockingly difficult. I kept finding five ways to do the same thing, each with its own set of weaknesses and corner cases. I wanted reusable styles and components. I was going to use the same sidebar on every page and there just was not a way. It makes sense why these things were hard in a language originally designed for text markup, but I felt that there had to be a more declarative and more pleasant way. So my goal was to create a better way to do GUI programming. I wanted to write front-end code that I was proud of.

Us: So why choose a functional language?

Czaplicki: I wanted to show that functional programming can be great for real problems. Many functional folks have a way of saying extremely interesting and useful things in a totally inaccessible and impractical way, and I wanted to fix this. I wanted to prove that functional programming actually helps you write nicer code. Elm's focus on examples, quick visual feedback, and shockingly short code are all meant to prove that purely functional GUIs are a good idea.

Us: What were your main influences?

Czaplicki: Haskell has been a big influence, but so have OCaml, SML, and F#. Syntax is very much like Haskell, though semantics are often closer to OCaml. I tend to say "Elm is an ML-family language" to get at the shared heritage of all these languages.

Stephen Chong and Greg Morrisett are my major influences in how I think about programming languages. With that foundation, I try to do a literature review for any new feature and end up looking at all sorts of languages. For example, Java and Python were extremely helpful for Elm's docs format, and Clojure and Scala are great resources on how to present a compile-to-VM language to people new to functional programming. The full list is quite long by now!

Us: What is the philosophy of the language?

Czaplicki: Balance simplicity and expressiveness. Introduce only the minimal set of features to make GUI programming a great experience. Static types, functional programming, and reactive programming are extremely important tools for writing short and reliable code, but it is a lot to learn all at once.

Not only does Elm need to make these things simple and accessible, it needs to make their value immediately obvious. Elm is not about being theoretically better, it is about being demonstrably better.

Us: What is your favorite language feature?

Czaplicki: I really love Elm's extensible records. This feature is based on Daan Leijen's ideas from Extensible Records with Scoped Labels, and because I was not involved in the theory work, it is something that delights me by balancing expressiveness and simplicity so beautifully. This is the kind of balance I hope to achieve when I design features.

Elm was built *from the ground up* to handle the most difficult aspects of user interface development. As you work through Day 2, look for ways that this new language helps you herd all of the elements of a great design into a coherent application.

Grappling with Callback Hell

Whether you're building a business application with user interface controls or a game, you need to be able to react to events. In fact, everything you do is a reaction to some event. The typical JavaScript program relies on sending events through callback functions, making programs much more responsive but at a cost. They're much too hard to read. Here's a typical example using the JQuery library with JavaScript that lets you grab the mouse position:

```
$(document).ready(function () {
    var position = {'x': 0, 'y': 0};
    $(document).bind('mousemove', function(event) {
        position = {'x': event.pageX, 'y': event.pageY};
    });

    setInterval(function () {
      // custom position code
    }, seconds * 1000);
});
```

Understanding that code takes a little experience. When the page loads, we get a ready callback. At that time, we bind the mousemove event to a function that sets a position variable. Then, at specific intervals, we have another callback function that uses position. Notice that our code binds anonymous functions to events. Said another way, *we're putting JavaScript in charge of the code's organization.* We call this inside-out programming strategy *inversion of control.*

For a feature so trivial, that code is much too complex, but it's a trade-off. We get better responsiveness since this program will change the mouse position every time the user moves the mouse. We trade away simplicity. The problem is that we really need both.

Avoiding Callbacks with Lifts and Signals

In Elm, we don't give up simplicity to get responsiveness. Instead of inversion of control, we'll use *signals* and a function called *lift*. A *signal* is a function representing a value that varies over time. The lift function applies a function to the value of a signal *each time the signal updates.* Let's try it out.

These programs will allow us to see how Elm handles user interaction without callbacks. For this part of the chapter, we'll use the Elm online editor[5] to try interactive programs without having to fire up your own server. You'll type code on the left, and see the results on the right. Let's start with a simple function to pick up the user's mouse position:

```
import Mouse

main = lift asText Mouse.position
```

Next, click the compile button. You'll see output that looks like this:

```
(29, 162)
```

That's much simpler. We import the Mouse module, and then declare the main function.

Conceptually, lift applies a function to a signal. Let's say the function is f, and the signal represents the value x that varies over time. Each time the signal updates, Elm will call f(x).

In the previous code, the Mouse.position signal returns a tuple containing the mouse position. Our function is asText, which converts to text. Mouse.position will "fire" whenever the mouse moves, and lift will call asText with the new mouse position. Interestingly, the result is a new signal! Rather than a callback, you have straight composition of functions. The result is revolutionary.

Looking at the bottom of the window, you can see that main is actually a signal—one that we display on the screen. That means Elm will update the window whenever the mouse position moves.

There are no callbacks, and no inversion of control. We just use a signal, convert to text, and lift the present value when the signal changes. Let's try another one. Let's use the count function, which counts the number of times a signal updates. Add count before the signal, and wrap it in parentheses, like this:

```
import Mouse

main = lift asText (count Mouse.position)
```

Navigate to the window on the right, move the mouse, and you'll see a number that quickly counts mouse moves:

```
246
```

---

5. http://elm-lang.org/try

We can simply change the signal to count mouse clicks:

```
import Mouse

main = lift asText (count Mouse.clicks)
```

In this case, the count function counts the number of signal updates, which are mouse clicks. You can start to see how we can write code that respects the rules of functional programming, but is still reactive and easy to understand. Let's see how keyboard signals would work:

```
import Keyboard

main = lift asText Keyboard.arrows
```

Compile it, click on the right-hand window, and press the up and right arrows. You'll see:

```
{ x = 1, y = -1 }
```

You can intuitively see exactly what's going on. lift updates the text when the signal changes, so we get a clean program that tells us the state of the arrow keys, in a form that we can easily use. Since we can compose with functions, we can get more sophisticated.

Combining Signals

Most user interfaces use more than one signal at once. For example:

- Find out where a user clicked
- Scroll based on window size and mouse position
- Find the value of input fields when the user clicks a mouse
- Drag and drop items

These problems are all combinations of signals. For more advanced applications, a simple lift is not enough. Several other functions help us combine signals in more sophisticated ways. One of the most common user interface problems is to find where a user clicks.

Let's use the function sampleOn. That function allows us to sample one signal when another updates, like this:

```
import Mouse

clickPosition = sampleOn Mouse.clicks Mouse.position
main = lift asText clickPosition
```

We build two signals, clickPosition and main. First, we create a signal with sampleOn. When the Mouse.Clicks signal updates, we'll sample the most recent Mouse.position.

The result is a new signal that returns a mouse position and changes whenever the user clicks a mouse. Next, we simply build our main signal. We lift asText onto our clickPosition signal. Simple. We can sample input controls in the same way.

Or, let's say you're implementing scrolling with a scroll bar. You need to find out how far down a page the mouse is, like this:

```
import Mouse
import Window

div x y = asText ((toFloat x) / (toFloat y))
main = lift2 (div) Mouse.y Window.height
```

Run it and scroll on the right-hand side to get something like this:

```
0.42973977695167286
```

This example uses lift2. Like lift, this function lifts functions onto signals, but uses two signals and two-argument functions.

First, to simplify type conversions, we create a version of division that takes integers and returns text. Next, we use lift2 to lift div onto two signals, Mouse.y and Window.height. Think about what a similar JavaScript program would look like. It doesn't take too many examples to see Evan's vision. *Monitoring user inputs is a functional job.*

Maintaining State

Let's use these same principles to produce an interactive experience. We'll work with an entry field, and update another part of the page. In functional languages like Elm, you have to learn tricks to handle state. We've seen how signals can help access things like the mouse position that changes over time, and how we use recursion to process lists. We manage state by the way we structure our functions. The fold functions, which you might know from Lisp or Haskell, are a good example. They take a two-argument function, an initial value, and a list. Here's an example of foldl in Elm:

```
> foldl (+) 0 [1, 2, 3]
6 : number
```

Here's what happens at each step:

- fold (+) 0 [1, 2, 3]. fold takes the initial value of the list, 1, and the accumulator, 0, and adds them together, returning 1, and uses that number, with the remainder of the list, calling fold again.

- fold (+) 1 [2, 3]. Elm takes the leftmost value of the list, 2, and the accumulator, 1, and passes those to the (+) function, returning 3.
- fold (+) 3 [3]. We call (+) with the accumulator 3 and the leftmost list element of 3, returning 6, and we're done.

Elm will let you fold from the left (foldl) or fold from the right (foldr). You might also want to fold a signal from the past, folding in the results of a signal. Elm provides the function foldp for that purpose, meaning fold from the past. Let's say we want to call a signal every time an arrow key is pressed. We want to count up with the right arrow or count down with the left arrow. foldp takes a function, an initial value, and a signal to solve that problem.

Here's the signal you can use:

```
import Keyboard

main = lift asText Keyboard.arrows
```

Press the left arrow, and you'll get { x = -1, y = 0 }; press the right arrow for { x = 1, y = 0 }. Now, we just need to accumulate state. We can use foldp, like this:

```
import Keyboard

main = lift asText (foldp (\dir presses -> presses + dir.x) 0 Keyboard.arrows)
```

Now, we create one signal with foldp. That signal adds the accumulator, called presses, to the x value from the signal of Keyboard.arrows. We can then lift that value onto the asText function. Now, when you run the application, you'll get a running total of presses. The left decrements the count, and the right increments the count.

Believe it or not, foldp is the foundation of our game, as you'll see on Day 3.

Working with Text Input

Functional languages are great at transforming text. Elm is excellent for capturing text too. Here's an example that takes some input, manipulates it, and puts it on the screen:

```
❶ import String
  import Graphics.Input as Input
  import Graphics.Input.Field as Field

❷ content = Input.input Field.noContent

❸ shout text = String.toUpper text
  whisper text = String.toLower text
  echo text = (shout text) ++ " " ++ (whisper text)
```

④ `scene fieldContent =`
```
    flow down
    [ Field.field Field.defaultStyle content.handle identity "Speak" fieldContent
    , plainText (echo fieldContent.string)
    ]
```

⑤ `main = lift scene content.signal`

Let's break that down.

❶ We import the libraries we'll need. String allows us to do string manipulation, and Graphics.Input gives us access to input fields.

❷ Next, we define a function to return an Input record, passing in the initial field content. We'll use Input records. This API will allow us to create records, which will let us access all of the data, signals, and functions we need.

❸ Next, we define a couple of simple functions for working with text, the shout and whisper functions. We use those to build an echo function to transform the text. These functions know nothing about user interfaces. They just work on raw String data.

❹ The next task is to build our layout, called scene. We use the flow function to specify our form, which will flow from the top down. Our form has two lines: a field and some text.

The field is an input control, expressed as the record that's returned by our content function. We pass in some configuration options defining the style, a handler from the input record, an id, a placeholder value, and a signal.

The next element of our layout is a line of text. We express the text as a signal that we create with the plainText function. Whenever fieldContent updates, our signal will fire and show the contents passed through our echo function.

❺ Finally, we create one last signal by lifting our content.signal onto scene. The signal will fire each time the user updates the entry field.

Whew. That's a lot of code packed into a short example. It may seem a little alien at first, but Elm's worldview is the perfect complement to web front-end programming. Each user interface is just a stream of transformed user inputs. Now that we've seen how text works, let's look at one more concept we're going to need for our game. Instead of working with text, we will draw shapes based on user input.

Drawing Shapes

In Elm, we can draw on the canvas with a full graphics library. We start with a collage with set dimensions, and then build shapes. We can transform the shapes by moving, scaling, or rotating them.

The figure shows a simple car. We'll describe it in terms of functions. As you'd expect, we'll use a combination of data structures and functions to do what we want.

```
elm/car.elm
carBottom = filled black (rect 160 50)
carTop =    filled black (rect 100 60)
tire = filled red (circle 24)

main = collage 300 300
       [ carBottom
         , carTop |> moveY 30
         , tire |> move (-40, -28)
         , tire |> move ( 40, -28) ]
```

First, we define a few basic shapes. We'll define the basic dimensions of the shapes, and by default they'll show up in the middle of the canvas. main is just a collage, which takes a width, a height, and a list of shapes, called forms in Elm. Each element of the list is just a shape. For example, carTop |> moveY 30 is just a rectangle moved 30 pixels vertically.

In this particular example, the figure is static. With Elm, animating that figure is nearly trivial. Say we have a rectangle with a form that looks like this:

```
filled black (rect 80 10)
```

When we build our game on Day 3, we'll need a paddle. We can animate the paddle by lifting Mouse.x onto the function that draws this paddle, like this:

```
elm/paddle.elm
import Mouse
import Window

drawPaddle w h x =
  filled black (rect 80 10)
    |> moveX (toFloat x - toFloat w / 2)
    |> moveY (toFloat h * -0.45)

display (w, h) x  = collage w h
       [ drawPaddle w h x ]

main = lift2 display Window.dimensions Mouse.x
```

Boom! Just like that, we have animation. We don't have to worry about drawing the paddle over time, or remember the previous location of the paddle. Instead, we just worry about drawing the paddle *right now*, and letting the user input determine where to move it. Now, you have all of the foundation you'll need to complete a game in Day 3. Let's recap.

What We Learned in Day 2

In Day 2, you learned about Elm's primary purpose. Previous languages focused on callbacks or simply single-threaded code to create programs that respond to users. The cost was complexity or unresponsive interfaces. Functional programming languages have traditionally struggled with user interfaces because processing user input often involved changing state.

Elm solves both problems with signals, which are functions that represent values that change over time. By viewing user input as functions rather than data, the same beautiful functional programming techniques that express complex computations can be brought to bear on complex user interfaces.

We learned to transform signals by lifting functions onto them with lift and lift2. Each time, the result is a new signal. We also used other functions to combine signals and functions such as foldp, which maintains a running accumulator, and sampleOn, which determines exactly when we sample.

Finally, we displayed some text and graphics. We also lifted a display function to move a paddle, which will come in handy when we work on our game.

Your Turn

Use the online editor[6] to solve these problems interactively.

Find...
- Examples of different signals available in Elm
- The relationship between lift and signals
- A signal that fires every second

Do (Easy):
- Write a signal to display the current mouse position, including whether a mouse button is pressed.

- Write a signal to display the y value of the mouse when the button is pressed.

---

6.   http://elm-lang.org/try

Do (Medium):

- Use lift and signals to draw your own picture at the current mouse position. Change the picture when a mouse button is pressed.

- Write a program that counts up, from zero, with one count per second.

Do (Hard):

- Use foldp to make the car move from left to right, and then right to left, across the bottom of the screen.

- Make the car move faster when the mouse is farther to the right, and slower when the mouse is farther to the left.

That's it for Day 2. Tomorrow, you're going to combine everything we've learned so far to write a game. We're going to go far beyond pong in this one, so fasten your seatbelt.

Day 3: It's All a Game

When I was in high school, I made extra spending money by writing games. We basically painted one screen after another in a loop, and the game went as fast as your hardware. The more complex the game, the slower it ran. These days, writing a game using conventional technologies is much tougher. The processors are much faster, so you need to spend more time dealing with timing and state. I quit writing games when I was in college. It just got too hard to crank out a game in an afternoon.

Until now. The game I wrote for this chapter is the first I've written in 20 years. The experience has been incredibly rewarding. The flow of this section is going to be a little different than most of the others in this book. I'm going to show you what a game skeleton looks like, we'll invent a game concept, and then we'll work through one giant example, about 150 lines long, piece by piece. When we're done, you will have a working game that you can customize. Hopefully, Elm will spark a new wave of game designers.

First things first, though. We need to start with a basic shell.

Describing a Skeleton

You've already seen how animation, user input, and graphics display work in Elm, so you probably know at least a little about what a game will look like. The basic strategy will be to build one time slice of the game. Then, we'll work on moving the game from one time slice to the next, based on user input. Using that strategy, all basic games will have the same basic components:

- A model—We'll build a data model of the game, including the user inputs and all data elements, player or computer controlled.

- A signal—The signal will combine the game state with user input signals and time.

- Step logic—We'll build a step function that will move the game to the next state based on the previous game state and the user inputs.

- Display logic—We won't worry about animation. We'll worry only about showing our game state, at a point frozen in time.

Keep in mind that all games have to do this work. It's just harder to express games in many other languages because the abstractions are not as clean. Let's take a look at a basic skeleton of our game, without any specifics attached.

Defining the Model

Here's the skeleton in code. As with most games in Elm, I've based the initial design on Evan's excellent game skeleton.[7] It's a free, open source project that you can use to get started. Alternatively, you can check out the many game examples at the Elm language site.[8] Let's check out my revised skeleton, piece by piece.

elm/skeleton.elm
```
module SomeGame where...

type Input = { ... }
type Player = { ... }
type Game = { player:Player, ... }
```

First, we model the game. Elm games are modules. Inside these you build a model of your game with simple data types. You can combine those simple types into higher level types. Generally, your model will represent the player, other computer-controlled elements, game state, and user inputs at one point in time. You're looking to collect everything you will need when it comes time to display the game, or to transition from one slice of time to the next.

Looping with Signals and foldp

Next, define a couple of signals. One will grab the user inputs we need, and the other will build each time slice based on the last one. As you can imagine, we'll use lift for the input and foldp to move from one slice to the next.

---

7.   https://github.com/evancz/elm-lang.org/blob/master/public/examples/Intermediate/GameSkeleton.elm
8.   http://elm-lang.org/Examples.elm

```
elm/skeleton.elm
delta = inSeconds <~ fps n
input = sampleOn delta (...)
main  = lift display gameState
gameState = foldp stepGame initialGameState input
```

delta is a signal (using the operator equivalent of lift, <~) that represents one slice of time. fps is a signal that means "frames per second." We're left with a signal that regularly updates every n seconds. Just like that, Elm has taken over the sensitive game timing so our math can focus on one point in time.

We then build another signal based on that one called input, which will capture all of the user input we need. gameState is a signal that builds the next state of the game based on user inputs and the previous game state. foldp is the perfect choice to do this work because it allows us to use the previous state in our definition of the next game.

main, then, needs only animate the game. That's easy since we can lift the gameState signal onto display. This code has a lot going on. Feel free to spend a little time with it to make sure you understand what's going on.

Stepping and Displaying the Game

Of course, stepping from one state to the next and displaying our game are the essence of our game and should command most of our attention. In Elm, they do. Further, both stepGame and display are simple functions that operate on one flat slice of time. We don't have to worry about input and output beyond its state at any instance of time. The framework lets us represent what is often the most difficult part of the game with a trivial four lines of code. Fantastic!

Describing Language Head

Before we start to code, we need to know one more thing. What are the rules of the game?

A strange language deserves an equally twisted game. We're going to build a game called Language Head. The object of the game is to bounce some balls across the screen, without letting each hit the ground. When a ball hits the ground, the game ends. The player

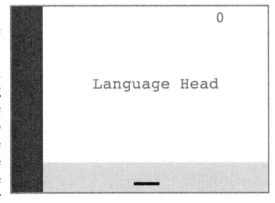

scores by staying alive and successfully getting a ball across the screen with a paddle they'll move with their mouse. There's a black line for a paddle on the bottom, a score on the upper right, and a primitive background, including a red rectangle representing a building on the left, and a gray area that will be our road on the bottom.

There's a twist. We're going to put the pictures of people on each ball, and call them heads. We'll drop more and more of them as the game goes on.

I'm going to break protocol for this chapter. Rather than work on this project iteratively, I'm going to tell you about each part of the completed game. Then, we'll talk about how to run the program, and you can take a well-earned break to play the game. Some of the parts will be a little long, but that's OK. We'll carve those long examples into shorter sections so you'll be able to see what's going on.

Modeling Language Head

Let's look at the first code section: the module definition and imports.

elm/game/languageHeads.elm
```
module LanguageHead where

import Keyboard
import Mouse
import Random
import Text
```

Longer Elm programs are broken down into modules. This module is called LanguageHead. We need mouse input for the paddle and keyboard input to capture the spacebar to start the game. We will also need a random signal to choose which head to present. All of the code for this whole game is in a single module.

Let's take a look at the data models.

elm/game/languageHeads.elm
```
❶ data State = Play | Pause | GameOver

   type Input = { space:Bool, x:Int, delta:Time, rand:Int }
   type Head = { x:Float, y:Float, vx:Float, vy:Float }
   type Player = { x:Float, score:Int }
   type Game = { state:State, heads:[Head], player:Player }

❷ defaultHead n = {x=100.0, y=75, vx=60, vy=0.0, img=headImage n }
   defaultGame = { state   = Pause,
                   heads   = [],
                   player  = {x=0.0, score=0} }
```

```
headImage n =
  if | n == 0 -> "/img/brucetate.png"
     | n == 1 -> "/img/davethomas.png"
     | n == 2 -> "/img/evanczaplicki.png"
     | n == 3 -> "/img/joearmstrong.png"
     | n == 4 -> "/img/josevalim.png"
     | otherwise -> ""
bottom = 550
```

This listing defines data types that describe our world. We first define data types, and then we declare some data that will come in handy when we introduce new data to the game. Let's look at it piece by piece.

❶ In short, we have an overarching Game model that contains the game State, user Input, all of the Heads, and the Player. The State is a primitive data type with the states we'll need: Play, Pause, and GameOver. The game will behave differently in each of these states.

The Player and Game types are pretty simple, but the Head type needs a little more explanation. We need to save not just the x and y coordinates (these are on a 800×600 grid, with the origin anchored on the top left), but also the velocity that the heads are moving across both dimensions. The y velocity will change over time to simulate gravity, flipping when any head bounces. We'll need this velocity as we step the game. We will also assign a random head image in img.

❷ In this section, we're done with *types*. We are building functions to return actual *data* for the initial state. defaultGame is simple as expected, but the heads have to have more logic built in because we are going to move them around. We define a default head. We include its starting coordinates, and set the vx to a constant. Ignoring the laws of physics, our heads will keep a constant x velocity (vx) because I am not smart enough to calculate wind resistance across the wide variety of hairstyles our heads could have. I'm looking at you, Evan. Our vy values start with a velocity of zero, but that will pick up once our artificial gravity kicks in.

Now that we've defined the model, it's time to define the signals that will drive our game.

Building the Game Signals

In this section, we handle all of the timing, the different user input states, the speed of the game, and the details that hold the application together from frame to frame. It's also the shortest section of our entire example. You can probably see where this is, um, headed. Elm is going to handle these details through signals. We'll just need to provide a little glue.

```
elm/game/languageHeads.elm
secsPerFrame = 1.0 / 50.0
delta = inSeconds <~ fps 50

input = sampleOn delta (Input <~ Keyboard.space
                              ~ Mouse.x
                              ~ delta
                              ~ Random.range 0 4 (every secsPerFrame))

main = lift display gameState

gameState = foldp stepGame defaultGame input
```

We first set the speed of the game. We define a function called secsPerFrame to return the size of each time slice. Next, we build a delta signal that updates 50 times per second. The <~ operator is shorthand for lift, so you could write inSeconds <~ fps 50 as lift inSeconds (fps 50). That means we're just going to get a float representing the number of seconds that have actually passed.

Next, we build our input signal. You'll see a new operator, the ~. (f <~ a ~ b) is equivalent to (lift2 f a b). Think of the squiggly arrow as signals flowing into the function. Using that operator, we pick off the various elements of the Input type, whether the spacebar is pressed, the x position of the mouse, and the total amount of time that's passed in this slice. We'll sample 50 times a second, based on the delta signal.

Finally, all that remains is to build our foldp loop. This recursive loop will build each successive Game based on the previous Game slice and user inputs. You can see that we're following the skeleton quite closely. The bulk of the code manages the creative side of the game, stepping and displaying each element. Herd on, Babe!

Stepping the Game

The trickiest part of this game is to manage all of the moving parts. We'll break this process into three major parts:

- *Stepping the game when we're in Play mode*—In this mode, we'll have to move the player's score and paddle. We'll also have to check to see if the game is over, and we'll need to move the heads around a bit.
- *Stepping the game when we're in Pause mode*—In this mode, the player has not yet started the game. We'll allow them to move the paddle and also to press the spacebar. Otherwise, there's not much work to do.

- *Stepping the game in GameOver mode*—We'll want to preserve the score, and we'll want to reset the player right before we restart the game. Otherwise, this mode is identical to the Pause mode.

There's a lot going on here, but the code is remarkably concise *because we don't have to worry about timing, animation, or managing user input.*

elm/game/languageHeads.elm

```
❶ stepGame input game =
    case game.state of
      Play -> stepGamePlay input game
      Pause -> stepGamePaused input game
      GameOver -> stepGameFinished input game

❷ stepGamePlay {space, x, delta, rand} ({state, heads, player} as game) =
    { game | state <-  stepGameOver x heads
           , heads <- stepHeads heads delta x player.score rand
           , player <- stepPlayer player x heads }

stepGameOver x heads =
    if allHeadsSafe (toFloat x) heads then Play else GameOver

allHeadsSafe x heads =
    all (headSafe x) heads

headSafe x head =
    head.y < bottom || abs (head.x - x) < 50
```

❶ Though we break it down into several different functions, stepGame is just a function. We take the input and game data types. We use case to branch on game.state, calling a function to step each possible game state.

❷ The first such function is stepGamePlay, which steps the game in Play mode. We update the game structure, calling a function to build each element of the game structure. stepGameOver will tell us if a head has crashed, stepHeads will manage any changes in the heads, and stepPlayer will handle changes in the paddle position and score.

The game is over when we experience a cranial catastrophe, meaning one head reached the bottom without a paddle. stepGameOver, then, is easy to write. We call a function called allHeadsSafe to see if any heads have reached the bottom without a paddle. That function will be true if headSafe head is true for every head in heads. headSafe needs only check to see if a single head has reached the bottom without the paddle close by (abs (head.x - x) < 50).

Now, we know enough to tell whether the heads are safe, so we can successfully transition to GameOver at the right time. Note that we don't care about any animation—we just check to see if all heads are safe at this point in time.

The next step is to move the heads according to the rules of the game. There are several steps to that process:

```
elm/game/languageHeads.elm
```

```elm
❶ stepHeads heads delta x score rand =
    spawnHead score heads rand
    |> bounceHeads
    |> removeComplete
    |> moveHeads delta

❷ spawnHead score heads rand =
    let addHead = length heads < (score // 5000 + 1)
      && all (\head -> head.x > 107.0) heads in
    if addHead then defaultHead rand :: heads else heads

❸ bounceHeads heads = map bounce heads

  bounce head =
    { head | vy <- if head.y > bottom && head.vy > 0
                   then -head.vy * 0.95
                   else head.vy }

❹ removeComplete heads = filter (\x -> not (complete x)) heads

  complete {x} = x > 750

❺ moveHeads delta heads = map moveHead heads

  moveHead ({x, y, vx, vy} as head) =
    { head | x <- x + vx * secsPerFrame
           , y <- y + vy * secsPerFrame
           , vy <- vy + secsPerFrame * 400 }
```

❶ The stepHeads function needs several arguments to do the entire job. The whole function is a function pipe, rolling the result of each function into the next. The result is a clear, concise representation of the data. We need to add heads when it's time with spawnHeads, bounce the heads when they reach the bottom with bounceHeads, remove heads that reach the right side of the window with removeComplete, and move the heads according to the rules of the game with moveHeads.

❷ We'll need to make sure the game has enough heads. addHead is a formula based on the score that determines how many heads are on the display. We add a head if there are not enough heads yet.

❸ Heads bounce when they get to the bottom, if they haven't already bounced. To bounce a head, we just make vy, the y velocity, negative if it's on the bottom. We also multiply by 0.95 when we bounce, so each bounce doesn't go quite as high as the last. It's a nice touch that looks a little more realistic.

❹ We remove all heads that are complete. A head is complete once it's reached the right-hand side, or head.x > 750.

❺ Each head has to move. We move the head in each direction based on the velocity per second, times the length of one time slice. We also adjust the y velocity to build in our gravity.

That's all there is to the head movement. We just adjust the next head list based on the previous list and the rules of the game. Next, we'll step the player data. We'll need to update the score and the paddle position.

elm/game/languageHeads.elm
```
stepPlayer player mouseX heads =
    { player | score <- stepScore player heads
             , x <- toFloat mouseX }

stepScore player heads =
    player.score +
    1 +
    1000 * (length (filter complete heads))
```

❶ Stepping the Player is comically simple. We just return a new player with the stepped score, and we capture the mouse position as a float. The float conversion will make it easier to display the paddle later.

❷ Our scoring system is simple. We give the player a point for each time slice and 1000 points for getting a head across the screen.

That's all for stepping the player. That was almost too easy. Let's finish up stepGame next. We can write the functions that step the game when it's in the Pause and GameOver states.

elm/game/languageHeads.elm
```
stepGamePaused {space, x, delta} ({state, heads, player} as game) =
    { game | state <- stepState space state
           , player <- { player |  x <- toFloat x } }

stepGameFinished {space, x, delta} ({state, heads, player} as game) =
    if space then defaultGame
    else { game | state <- GameOver
                , player <- { player |  x <- toFloat x } }

stepState space state = if space then Play else state
```

❶ A game in the Pause state will need to step the state based on the space
bar so players can start the game, and also update the paddle position
so the player can move the paddle even if the game is paused.

❷ A game in the Finished state needs to reset to a defaultGame when the user
presses the spacebar, or just replace the player's mouse position.

❸ Stepping the state involves simply transitions to Play when space is true.

Let's review what happened here. We used signals to allow us to grab the
current user inputs we needed: the size of our time slice, the mouse x position,
and whether the spacebar was pressed. We packaged those up in an Input
data type. Then, we passed that input and the Game record we produced in
the previous time slice into stepGame. Based on that data and the rules of the
game, we built a new Game record.

Next, we can display the Game record and then we can let the heads fly.

Displaying the Game

We're going to use many of the same techniques you learned in Day 2 to display the Game record we produced in Day 1. The code looks a lot like you'd
see in any graphics library:

elm/game/languageHeads.elm
```
display ({state, heads, player} as game) =
   let (w, h) = (800, 600)
   in collage w h
        ([ drawRoad w h
        , drawBuilding w h
        , drawPaddle w h player.x
        , drawScore w h player
        , drawMessage w h state] ++
        (drawHeads w h heads))

drawRoad w h =
   filled gray (rect (toFloat w) 100)
   |> moveY (-(half h) + 50)

drawBuilding w h =
   filled red (rect 100 (toFloat h))
   |> moveX (-(half w) + 50)

drawHeads w h heads = map (drawHead w h) heads

drawHead w h head =
  let x = half w - head.x
      y = half h - head.y
      src = head.img
```

```
    in toForm (image 75 75 src)
        |> move (-x, y)
        |> rotate (degrees (x * 2 - 100))

❹ drawPaddle w h x =
      filled black (rect 80 10)
      |> moveX (x +  10 -  half w)
      |> moveY (-(half h - 30))

   half x = toFloat x / 2

❺ drawScore w h player =
      toForm (fullScore player)
      |> move (half w - 150, half h - 40)

   fullScore player = txt (Text.height 50) (show player.score)

   txt f = leftAligned << f << monospace << Text.color blue << toText

❻ drawMessage w h state =
      toForm (txt (Text.height 50) (stateMessage state))
      |> move (50, 50)

   stateMessage state =
     if state == GameOver then "Game Over" else "Language Head"
```

❶ First, we write the main display function. This function draws a collage with parts we build in other functions. We'll draw the building on the left, the road on the bottom, the paddle, the score, a message, and all of the heads. To keep this code short, we are hard-coding the display size to 800 by 600, but it's possible to use lift2 to use both the Window.dimensions signal and the gameState signal at the same time.

The collage takes forms that originate in the center of the canvas. You'll move each element to where you want it after you create it.

❷ The background elements are simple. The building is just a vertical rectangle that we move to the left, and the road is a horizontal rectangle that we move down.

❸ The drawHeads function just maps the drawHead function onto the heads list. Remember, collages take shapes called forms. Since heads are images, we need to reference the head's source image (you'll have to copy them from the book's source code), and convert that image to a form. Then, we do a little math to make sure the heads move to the right form on the page. A collage anchors the origin at the bottom left, so we do need to reverse the y position. Also, since the heads are initially drawn in the center of the canvas, we need to adjust for that with our move function. For good measure, we rotate the head based on the x coordinate. I hope Joe doesn't get too dizzy.

❹ Paddles are just rectangles, moved to the bottom of the canvas, and adjusted for the Mouse.x position and the central location on the page.

❺ Working with text in Elm is a little tricky. We have a couple of conversions to do. We need to make sure we're working with text elements, and we need to convert those to forms. I'm not going to go into too much detail here, because it deals with many data types we've not yet introduced. At a high level, these functions convert strings to text objects with the font, color, and size that we want. Then, they translate that text into forms that will work in our collage.

❻ The last element to display is a message for the game. We'll show either the string "Language Head" or the string "Game Over", based on the game state.

And that's all there is to it! To start the game, put your source code in a game directory. Also in that directory, put an img directory with all of the head images you referenced in the source. If you'd like to use our heads, you can copy them from the book's source code (see the Online Resources section of the Preface). Finally, navigate to your game directory and start your local Elm server, like this:

```
> elm-reactor
Elm Reactor 0.1, backed by version 0.13 of the compiler.
Listening on http://localhost:8000/
```

Then press the spacebar to start the game! You'll see something like this image.

There you have it. We wrote a full game in fewer than 150 lines of code. The design also allows us to add many different bells and whistles without customary callbacks and the hallmark complexities of JavaScript approaches.

What We Learned in Day 3

Day 3 showed a single extended example of using Elm to build a game. We chose this problem because it wraps up many of the most demanding problems in user interface design. This example includes interacting with the mouse and keyboard; working with text and images; using animation, including simulated gravity; image presentation and manipulation; and more. By shaping the game with signals and functions, Elm allowed us to live in the realm of functions.

Elm's structure let us simplify the most sophisticated problems, like the interplay between objects on the screen, scoring, and our simulated physics. If Elm can handle games with such grace and dexterity, other user interface problems should be a breeze.

Your Turn

Find...
- Evan's excellent blog post on the implementation of Pong in Elm
- Game contributions from the Elm community
- More about dealing with Text on HTML pages in Elm

Do (Easy):
- Provide another message that asks the user to press the spacebar to start.
- Make the heads bounce more times as they cross the screen.
- Make the road look more like a road and the building look more like a building.

Do (Medium):
- Add some random elements to when heads get added so that all of the games are no longer the same.
- Make the game choose a random head from a list of graphics.
- Don't allow another head to be added too closely to an existing head.
- Show a different kind of head when one reaches the bottom.

Do (Hard):
- As written, the game allows heads to be added so that they reach the bottom at potentially the same time. Prevent this from happening.
- Add other features that show up at different score increments. For example, bounce the heads up in the air, wherever they are, when the user presses a key. This will let the user survive when two heads reach the bottom at the same time.
- Give the user three lives. Add additional lives when the user hits a certain score.
- Provide a better formula for when to add additional heads.

- Add heads at predetermined spacings.
- Add another paddle users could move with the A and D keys, or arrow keys. Two paddles and more heads!

Wrapping Up Elm

You've now used Elm to solve a demanding user interface problem. You've also seen the concept of reactive programming, expressed in terms of signals. Reactive programming with functional languages will revolutionize the way we build user interfaces in the browser. The revolution is already started.

Strengths

Elm's primary strengths are the type system and reactive concepts for dealing with events. The result eliminates two of the biggest JavaScript problems: the weak typing model and "callback hell." The callback model is especially significant.

Also, Elm brings many of the advanced Haskell features to the browser. The type model—partially applied functions and currying—allows much more sophisticated programming, and allows the compiler to capture more errors. Several different Haskell alternatives have shown up here and there, but only Elm seems to be getting much traction.

Weaknesses

Elm may be hard for novices to learn. As with most Haskell-like implementations, it's easy to get lost with the type conversions. You're not just worrying about data types. Signals bring functional types into the mix, and the concepts are conceptually difficult.

Elm is also quite young. It will be some time before we know whether Elm will gather enough critical mass to break out beyond the emerging languages camp.

Final Thoughts

With Elm alone, you can tell a great deal about language evolution. We're seeing a movement toward reactive concepts in the user interface, and we are seeing the Haskell type system have an increasingly profound impact on emerging languages.

When something is right, you can feel it. To me, a whole lot of Elm feels right. It may not be the final winner, but these concepts are helping the industry head in the right direction.

CHAPTER 4

Elixir

by Bruce Tate

Languages that provoke the strongest reactions in me are all strongly opinionated. Ruby provided plenty of sugar, insulating me from tedium and letting me focus on a task. Others find the language structure haphazard and frustrating. Scala's strong typing structures work well for some, but for me managing types across two major programming paradigms built an intellectual wall that proved too steep for me to climb.

Elixir was love at first sight. I was looking for a functional language that handled distribution, had plenty of sugar to eliminate tedious repetition, and allowed me to grow the language through metaprogramming. After a couple of sips of Elixir, I found all of these features and more. Each new language is a love-hate relationship.

Think Wolverine, the surly vigilante. You love him or hate him. With a souped-up skeleton he didn't actually grow, this brooding antihero has the remarkable ability to regenerate when things go wrong. Let him crash. He'll respawn.

As you might expect, you'll notice plenty of strong opinions as we dive in:

- Elixir embraces and extends Erlang's message passing actor model.
- You get Lisp-like, real macros without all the parentheses and prefix notation, for better and for worse.
- Gone are Erlang's constricting single assignment variables and alien syntax.

From that list alone, you're probably already forming some of your own opinions. Let's accelerate that process and dive right in.

Day 1: Laying a Great Foundation

Our speed tour will focus on the three biggest influences on Elixir: Ruby, Lisp, and Erlang. Day 1 will show you where Ruby's influence begins and ends. I'll walk you through the basic building blocks of the language, while taking an informal look at operators, simple types, and expressions. Then, we'll look at functions and modules. Finally, we will work with collections of things and craft together some simple programs with recursion. That's a lot to handle, but to get to know this rich language, we'll have to move fast.

Day 2 will bring forth the strong Lisp influences on the abstract syntax tree (AST), the foundation for Elixir's macro system. We'll focus most of our attention on building a macro to represent a state machine in code.

We'll finish our tour by looking into Erlang influences in Day 3. The third day will a little shorter, because in Days 1 and 2 we have to lay a lot of language foundation to handle the rich macro material. We'll use our state machine in a concurrent, distributed application.

Rarely will you get the opportunity to explore so closely the influences of one language on another. It's going to be a long first day, so let's get started.

Installing Elixir

Elixir is a language based on Erlang (*Programming Erlang: Software for a Concurrent World [Arm07]*), which we covered in the first *Seven Languages* book (*Seven Languages in Seven Weeks: A Pragmatic Guide to Learning Programming Languages [Tat10]*). You'll need to install Erlang.[1] I'm using 17.1, and you'll need version 17.0 or later.

Next, you'll install the language and environment. Find them on the language's Getting Started page.[2] I used Homebrew, version 0.14, but everything should work on Elixir version 1.0. Syntax is changing quickly, so if you decide to use a later version, you'll need to pay attention to changes in syntax.

Once you've installed it all, fire up Interactive Elixir (iex) like this:

```
> iex
Erlang/OTP 17 [erts-6.1] [source] [64-bit] [smp:8:8]
[async-threads:10] [hipe] [kernel-poll:false]

Interactive Elixir (1.0) - press Ctrl+C to exit (type h() ENTER for help)
iex(1)>
```

---

1. http://www.erlang.org/download.html
2. http://elixir-lang.org/getting_started/1.html

So...It's Ruby++, Right?

Since José Valim, creator of Elixir, was a member of the Ruby on Rails core team, many people viewed his new language with Ruby-colored glasses. Syntactically, you can see more than a coincidental similarity. Try to see what reminds you of Ruby:

```
iex> IO.puts "It's B-29s, bub."
It's B-29s, bub.
iex> 4
4
iex> 4 != 5
true
iex> 4 > 5 and 6 > 7
false
iex(2)> Enum.at [], 0
nil
iex> :atom
:atom
```

Like Ruby and many modern languages, Elixir programs are made up of simple data types, operators, and functions that roll up into expressions. The special values nil, true, and false all mean what you think, and are named just as they are on the Ruby side. Elixir also copies Ruby's syntax for symbols instead of Erlang's atoms.

```
iex> if 5 > 4, do: IO.puts "You wanted the truth!"
You wanted the truth!
:ok
iex> if nil, do: IO.puts "You wanted the truth!"
nil
:ok
```

:ok is a typical Elixir return code. Like Ruby, Elixir has do/end syntax for simple control structures. Like Ruby, Elixir also has one-line syntax for if expressions. Like Ruby, Elixir has so-called "truthy" expressions. nil and false are false; everything else is true. Strings have some familiar sugar, too:

```
iex> "Two plus two is #{2 + 2}"
"Two plus two is 4"
```

Elixir's string interpolation drops a string representation of an expression into the string you specify. There are other similarities to Ruby on the string side. They can contain escape sequences for unprintable characters such as newlines and tabs; Elixir allows for multiline representations called heredocs, and you'll find C-style sigils, a syntax for formatting literals.

No, Not Ruby

Although the syntax might be familiar to Ruby developers, under the hood, things are remarkably different. Elixir is a functional language. The base types are not objects, and the base types are immutable. You can't change a list or a tuple after you've defined it the first time.

It's best to think of Elixir as a language *whose syntax is influenced by Ruby*. The similarities end there. Take the = operator, for example:

```
iex> i = 5
5
iex> 10 = i
** (MatchError) no match of right hand side value: 5
```

It may look like an assignment here, but it's not. If you learned Erlang in *Seven Languages*, you recognize the = operator as a pattern match. Said another way, the interpreter asked the question "Do the values on the left side match the values on the right?" If necessary, the interpreter assigns unbound variables on the left to match values on the right. Let's push pattern matching a little further.

Tuples are collections of fixed size. You can have a two-tuple representing a city and state, like this:

```
iex> austin = {:austin, :tx}
{:austin, :tx}
iex> is_tuple {:a}
true
```

austin is a variable, and we assign a tuple with two atoms, :austin and :tx. Elixir makes the left side match the right by assigning {:austin, :tx} to the variable austin. In this case, we matched the whole tuple. We can also use matching to access both elements of the tuple individually, or using wildcards, we can access either element in isolation. This concept, called *destructuring*, is critical.

```
iex> austin = {:austin, :tx}
{:austin, :tx}
iex> {city, :tx} = austin
{:austin, :tx}
iex> city
:austin
iex> {city, :ok} = austin
** (MatchError) no match of right hand side value: {:austin, :tx}
iex> {_, big_state} = austin
{:austin, :tx}
iex> big_state
:tx
```

Nice. In this way, you'll use Elixir to trivially pack and unpack complex data structures just as you did this one.

So what was all of that noise about surly and opinionated?

In functional languages like Erlang, multiple assignment just won't work. You can assign a given variable a value exactly once. That practice means that these languages are immune from many of the problems related to mutable state or multiple assignment. To handle this language limitation, you'll see developers use different variable values on the left-hand side for each assignment, and keeping track of those changing values can be tedious and error prone as code evolves, like this:

```
...
Price = Catalog.lookup(Item)
Price2 = Price * Quantity
Price3 = Price2 + Price2 * Tax
...
```

Elixir's approach looks a little more like the imperative style of Ruby or Java:

```
...
price = Catalog.lookup(item)
price = price * quantity
price = price + price * tax
...
```

Some card-carrying Erlang developer now knows exactly what I mean by opinionated. In fact, his thoughts could be sliding into black rage because *functional programming should not allow reassignment*. We can only hope that he doesn't have adamantium blades for fingernails and the ability to respawn.

That code looks suspiciously like mutable state, but really, it's not. The compiler is playing a game here. The compiler marks each new price as price' internally, and for each subsequent access. In fact, the compiler is doing implicitly exactly what the original Erlang program does by hand. The result is that internally, there's no mutable state at all.

This language feature expresses an opinion. Does this trick actually make code more expressive, or does it take you down the slippery slope toward mutable state and obscure what's actually happening? Decide for yourself.

The primary Ruby influence, though, isn't mutability, or 'true's and 'nil's. It's *intelligent sugar*. You express powerful idioms in a way that communicates to both you and the compiler. The debate is how far syntactic sugar should go.

Elixir is about as much like Ruby as Java is like JavaScript. From here on, put Ruby out of your head completely, and enjoy the new path Elixir is cutting.

Writing Functions

So far, we've seen how some basic types and expressions work, and that the language relies heavily on pattern matching to accomplish basic tasks. It's time to add the basic building block of all functional languages, the function. Elixir has plenty of different options for declaring and consuming functions. We're going to start simple, with unnamed or *anonymous functions* and then ramp up to named functions in modules. We can assign a function to a variable like this:

```
iex> inc = fn(x) -> x + 1 end
#Function<6.80484245 in :erl_eval.expr/5>
iex> inc.(1)
2
```

When you invoke an anonymous function, you need a . character before your arguments. This double_call is a higher order function:

```
iex> double_call = fn(x, f) -> f.(f.(x)) end
#Function<12.80484245 in :erl_eval.expr/5>
iex> double_call.(2, inc)
4
```

As expected, we called inc.(inc.(2)) and got 4. As you might imagine, you'll be working with functions more than any other language construct. Here's a shorthand way for declaring a function to add two numbers:

```
iex> add = &(&1 + &2)
&Kernel.+/2
iex> add.(1, 2)
3
```

Beautiful. We just used &1 and &2 as placeholders for our arguments. Now that we have an add, we can use it to declare other functions that build on it.

```
iex> inc = &(add.(&1, 1))
 #Function<6.80484245 in :erl_eval.expr/5>
iex> inc.(1)
2
iex> dec = &(add.(&1, -1))
 #Function<6.80484245 in :erl_eval.expr/5>
iex> dec.(1)
0
```

inc and dec are examples of partially applied functions. As you learned in Elm, these functions take existing functions and apply only a subset of arguments to them. For example, inc is a partially applied function, applying the second argument and leaving the first unapplied.

Composing with Pipes

Functional programming is about building functions that work together. One of the most important compositions is running functions in sequence, matching up inputs and outputs. Let's express two steps forward and one step back with inc and dec:

```
iex> x = 10
10
iex> dec.(inc.(inc.(x)))
11
```

We started with x = 10. A step forward is an inc and a step back is dec. If you start from the inside and work your way out, you can see that we are actually doing inc, inc, and dec. But the intention is not clear. Let's remedy that.

```
iex> 10 |> inc.() |> inc.() |> dec.()
11
```

That's much clearer. These pipes work just like they do in Factor or Elm. Elixir evaluates the pipe from left to right, passing the expression on the left-hand side of the pipe as the first argument of the function on the right. If you had two named functions, inc and dec, you could strip away even more syntax with 10 |> inc |> inc |> dec. The pipe operator translates the obtuse inside-out representation to a simple and direct statement of what our program accomplishes. Clojure developers, think ->.

You'll find that the pipe operator is perhaps the most important operator in the language in the same way that Unix shell languages rely on the | operator. It allows you to express ideas in the same way that you're used to consuming information: from left to right, with inputs on the left contributing to the process on the right. You can make complex problems simpler by expressing them as a pipe of simpler functions.

As we continue to work with bigger and bigger building blocks in the language, we go from the function to the *module*. In the next section, we'll organize named functions into modules.

Using Modules

Elixir programmers group functions, macros, and other constructs into modules. Learning Elixir is easier if you think of a module definition as plain, old executable code rather than a series of function definitions. Take a look:

```
iex> defmodule Silly do
...>    IO.puts "Pointless existence"
...> end
Pointless existence
{:module, Silly, ..., :ok}
```

Notice that the compiler ran the module, and printed the expression Pointless existence. You can see that as Elixir is loading the module, it will just execute each line, in sequence. Most of the time, those lines will define other functions or modules.

For now, think of modules as specialized functions that generate code at compile time. defmodule is a macro that defines a module, and def is a macro that defines functions. Keep this knowledge in the back of your mind as we walk through these basic examples.

Named Functions

Let's create some modules to do elementary geometry. We'll start with some simple functions to compute the area and perimeter of a rectangle. You might start with a couple of functions that each take parameters h and w, like this:

```
defmodule Rectangle do
  def area(w, h), do: h * w
  def perimeter(w, h), do: 2 * (w + h)
end
```

We call the defmodule function, which defines a module. We provide a block that calls the def function twice, creating two functions within the module.

area and perimeter are functions you'd expect to apply to a rectangle, so we can improve on the API. Instead of passing in individual dimensions, let's pass in a tuple with two dimensions that represents our rectangle, like this:

elixir/geometry.exs
```
defmodule Rectangle do
  def area({h, w}), do: h * w

  def perimeter({h, w}) do
    2 * (h + w)
  end
end
```

That's much better. Now, the API is Rectangle.area(shape), where shape is a two-tuple that represents a rectangle with width and height. The API clearly expresses our intentions. We use pattern matching to pick off each dimension, and then use those dimensions in a calculation.

Do Blocks

Do blocks group lines of executable code together. They act like a single function. Notice we're using two forms of do/end, one expressed on multiple lines, like this:

```
def f do
  IO.puts "Block form"
end
```

Alternatively, you could use a one-line version of the function, like this:

```
def f(x), do: IO.puts("Key/value form")
```

Wrap them in a module to execute them in the console. Internally, both of these forms are represented in the same way.

Let's push on. We can add a few similar methods to calculate metrics for a square. Just for fun, we'll allow two representations for a square {w}, where w is the width of one side, and {w, h}. Take a look:

```
elixir/geometry.exs
defmodule Square do
  def area({w}), do: Rectangle.area({w, w})

  def area({w, h}) when w == h do
    Rectangle.area({w, w})
  end

  def perimeter({w}) do
    Rectangle.perimeter({w, w})
  end

  def perimeter({w, h}) when w == h do
    Rectangle.perimeter({w, w})
  end
end
```

You can see a couple of new features here. First, we have the same function name for area and perimeter used twice. The area function is a single function called Square.area/1, and our clauses describe the behavior the function will have based on what you pass in. Elixir will execute the first function that matches the argument list, so our code uses pattern matching to differentiate the square and rectangle forms.

Notice also the when clauses, called *guards*. If an inbound argument does not satisfy the condition specified in the guard, it falls through to the next definition. In this case, if the argument doesn't match the first or second, it will throw an error.

Tack on some print expressions to the bottom of geometry.exs, like this:

elixir/geometry.exs
```
r = {3, 4}
IO.puts "The area of rectangle #{inspect r} is #{Rectangle.area r}"

s = {4}
IO.puts "The area of square #{inspect s} is #{Square.area s}"


IO.puts "The area of rectangle #{inspect r} is #{Square.area r}"
```

EXS files are scripts; they're compiled on the fly. You'll use them for things like test cases. You can run geometry.exs like this:

```
> iex geometry.exs
Erlang 17.0 (erts-6.1) [source] [64-bit] [smp:8:8]
[async-threads:10] [hipe] [kernel-poll:false]

The area of rectangle {3, 4} is 12
The area of square {4} is 16
** (FunctionClauseError) no function clause matching in Square.area/1
    geometry.exs:13: Square.area({3, 4})
    geometry.exs:38: (file)
    src/elixir_lexical.erl:18: :elixir_lexical.run/2
    /private/tmp/elixir-nEKc/elixir-0.11.0/lib/elixir/lib/code.ex:307:
    Code.require_file/2
```

Elixir executed Rectangle.area/2, and then Square.area/1. Next, the script asked for the area of {3, 4}. Elixir faithfully tells us that there's no matching clause for our square of {3, 4}. We called function Square.area/1. That function had two clauses. The first clause doesn't match because our tuple is a two-tuple, and the clause matches a one-tuple. The second matches but does not satisfy the guard clause because 3 != 4.

So far, so good. Now that you have modules, named functions and pipes, you can break bigger ideas into smaller functions, roll those functions up into a module, and compose them again with pipes. This is the primary strategy you'll use to attack larger problems.

The next step is working with some richer data structures. You've seen tuples, which we will typically use for fixed-length heterogeneous data. You also learned how to match individual elements in a tuple. Let's move on to using maps and lists.

Using Maps

Maps associate keys with values. To avoid confusion with tuples, include an extra % before the initial curly brace, like this:

```
iex> language = %{ :name => "Elixir", :inventor => "Jose"}
%{inventor: "José", name: "Elixir"}
iex> language[:name]
"Elixir"
iex> language.inventor
"José"
```

Key-value pairs are expressed with key => value. We accessed the fields two different ways. The second is sugar for the first. Notice the shortcut syntax returned by iex. If your keys are atoms, you can use a shortcut syntax that moves the atom's colon to the end of the atom.

Sometimes, you might have a map with nested values. Because Elixir is a functional language, we don't edit values in place, so replacing some value buried in a nested structure might be tedious:

```
iex> book = %{title: "Programming Elixir",
...>          author: %{first: "David", last: "Thomas"}}
%{author: %{first: "David", last: "Thomas"}, title: "Programming Elixir"}
iex> %{book: book.title, author: %{ first: "Dave", last: book.author.last}}
%{author: %{first: "Dave", last: "Thomas"}, title: "Programming Elixir"}
```

Elixir offers a shortcut syntax to return a new map with just one part updated, like this:

```
iex> put_in book.author.first, "Dave"
%{author: %{first: "Dave", last: "Thomas"}, title: "Programming Elixir"}
```

Now, we can trivially make a new copy of any map with only a single item updated. This feature takes some of the sting out of the lack of edit-in-place semantics.

Of course, maps would not be complete without pattern matching:

```
iex> %{ author: %{ last: "Thomas"}, book: title} = book
%{author: %{first: "David", last: "Thomas"}, book: "Programming Elixir"}
iex> title
"Programming Elixir"
```

Perfect. This kind of deconstruction can save you a tremendous amount of time. With our quick tour of maps out of the way, let's move on to lists.

Representing Lists

Lists are the primary variable-length structure in Elixir and are implemented as linked lists internally. Lists are enclosed in brackets and separated by commas, like this:

```
iex> list = [1, 2, 3]
[1, 2, 3]
```

This list is not an array, though:

```
iex> list[1]
** (FunctionClauseError) no function clause matching
  in Access.List.access/2
```

That last line of code doesn't do what you think it does! Elixir lists are actually *linked lists.* You'll build and access them from the front, or head, because the internal representation makes it more efficient that way.

Internally, some data structures are lists, and others aren't:

```
iex> is_list list
true
iex> is_tuple list
false
iex> is_list "string"
false
iex(27)> is_list 'char'
true
iex> is_list %{one: 1, two: 2}
false
```

Lists and char lists are lists; tuples and strings are not. We delimit char lists with single quotes, and they are not the same as strings. (We'll use strings in this book because they are more efficient and better support international encodings.) As with all Elixir types, both are immutable.

You can't add to a list once it's been defined, but you can return a new copy of the list with a prepended item. | is the construction operator—use it to add a single item, more than one item, or another list.

```
iex> [0 | list]
[0, 1, 2, 3]
iex> [0 | []]
[0]
iex> [[4, 5, 6] | list]
[[4, 5, 6], 1, 2, 3]
iex> [4, 5, 6 | list]
[4, 5, 6, 1, 2, 3]
```

Let's do some basic pattern matching with lists:

```
iex> list = [:wolverine, :magneto, :cyclops]
[:wolverine, :magneto, :cyclops]
iex> [x, y, z] = list
[:wolverine, :magneto, :cyclops]
iex> {x, y, z}
{:wolverine, :magneto, :cyclops}
iex> [x, y] = list
** (MatchError) no match of right hand side value: [:wolverine, :magneto, :cyclops]
```

If you don't use the | operator, matching works just as it does with tuples. If the list count doesn't match on both sides, the expressions won't match. Lists get more interesting when you throw in the | operator. With functional languages, pattern matching usually means matching the head and tail. As in Prolog and Erlang, list matching is just construction in reverse:

```
iex> [head|tail] = list
[:wolverine, :magneto, :cyclops]
iex> {head, tail}
{:wolverine, [:magneto, :cyclops]}
iex> [first, second | tail] = list
[:wolverine, :magneto, :cyclops]
iex> {first, second, tail}
{:wolverine, :magneto, [:cyclops]}
```

Now we can match lists of arbitrary length. Remember, internally lists are implemented as linked lists and accessed strictly head first. This method of matching means we'll naturally build algorithms that attack lists *head first*. Now, let's look at some more advanced matches:

```
iex> [first] = []
** (MatchError) no match of right hand side value: []
iex> [first, second] = list
** (MatchError) no match of right hand side value: list
iex> [first, second | _] = list
[:wolverine, :magneto, :cyclops]
iex> {first, second}
{:wolverine, :magneto}
iex> [_, second|_] = list
[:wolverine, :magneto, :cyclops]
iex> second
:magneto
```

The _ operator allows us to match an arbitrary item, or any trailing list of items on the right-hand side of the |. Also, notice that [] matches only an empty list. You can use wildcards in combination to match an arbitrary group of elements at the head of a list.

Recursion over a list will normally involve two forms of a function. The first form will match the head and tail. The second will match an empty list. Put the following into a file called print.exs.

```
elixir/print.exs
defmodule ListExample do
  def print([]), do: :ok
  def print([head|tail]) do
    IO.puts head
    print tail
  end
end

ListExample.print([:storm, :sabretooth, :mystique])
```

That's classic list traversal. For the most part, you won't be writing your own recursive functions. You'll use libraries to do that for you. Several libraries will help you work with lists, but the primary one is Enum. You could easily implement this program with Enum.each/2, which passes each element of a list to a function, like this:

```
iex> Enum.each list, &(IO.puts &1)
wolverine
magneto
cyclops
:ok
```

A function to print an arbitrary list, then, would look like this:

```
def print(x), do: Enum.each( x, &( IO.puts &1 ) )
```

Enum has the libraries you've come to expect for dealing with functions. I won't bore you with a full list, but we'll walk through a few of them to see how it all works:

```
iex> Enum.filter [1, 2, 3], &(&1 > 1)
[2, 3]
iex> Enum.reduce [1, 2, 3], &(&1 + &2)
6
iex> Enum.any? [1, 2, 3], &(&1 > 2)
true
iex> Enum.all? [1, 2, 3], &(&1 > 2)
false
iex> Enum.zip [1, 2, 3], [4, 5, 6]
[{1, 4}, {2, 5}, {3, 6}]
```

For a more complete list, check out the Elixir Enum documentation.[3]

Functions are fundamentally transformations. It's not surprising that you'll often want to do multiple transformations at once, such as a filter and a map. Elixir has a tool to do just that: the *for comprehension*.

For Comprehensions

Each for comprehension has a generator step, a filter step, and a map step. You can omit the filter step. The comprehension generators can work on anything implementing Enumerable—enums, maps, and so on. The simplest form of a generator takes an element from a list:

```
iex> for x <- [1, 2, 3], do: x
[1, 2, 3]
```

If you specify more than one generator, the comprehension will find all possible combinations of both:

```
iex> for x <- [1, 2], y <- [3, 4], z <- [5], do: {x, y, z}
[{1, 3, 5}, {1, 4, 5}, {2, 3, 5}, {2, 4, 5}]
```

You can also filter your generators:

```
iex> for x <- [1, 2], y <- [3, 4], z <- [5], x + y < 5, do: {x, y, z}
[{1, 3, 5}]
```

The comprehension is an extremely powerful tool for expressing transformations of any kind. Here's an example of an ironically named "Quicksort":

```
elixir/quicksort.exs
defmodule QuickSort do
  def sort([]), do: []
  def sort([head|tail]) do
    sort( for(x <- tail, x <= head, do: x) ) ++
    [head] ++
    sort( for(x <- tail, x > head, do: x) )
  end
end

IO.inspect QuickSort.sort([5, 6, 3, 2, 7, 8])
```

One Quicksort step will take the head of a list and the remainder. Simply put, each step will return a sorted list of all numbers in the list less than the head, plus a list containing only the head, plus a sorted list of all the numbers in a list greater than the head. The for comprehension does most of the work. It has a generator, x inlist tail, a filter, x < head, and a transformation step, do: x.

We've taken a quick pass through representing lists. Now, we'll learn to handle key-value pairs in Elixir.

Keyword Lists

Before Erlang added maps in late 2013, the language used lists of key-value pairs to express associations. Elixir also supports keyword lists, like this:

```
iex> powers = [{:wolverine, [:regeneration, :claws]}, {:sway, [:time_control]},
                {:iceman, [:freeze]}]
[wolverine: [:regeneration, :claws], sway: [:time_control], iceman: [:freeze]]
iex> Keyword.get powers, :wolverine
[:regeneration, :claws]
```

The same shortcut syntax that works with maps also works with keyword lists, for example, [key: :value]. For the most part, you'll prefer maps to keyword lists.

Function Sugar

Before we finish Day 1, let's take a look at some of the variations of functional definitions that you'll see. Elixir allows you to specify default values for arguments. This is what the syntax would look like:

```
iex> defmodule Secret do
...>    def hanger(x \\ 18), do: x
...> end
```

Simple enough. That module declares two functions: hanger/0 and hanger/1.

You can combine keyword lists with optional arguments to declare functions with options on the end, like this:

```
def draw(square, options \\ [])
```

When the last argument of a function is a list, you can omit the enclosing brackets, like this:

```
draw my_square, color: "FFFFFF", width: "10px"

def some_function(), do: this_is_an_option
```

Now you know where the one-line version of the do/end block comes from! It's just a keyword list as the trailing argument, allowing omitted brackets. You'll see us take advantage of this syntax often when we do metaprogramming in Day 2.

What We Learned in Day 1

Day 1 was a busy one. We spent most of the day working with the features that make Elixir a great general-purpose language. We learned about some of the foundational concepts that Elixir shares with Ruby:

- The basic syntax is heavily influenced by Ruby.
- Expressions track more closely to Ruby than Erlang.
- The expression of code blocks as do/end and def/do/end is familiar.

While many of the concepts may seem familiar, Ruby developers will notice some striking differences:

- Elixir is a pattern matching language, from the inside out.
- In Elixir, you work with data structures such as lists and structs directly instead of objects.
- The Erlang influence in functional declarations is pronounced, permitting multiple function bodies with the same name.

To wrap up the day, you're going to finish up Day 1 writing some functions and working with maps and lists. Tomorrow, we're going to dive into the Erlang side of this split personality.

Your Turn

It's your first day in Elixir. You know the drill. These questions will help you learn your way around and present you with a few problems at different skill levels.

Find...

Elixir is a name that is picking up traction quickly, but if you're interested in finding the language quickly, you should search for "elixir language" rather than just "elixir".

- The Elixir language home page, which is connected to some Wiki articles
- An article about using Elixir's build tool, Mix
- The Elixir project on GitHub, where you can report an issue
- The functions supported by Enum, List, and String
- Elixir mailing lists, where you can ask questions
- A way to call Erlang libraries from Elixir

Do (Easy):

- Express some geometry objects using tuples: a two-dimensional point, a line, a circle, a polygon, and a triangle.
- Write a function to compute the hypotenuse of a right triangle given the length of two sides.
- Convert a string to an atom.
- Test to see if an expression is an atom.

Do (Medium):

- Given a list of numbers, use recursion to find (1) the size of the list, (2) the maximum value, and (3) the minimum value.
- Given a list of atoms, build a function called word_count that returns a keyword list, where the keys are atoms from the list and the values are the number of occurrences of that word in the list. For example, word_count([:one, :two, :two]) returns [one: 1, two: 2].

Do (Hard):

- Represent a tree of sentences as tuples. Traverse the tree, presenting an indented list. For example, traverse({"See Spot.", {"See Spot sit.", "See Spot run."}}) would return:

```
See Spot.
  See Spot sit.
  See Spot run.
```

- Given an incomplete tic-tac-toe board, compute the next player's best move.

Day 2: Controlling Mutations

In Day 1, you learned about the hardened skeleton—the language features that make such an excellent general purpose language—and that the syntax, filled with sugar to simplify recurring idioms, is opinionated and rich. Even if Elixir were just a general-purpose language with no bells and whistles, it would be attractive.

Today, you're going to learn to grow your own mutations, without radiation exposure. We'll roll our own mini-language, building a state machine with Lisp-style macros. Before we do that, we're going to have to lay a little more foundation. We'll work with Mix to manage our application build process, and we'll learn to use structs. Then, we'll dive head first into macros.

Mix

The first examples in this chapter were all in the console. As our ideas got too big to express on a line or two, we used scripts. For the next few examples, we're going to want to compile our code, which may be based on dependencies. We'll use Mix for that task. If you've got Elixir, you've got Mix. If you're ever lost, you can see what's available by running mix help.

Mix is Elixir's build tool, like make for C, rake for Ruby, or ant for Java. You'll use mix to create a project with a uniform structure and to maintain your dependencies. Let's create a new project. Navigate to a directory where you want your new project to be and type mix new states --sup (we pass --sup to generate a supervisor tree that we will need in Day 3):

```
> mix new states --sup
* creating lib
* creating test
...

Your mix project was created with success.
...
```

Mix created a project called states in its own directory and a number of files underneath. Your tests will go in test, your source files will go in lib, and the file describing your application and dependencies will go in mix.exs. To make sure things are working, change into the states directory, compile the default application, and run tests, like this:

```
> cd states
> mix test
Compiled lib/states.ex
Generated states.app
.

Finished in 0.02 seconds (0.02s on load, 0.00s on tests)
1 tests, 0 failures
```

Mix compiled the file because it tracks dependencies between tasks. It also provides good support for your custom tasks.

Our tests are clean and green. Each . represents a test. Let's put this new structure to use. We're going to build a state machine.

From Concrete to Meta

Metaprogramming uses programs to write more sophisticated programs. In this section, we're going to build a concrete state machine that will work fine but that might be difficult to reuse. Then, we'll take that concrete implementation and use metaprogramming to morph it into something more abstract and flexible.

Sometimes, the best way to do metaprogramming is to build a simple tool that implements the code you want your metaprogramming platform to build. Said another way, if we want to build a generic *state machine builder*, we start by building a *single state machine*.

First, let's review. Abstractly, a state machine is a graph where the nodes are states and the connections are events. Triggering an event moves the state machine from one state to the next. Concretely, think of a state machine as a set of rules that move from one state to another. We have to work with four pieces, then:

- Our state machine data. This will be some kind of data structure describing our state machine.
- Our state machine behavior. This will be a module with functions attached.
- Our application data. This will be some data structure with a state.
- Our application behavior.

For example, let's write a state machine for an old-school brick-and-mortar video store. A state machine works well for us because:

- Videos in a store have concrete states to represent.
- The rules for transitioning between states are well defined.
- We might want to execute complex application logic when the video transitions from one state to another.

A state machine will help us organize code and manage change. Here's the basic state machine for our simplistic old-school video store. It has three states: available, rented, and lost.

When a new video arrives on the shelves, it will go into the available state. When a customer rents a video, it goes to the rented state. When the customer returns a video, it will go back to available. Lose a video, and it goes to lost. At that point, let's assume that our customer must buy the video, so there's no return to any other state.

Let's start with the data structure for a video first. We could use maps, but since videos will each have a fixed structure, we'll use a data structure with a fixed number of named fields called *structs*.

Naming Fields with Structs

A struct is like a map with a fixed set of fields with the ability to attach behavior in the form of functions. We're going to use a struct to represent our video. To keep things simple, assume there's one video per title. We'll represent each video with a state and a title. Place the following in states/lib/video.ex:

```
elixir/day2/states/lib/video.ex
defmodule Video do
  defstruct title: "", state: :available, times_rented: 0, log: []
end
```

And take it for a spin:

```
> iex -S mix
```

I started the console via iex -S mix. Mix compiled the file and then loaded the application modules. Now, I can use the console *in the context of my project.*

```
iex> vid = %Video{title: "The Wolverine"}
%Video{title: "The Wolverine", state: :available}
iex> vid.state
:available
```

I created a new struct with the constructor %Video{}. Struct syntax works like maps with the name of the struct between the % and {. Notice that I specified a title but picked up the default value for state.

Structs are just maps—create, update, and pattern match using the map syntax. Define them in modules, and include the functions that work on them.

Like everything else in Elixir, structs are immutable. You can create a new copy of a struct with one or more fields changed like this:

```
iex> checked_out = %Video{vid | state: :rented}
%Video{title: "The Wolverine", state: :rented}
```

Structs are sometimes safer than maps because they will allow only keys you specify in the formal definition:

```
iex(6)> checked_out = %Video{vid | staet: :rented}
** (CompileError) iex:6: unknown key :staet for struct Video
    (elixir) src/elixir_map.erl:169:
    ...
```

Now that we have a strategy for representing our application data, let's move on to application behavior.

Creating Concrete Behavior

As we flesh out our video store, we'll need three basic modules:

- VideoStore will have the implementation of business logic.
- VideoStore.Concrete will have the video store's state machine, and state-machine behavior specific to that video store.
- StateMachine.Behavior will have generic state-machine behavior that we'll reuse.

Our concrete video store will have application-specific behavior, lists that represent our state machine, and generic state-machine behaviors. First, a real video store will likely have some business logic that occurs whenever the video enters a new state. We'll capture each of these in a function.

We'll build something concrete, extract common ideas, and then generalize a state machine API. We'll reuse the functions in VideoStore and StateMachine.Behavior. Eventually, we'll look for patterns in VideoStore.Concrete that we can exploit with our state machine macros.

First, let's build that business logic. Initially, we'll build the code that will execute whenever a customer decides to rent, return, or lose one of our videos. Put the following in states/lib/video_store.ex:

```
elixir/day2/states/lib/video_store.ex
defmodule VideoStore do
  def renting(video) do
    vid = log video, "Renting #{video.title}"
    %{vid | times_rented: (video.times_rented + 1)}
  end

  def returning(video), do: log( video, "Returning #{video.title}" )

  def losing(video), do: log( video, "Losing #{video.title}" )

  def log(video, message) do
    %{video | log: [message|video.log]}
  end
end
```

For now, we'll record interactions on a video much like a librarian would on a book's library card. We'll count the number of times a video is rented. You see just four functions: one to do the logging, and one for each of the events on our state machine.

Modeling the State Machine

So far, we have only created a video struct to preserve our state. Now, we'll need to work out how the state machine works. Here's how we'll build it:

- The state machine will be a keyword list of the form [state_name: state].
- Each state will have a keyword list of events, keyed by event name, with each event having a name, the transition, and a possible list of callbacks.

The state machine is a straight-up keyword list of states, and the events are keyword lists as well. We don't need to write any code, but we're armed with what we'd like our API to look like.

We'll be able to define a state machine like this:

```
[ available: [
    rent:   [ to: :rented,    calls: [&VideoStore.renting/1]]],
  rented: [
    return: [ to: :available, calls: [&VideoStore.returning/1]]],
    lose:   [ to: :lost,      calls: [&VideoStore.losing/1]]],
  lost: [] ]
```

We have three states: available, rented, and lost. Each has an associated list of events. Let's write the functions that will do the bulk of the work.

Adding State-Machine Behavior

Our state machine will allow an application to fire an event on some struct with a state. Firing that event will transition the state machine to a new state, and perhaps fire some callbacks as well.

Put the following in states/lib/state_machine_behavior.ex. We'll start with a function called fire that will fire an event, and another called activate that will invoke all of the user-defined functions associated with an event. Our goal is to add code that we'll be able to use directly when we create our state machine macros. The functions are short and simple:

```
elixir/day2/states/lib/state_machine_behavior.ex
defmodule StateMachine.Behavior do
  def fire(context, event) do
    %{context | state: event[:to]}
    |> activate(event)
  end

  def fire(states, context, event_name) do
    event = states[context.state][event_name]
    fire(context, event)
  end

  def activate(context, event) do
    Enum.reduce(event[:calls] || [], context, &(&1.(&2)))
  end
end
```

Since functional languages are immutable, a recurring pattern is to pass around some data structure using transforming functions that return new copies that evolve over the life of the program. We'll call this evolving state the context. All of our state machine APIs will take a context struct, transform it, and pass the transformed version to the next function in the chain. One of the fields in our context will be state. This is what the functions do:

1. Our first job is to fire an event. It is easier to define that function in terms of an event and the context. The job of fire is straightforward: update the context with the new state, and then apply all of the functions provided in event.calls.

2. We provide an alternative API for convenience, one that does not require an event lookup. We just look up the event and call the other fire API.

3. The activate function chains together each function in activate as if it were a pipe. Each function takes the previous context, transforms it, and passes it to the next function. Enum.reduce provides this service. For the anonymous function &(&1.(&2)), &1 is a function from event.calls, and &2 is the result returned from the last function call (or simply context for the first call).

We could write a test of the functions so far, but the video store we'll define in the next step will provide a far better testing opportunity. Let's push on.

Looking for Patterns

The next step is to provide the pieces of the video store that implement one specific state machine. We've come to the point where we need to think a little bit about what we'll use to represent our state machine itself. As I build a language, I prefer to rely on basic data structures, especially keyword lists, wherever possible. We'll tweak that language a little later when we are ready to code individual macros. With that in mind, let's look at the state machine features.

```
elixir/day2/states/lib/video_store_concrete.ex
defmodule VideoStore.Concrete do import StateMachine.Behavior
  def rent(video),   do: fire(state_machine, video, :rent)
  def return(video), do: fire(state_machine, video, :return)
  def lose(video),   do: fire(state_machine, video, :lose)
  def state_machine do
    [ available: [
        rent:   [ to: :rented,    calls: [&VideoStore.renting/1]   ]],
      rented: [
        return: [ to: :available, calls: [&VideoStore.returning/1] ],
        lose:   [ to: :lost,      calls: [&VideoStore.losing/1]    ]],
      lost: [] ]
  end
end
```

❶ You can trigger an event on a state by simply calling a function. The context has the state name, and the function bodies have the state machine and the event names. This function is simply a convenience so that users of the class can access basic business functionality.

❷ This function actually specifies the state machine as keyword lists. The outermost keyword list has pairs that represent {state_name, event_keyword_list}. The next level is a keyword list of events that looks like {event_name, event_metadata}. The innermost list has the event metadata that expresses the new state (to: new_state) and a list of functions that allow customized behavior as the states change (calls: [callback_functions]).

Let's pause to make a few observations. First, the specification of states is a little awkward because the data structure must do too much of the work. It would help us to have a macro expressing each individual state.

Second, you can see the duplication in the callback functions. We should try to create those from our macros. Keep those thoughts in the back of your mind as we build out the concrete version of the state machine. Right now, it's time for some tests.

Writing Tests

I get nervous if I'm building something substantial and I get too far before writing a test. There's not too much to test yet, but that will change quickly. Put the following code in states/test/concrete_test.exs:

```
defmodule ConcreteTest do
  use ExUnit.Case
  test "should update count" do
    rented_video = VideoStore.renting(video)
    assert rented_video.times_rented == 1
  end

  def video, do: %Video{title: "XMen"}

end
```

This file looks a little different than traditional modules. First, you see the use macro that includes our macros. Also, the test looks different. You'd expect to see def of some kind at that level. test is actually a macro. A macro takes valid Elixir code and transforms it. In this case, the test macro is actually declaring a function with an API that we would find repetitive and awkward.

Macros actually get defined at an explicit point in compilation called *macro expansion time*. Their domain is the AST. To see what the syntax tree looks like, in the console use quote:

```
iex> quote do: 1 == 2
{:==, [context: Elixir, import: Kernel], [1, 2]}
```

The quote command shows you the internal representation of Elixir code. Here, we're using quote to look at the syntax tree. In fact, that's exactly what the assert macro does. It looks at the quoted expression you pass in, so it can tell what comparison you're using. For a failed comparison, assert will give you a rich message, like this:

```
1) test should update count (ConcreteTest)
   ** (ExUnit.ExpectationError)
               expected: 1
     to be equal to (==): 2
   at test/concrete_test.exs:5
```

In fact, every row in the AST is a three-tuple. It has an operator, some metadata, and an argument list. The second element has contextual metadata, and we're not going to worry about it here. Focus on the first and last elements. This simple format is exactly what makes Elixir such a strong metaprogramming language.

Implementing should with Macros

Now, we'll use quote to actually inject our own code. Since we're just dealing with lists and tuples, it's easy. I'm a fan of using "should" to describe test expectations. That means that every test will start with test "should..." but that syntax is repetitive. Let's fix that. Let's tell the Elixir compiler to look for the word should and replace it with our own macro.

The existing test macro takes a name and a do block. As a do block is just a keyword list, we'll express it with options, and make our own macro that calls the test macro. Add the following to the top of states/test/test_helper.exs:

```
defmodule Should do
  defmacro should(name, options) do
    quote do
      test("should #{unquote name}", unquote(options))
    end
  end
end
```

This code tells the compiler the following:

"As you are building the AST for this program, whenever you see the word should, replace it with everything inside the quote do block."

Think of quote as diving one level deeper into the program.

Our program is an onion that has layers: programs are writing programs. When we're inside this quote, we're actually writing the code that will replace should.... This replacement happens in a pre-compile step called *macro expansion time.* We're one level deeper into the onion. The problem is that by the time the code executes, the keyword name and the keyword options will both be undefined. Our test macro doesn't understand name or options at all. It's one level up. We have to go up and get it.

Think of unquote as climbing one level out of the onion that is your program.

When we use unquote, we climb up one level outside of the quote. We can now see everything that the should macro defines, including name and options. When we unquote those, we say to the compiler, "Add the value of name and the value of options as you find them, one level up."

Now, we can change our tests to use the new structure, like this:

```
import Should
use ExUnit.Case

should "update count" do
...
```

And run your tests. You'll find them clean and green. A few lines of code, and we've streamlined the testing API. That's the power of macros.

Writing More Tests

Make concrete_test.exs look like this:

```
elixir/day2/states/test/concrete_test.exs
defmodule ConcreteTest do
  use ExUnit.Case
  import Should

  should "update count" do
      rented_video = VideoStore.renting(video)
      assert rented_video.times_rented == 1
  end
  should "rent video" do
    rented_video = VideoStore.Concrete.rent video
    assert :rented == rented_video.state
    assert 1 == Enum.count( rented_video.log )
  end
  should "handle multiple transitions" do
    import VideoStore.Concrete
    vid = video |> rent |> return |> rent |> return |> rent
    assert 5 == Enum.count( vid.log )
    assert 3 == vid.times_rented
  end

  def video, do: %Video{title: "XMen"}
end
```

Now, you can finally see why we've been working on a state machine. The should macro makes our tests easy to understand, and the state machine is a great abstraction for handling transitions of state in a functional system. Elixir's pipe operator shows any users of this code exactly what's happening.

We have successfully built out an application with a state machine. That's not the point of this day, though. We'd like to allow *anyone* to plug in his or her own state machine, without duplicating effort.

We can't put it off any longer. It's time to tame the macro beast.

Writing a Complex Macro

If we were to attack a state machine without macros, we'd need to write many similar functions that looked almost alike. Macros will let us build function templates that declare those similar functions for us. There's a cost, though. You need to be able to handle another level of complexity.

We'll manage our macro just as we'd manage any other complex task. We'll start with the entire problem and break it down into smaller function calls. First, let's decide exactly how our macro should look. Here's our target API:

```
use StateMachine

state :rented,
        [ return: [to: :available, calls: [&renting/1]],
          lose:   [to: :lost] ]

state :lost, []
```

You can already see how the macros will help us. Our users can break down the definition of a machine into clearly defined parts. Instead of using *functions at runtime* to do the work, we'll use *macros at compile time*. Using this strategy, we can build templates that generate similar functions across many different applications. Using a little metadata, we'll be able to generate all of the code that will let us manage a state machine for our application.

We have one main macro to build: the state macro. It will take a state name and a keyword list of events. We'll need a few new tools as we build, but that will be no problem.

Understanding Compile-Time Flow

If thinking this way is a little troubling, understand this first. Elixir evaluates functions at *execution time*, whereas macros execute at *compile time*:

```
iex> defmodule TestMacro do
...>    defmacro print, do: IO.puts( "Executing..." )
...> end
{:module, TestMacro, ..., {:print, 0}}
```

Simple enough. We've defined a one-line macro that will print "Executing...".
Now, let's use it.

```
iex> defmodule TestModule do
...>    require TestMacro
...>    TestMacro.print
...> end
Executing...
{:module, TestModule, ..., :ok}
```

That "Executing..." message confirms macros run at compile time. Specifically,
one of the compile steps is macro-expansion. Then, the compiler continues,
with any expanded macro code *injected* into the compilation. When you see
quote and unquote, don't get confused. Those functions make it easy to reason
about the code Elixir is injecting at compile time, no more and no less.

Building a Skeleton

Like Wolverine, we'll start with a strong skeleton based on the simplest tasks.

You might have noticed that we had to fully qualify the macro print with Test-
Macro.print. That API would get tedious. Sure, we could solve this problem with
an import directive, but we don't want the consumers of our API to have to
manually require dependencies for our macros. We can handle the imports.
The magic directive for this purpose is use.

import makes a module available for consumption. require lets you use functions
in a module as if they were scoped locally. Both are compile-time behaviors.

The use directive is different. The use macro will let us specify behavior that
we want to happen *when a user includes our module, before compile time*. use
will call the macro __using__. We'll also stub out the other functions we'll need.
Here's our initial skeleton, in states/lib/state_machine.ex:

```
defmodule StateMachine do
❶   defmacro __using__(_) do
      quote do
        import StateMachine
        # initialize temporary data
      end
    end
❷   defmacro state(name, events), do: IO.puts "Declaring state #{name}"
    defmacro __before_compile__(env), do: nil
  end
```

So far, we're just working with the mechanical devices of building a macro. We're not actually doing much work yet. Still, let's take a brief look at what's going on. We'll add detail and depth as we go.

❶ A call to use StateMachine will trigger this _using_ macro. So far, we're just importing the StateMachine API, so our consumers won't have to type out StateMachine.state to invoke our macro.

❷ This function will eventually specify the state machine as keyword lists. The outermost keyword list has pairs that represent {state_name, event_key-word_list}. The next level is a keyword list of events that looks like {event_name, event_metadata}. The innermost list has the event metadata that expresses the new state (to: new_state) and a list of functions that allow customized behavior as the states change (calls: [callback_functions]). For now, we simply stub it out.

It's too early to write any tests, but we can at least put our skeleton through its paces. Open the console with iex -S mix or compile the file from the console, and try it out

```
iex> c "state_machine.ex", "states/lib"
states/lib/state_machine.ex:9: warning: variable events is unused
states/lib/state_machine.ex:10: warning: variable env is unused
iex> defmodule StateMachineText do
...>    use StateMachine
...>    state :available, []
...>    state :rented, []
...>    state :lost, []
...> end
Declaring state available
Declaring state rented
Declaring state lost
{:module, StateMachineText, ... :ok}
```

You can see that we're on the right track because we get a diagnostic message for each state as Elixir compiles the module. Let's work on the temporary variables that will hold the state. To do this, we'll use module attributes.

Understanding Compile-time Flow, Part 2

As we put a little more flesh on the skeleton, we'll also beef up your understanding of compile-time flow. In this section, we're going to need *module attributes*, or compile-time variables expressed as @variable. At macro expansion time, Elixir does all of the following:

• An application's module includes the macro's module with use.
• The compiler executes the _using_ function, injecting some setup code.

- The compiler then processes the file, making any macro substitutions that it encounters.
- Individual macros may interact with module attributes to work together.
- The compiler then looks for the function identified by the @before_compile module attribute and executes it, potentially injecting more code.

Now, it's time to see our full macro at work. Hide the annotations as you read through the code. See if you can identify each of these steps. This is the full macro:

elixir/day2/states/lib/state_machine.ex

```elixir
defmodule StateMachine do
  defmacro __using__(_) do
    quote do
      import StateMachine
      @states []
      @before_compile StateMachine
    end
  end

  defmacro state(name, events) do
    quote do
      @states [{unquote(name), unquote(events)} | @states]
    end
  end

  defmacro __before_compile__(env) do
    states = Module.get_attribute(env.module, :states)
    events = states
             |> Keyword.values
             |> List.flatten
             |> Keyword.keys
             |> Enum.uniq

    quote do
      def state_machine do
        unquote(states)
      end

      unquote event_callbacks(events)
    end
  end

  def event_callback(name) do
    callback = name
    quote do
      def unquote(name)(context) do
        StateMachine.Behavior.fire(state_machine, context, unquote(callback))
      end
```

```
      end
  end

  def event_callbacks(names) do
    Enum.map names, &event_callback/1
  end

end
```

❶ Our _using_ function is finally complete. We're initializing module
attributes for a list of states so that the compose operator will work correctly. We also instruct the compiler to call _before_compile_ after macro
substitution but before compilation.

❷ We use simple list construction to add each state to the head of our list.
Notice there's no = sign. Module attribute assignment is not a match
expression, as the runtime = would be.

❸ Our _before_compile_ function is now doing the lion's share of the work.
We read the value of our module attributes into states. Next, we start with
all states. We pipe to Keyword.values to get all of the events, pipe those to
List.flatten so we have a uniform list of events, and pipe that flattened list
to Keyword.keys to get a list of all names.

❹ Finally, we inject some code. Since states was defined up one level, we
must unquote it. This function is simple since we're just returning the
state machine structure.

❺ Building the callbacks is a slightly bigger job, so we call a function to do
that work. Since that function is defined one level up (as is events), we
unquote them.

❻ event_callback defines a single callback. Each callback defines a function
that invokes fire. Using these, a consumer can easily fire state machine
events through simple function calls.

Using Our State Machine

We finally get to see this skeleton dance. We can now tweak VideoStore to use
our new version of the API. Let's make a copy of it so you can study the old
version and the new. Copy video_store.ex to vid_store.ex. The new file will be our
dynamic state machine. We can just add this code to the top of VidStore, and
the macro will do all of the work for us, creating everything that was in Con-
creteVideoStore dynamically. Copy video_store.ex to vid_store.ex, and then change
the top of vid_store.ex to look like this:

```
defmodule VidStore do
  use StateMachine

  state :available,
    rent: [ to: :rented,       calls: [ &VidStore.renting/1 ]]

  state :rented,
    return: [ to: :available, calls: [ &VidStore.returning/1 ]],
    lose:   [ to: :lost,       calls: [ &VidStore.losing/1 ]]

  state :lost, []

  ...
```

Ah. That's much better. The state machine reads as cleanly as a book. Now, any application can make use of our state machine's beautiful syntax. Take your tests for a spin to make sure they still pass.

While you're at it, create a test called vid_store_test.exs that uses the VidStore API. Make sure all tests are green! Remember, you won't need anything in the Concrete module because our state machine now creates all of that code dynamically.

We're not done with this video store yet. We'll build onto vid_store in Day 3 to make the file both distributed and concurrent using Elixir's macros for Erlang's OTP library.

What We Learned in Day 2

We packed a lot into Day 2. First, we learned to create projects with Mix. Then, we learned to create maps with named fields, called structs. We then built two versions of a state machine, a concrete one and a dynamic one. The second version used a generic state machine language that we created with Lisp-style macros.

We saw that Elixir expressions all reduce to the same structure: a three-tuple with a function name, metadata, and the function arguments. Our state machine macros used a wide range of tools:

- Our users consume our macros with the use command.
- Within our macro module, we imported our macro file and set up some variables within the __using__ macro.
- We introduced a state macro so our users could create a state.
- We used module attributes to compute a running list of states.
- We added __before_compile__ behavior to our macro to round out our macro.

When we were done, we had a unified strategy for conveniently and concisely representing a state machine. The Lisp-like syntax tree, quote and unquote, made it all possible, but the end result was syntax that was anything but Lisp-like.

Your Turn

In this set of exercises, you're going to look at some existing Elixir modules and how they work. You'll also try your hand at extending our macros.

Find...

- The elixir-pipes GitHub project. Look at how the macros improve the usage of pipes. Look at how pipe_with is implemented.
- The supported Elixir module attributes.
- A tutorial on Elixir-style metaprogramming.
- Elixir protocols. What do they do?
- function_exported? What does that function do? (You will need it for one of the next problems.)

Do (Easy):

- Add a find state to the state machine that transitions from lost to found. Add this code in both the concrete and abstract versions of your state machine. Which is easier, and why?

Do (Medium):

- Write tests for VidStore. What was different, and what was the same?

Do (Hard):

- Add before_(event_name) and after_(event_name) hooks. If those functions exist, make sure fire executes them.
- Add a protocol to our state machine that forces a state machine struct to implement the state field.

Day 3: Spawning and Respawning

In Day 2, you effectively redefined the Elixir language, adding your own syntax for expressing state machines. That's heady stuff. Today, you're going to use macros and Erlang's OTP to build an application that you can fully distribute. Before we get started, let's hear from José Valim, the creator of Elixir, and learn what he was thinking when he created the language.

Us: What language did you use before Elixir?

Valim: My main language before Elixir was Ruby. However, I have always been curious and interested in other languages and paradigms, so I am always reading and building prototypes in different languages. Although they rarely make it to production, it is always a very fun learning exercise!

Us: Why did you move on?

Valim: Lack of better tools for concurrency was the main reason why I moved on. Boxes with 16 and more cores have become commodity hardware, and traditional languages do not provide the proper abstractions to use this hardware efficiently in large scale.

I've found the opposite scenario in the Erlang VM, where concurrency is the norm and developers are used to writing distributed, fault-tolerant applications. And that was the trigger for Elixir.

Us: What were Elixir's main influences?

Valim: Erlang is definitely the main influence in the language. Most of Elixir's semantics are shared with the Erlang language since both run in the same virtual machine. However, the parts that do differ are highly inspired by languages like Lisp, Ruby, and Clojure.

For example, one of the first language decisions was to provide metaprogramming functionality via macros, as seen in Lisp. However, back then, we already had two Lisps running in the Erlang VM (Joxa and LFE) and I really wanted to explore the feasibility of a macro system on top of non-Lisp syntax. So we came up with a quite uniform syntax representation and borrowed from Ruby and Erlang to make common idioms more elegant.

Developers should also see minor influences from other languages, like a focus toward documentation and doc tests functionality coming from Python. Some great language developers came before me. I try to learn from them all.

Us: What's your favorite feature?

Valim: That's a very hard question. We have inherited excellent functionalities by simply running in the Erlang VM, like pattern matching and message passing, which would definitely be at the top of the list. But if we are considering only what Elixir brings to the game, I would definitely pick protocols, which add dynamic polymorphism to the language. Protocols allow library developers to specify interfaces which can be implemented and extended by any user to their own data types. They seem the perfect balance in between dynamic OO languages (where no interface is specified) and static interfaces (which are a design-time choice).

Us: What would you do differently if you had the opportunity to start over?

Valim: I would have tackled fine-grained constructs for concurrency earlier on. The Erlang VM provides a simple and great foundation for concurrency based on very few constructs: processes, message passing, monitoring, and so on. However, *those constructs are building blocks, so sometimes it is hard to communicate intent because we don't have names for common patterns. How do you call the action of spawning a process to compute some work and reading its value later on? Some languages call it promises, others call it tasks. But we call it "spawning a process to compute some work and reading its value later on."*

I believe the language and the ecosystem would greatly benefit if the language provided a few common patterns. The upside is that, due to the foundation provided by the VM, those constructs are quite easy to implement. So it is more of a community effort in identifying the common needs and patterns than a technological one.

Clearly, Erlang was a strong influence on the language. Actors and concurrency are among the most important and influential features in the language. We'll get to use them to take our state machine to the next level. Let's roll!

Spawning Processes

Just like Erlang, Elixir makes it easy, even trivial, to spawn processes and communicate between them. You can use processes in the console. For now, we'll use a simple anonymous function in the console. Look for the send function in the following code:

```
iex> ball_glove = fn -> receive do
...>    {:pitch, pitcher} ->
...>      send pitcher, {:catch, self()}
...> end
...> end
 #Function<20.80484245 in :erl_eval.expr/5>
iex> catcher = spawn ball_glove
 #PID<0.51.0>
```

First, we declare an anonymous function. Every process has an *inbox*. All communication between processes uses this inbox as a queue. The receive function receives messages from the inbox. In this case, we match messages of the form {:pitch, _}. We grab the second part of the two-tuple, and it matches to pitcher. That's the identifier of the process that sent this message. We use it to send a message back to pitcher.

Then, we spawn a process that executes ball_glove. We grab the process id (or pid, for short) and match it to catcher. Now, we're ready for the other side of this game of catch.

```
iex> send catcher, {:pitch, self()}
{:pitch, #PID<0.40.0>}
iex> receive do
...>    {:catch, pid} ->
...>      IO.puts "Caught it!"
...> end
```

```
Caught it!
:ok
```

Simple and clean. We send a :pitch message to catcher, and the catcher replies with :catch. That's a classic *actor* model for concurrent programming. You can see just how convenient Elixir processes can be.

Understand that Elixir processes, like Erlang processes, are also *cheap.* They cost next to nothing to create. Erlang and Elixir programmers often use processes like OOP programmers use objects.

Elixir uses processes as the basic primitive for building useful abstractions. For example, Elixir provides tasks, which starts another process and waits until a result from that task is available. You can start a task in another process, continue to work in your current thread, and await the result, like this:

```
iex> claim_slip = Task.async(fn -> IO.puts("park the car") end)
park the car
%Task{pid: #PID<0.98.0>, ref: #Reference<0.0.0.370>}
iex> IO.puts "run around town"
run around town
:ok
iex> Task.await claim_slip
:ok
```

You can actually run around town while the valet parks the car because the task runs in another process. You can pick up your car immediately, or wait until you're ready. Elixir also provides Agents and Event managers, but we will focus on two abstractions for now, GenServer and Supervisors, which are rooted in Erlang OTP and are the foundation for building distributed and fault-tolerant applications.

Building an OTP Application

We've seen how to build trivial concurrent applications, but the devil is in the details. To finish that application, we'd have to handle crashes and errors, cleaning up resources and handling respawning or reporting. Elixir provides a better way through Erlang's OTP.

Erlang's roots are deep in the telecom field. Back when OTP was created, the acronym stood for Open Telecom Platform. Now, it's just called OTP. Elixir macros on top of the Erlang OTP libraries make it easy to distribute your applications to the web. Let's create a simple in-memory database for our video store using Elixir's convenient wrappers around Erlang's OTP.

As you've seen, it's common practice to separate behavior and state in Elixir. As you might imagine, the same is true of Erlang too. We're going to use a behavior called GenServer. In this case, Gen stands for Generic, and it separates the "same-for-every-application" features from your specific application features, like our state machine. This is what we will need to get started.

- GenServer is a behavior with some macros to keep things simple. We'll need to import them.
- We will need to initialize the state of our video store.
- We will need a callback to add videos to the store. We'll use an asynchronous cast OTP function.
- We will need a callback to fire our state machine events on a video. We'll use a synchronous call OTP function.
- We'll add a function called start_link that will make it easier to restart, should it ever crash.

Now that you've seen the overview, let's take a look at the code. Put the following in lib/states/states_server.ex:

```
elixir/day3/states/lib/states_server.ex
defmodule States.Server do
❶  use GenServer
   require VidStore

❷  def start_link(videos) do
     GenServer.start_link(__MODULE__, videos, name: :video_store)
   end

❸  def init(videos) do
     { :ok, videos }
   end

❹  def handle_call({action, item}, _from, videos) do
     video = videos[item]
     new_video = apply VidStore, action, [video]
     { :reply, new_video, Keyword.put(videos, item, new_video) }
   end

❺  def handle_cast({ :add, video }, videos) do
     { :noreply, [video|videos] }
   end
end
```

This code is remarkably compact. Let's take a look at what is happening.

❶ GenServer has macros, so we announce our intent to use them with use. We will also use the state machine, so we require that behavior as well. The GenServer works by specifying a generic OTP behavior where the user fills in a few callbacks, GenServer will also provide default implementations for the callbacks so you only need to implement the callbacks you need. We're using two: handle_call and handle_cast. We use Call to return a specific video, and use Cast when we don't care about the result.

❷ This callback does application-specific initialization. In this case, you can pass in a video dictionary or an empty list. We won't use this function right away, but when we decide to add a supervisor, it will come in handy.

❸ This callback initializes our server to the value of videos.

❹ We get a video from the keyword dictionary, invoke a state machine event using apply, and then replace the existing video in the keyword list with our new one. apply is new, but don't get confused. It just calls a function on a module with the given argument list. In this case, action is one of our state machine callbacks.

The arguments are simple. The first inbound argument is provided by the user. The second is information about the calling process. The third is the revised state of the server. OTP takes care of managing state for us! Note that this call is synchronous. We'll get the value of the transformed video back. OTP will take care of managing state for us.

❺ The final callback, handle_cast, is almost as simple as init. Look at the returned tuple—this callback sends no reply to the client. The structure of handle_cast is nearly identical to handle_call, except that there is no return value to set. We add our new video to the list with simple list construction.

Using OTP from the Console

Mix is going to take care of most of the dirty work for us. The console work will be near trivial. Let's check it out. First, start the console with iex -S mix. Then, start the server with States.Server.start_link. You'll want to match on {:ok, pid} to capture the inbound pid, like this:

```
iex> {:ok, pid} = States.Server.start_link([])
{:ok, #PID<0.157.0>}
```

The arguments are the module implementing our store initial video store and options. Now we can interact with the server by sending call and cast messages. We'll create a couple of videos for our store.

```
iex> wolverine = %Video{title: "Wolverine"}
%Video{title: "Wolverine", state: :available, times_rented: 0, log: []}
iex> xmen = %Video{title: "X Men"}
%Video{title: "X Men", state: :available, times_rented: 0, log: []}
```

A call to cast with our tuple adds the two videos to our distributed server:

```
iex> GenServer.cast(pid, { :add, {:wolverine, wolverine} })
:ok
iex> GenServer.cast(pid, { :add, {:xmen, xmen} })
:ok
```

It can't be that easy, can it? Let's interact with our state machine:

```
iex> GenServer.call(pid, {:rent, :xmen})
%Video{title: "X Men", state: :rented, times_rented: 1, log: ["Renting X Men"]}
iex> GenServer.call(pid, {:return, :xmen})
%Video{title: "X Men", state: :available, times_rented: 1,
 log: ["Returning X Men", "Renting X Men"]}
iex> GenServer.call(pid, {:rent, :xmen})
%Video{title: "X Men", state: :rented, times_rented: 2,
 log: ["Renting X Men", "Returning X Men", "Renting X Men"]}
```

That's amazingly simple. We've built a fully distributed server with very little effort. Erlang let us wrap up a generic OTP behavior, and Elixir macros insulated us from the boilerplate.

Further, our advantages will extend beyond our video store. If we want to use this pattern in other applications, we can use the GenServer macros that were provided by Elixir and the StateMachine macros that we wrote ourselves.

Supervising for Reliability

If you're a Ruby or Java coder, you might have used tools that restart dead servers when they start. Deploying those applications is black magic. With Elixir, this kind of supervision is baked into the language. When you used mix new --sup to create States, it created two files for you: a supervisor and an application. They will do most of the work, but we'll have to tweak them a little. Change states/lib/states.ex to look like this:

```
elixir/day3/states/lib/states.ex
defmodule States do
  use Application

  # See http://elixir-lang.org/docs/stable/elixir/Application.html
  # for more information on OTP Applications
  def start(_type, videos) do
    import Supervisor.Spec, warn: false

    children = [
      # Define workers and child supervisors to be supervised
      worker(States.Server, [videos])
    ]
```

```
    # See http://elixir-lang.org/docs/stable/elixir/Supervisor.html
    # for other strategies and supported options
    opts = [strategy: :one_for_one, name: States.Supervisor]
    Supervisor.start_link(children, opts)
  end
end
```

The worker function insulates us from boilerplate that we don't see. We access the supervision behavior through the import Supervisor.Spec expression. The children defines the processes we want to supervise. start_link spawns and links the supervisor process to our States server. init fires any child processes, passing through the initial video library, which is initially an empty keyword list.

The application monitors the supervisor. When a supervisor goes down, the application will act accordingly. We need to do one more thing. We need to tell Mix how to initialize our application. Now, when you start iex -S mix or Application.start, it will actually start your full OTP application. You'll be able to put :video_store through its paces simply by using GenServer commands, like this:

```
iex> GenServer.cast :video_store, {:add, {:xmen, %Video{title: "X men"}}}
:ok
iex> GenServer.call :video_store, {:rent, :xmen}
%Video{title: "X men", state: :rented, times_rented: 1, log: ["Renting X men"]}
```

You can crash the server by passing a command that doesn't exist:

```
iex> GenServer.call :video_store, {:crash, :xmen}

=ERROR REPORT==== 9-Aug-2014::23:57:43 ===
** Generic server video_store terminating
** Last message in was {crash,xmen}
...
```

The supervisor will create a new one:

```
iex> GenServer.cast :video_store, {:add, {:et, %Video{title: "ET"}}}
:ok
```

We're up and running again. If we wanted to, we could capture the existing state at the time of the last crash.

And there you have it. We've got three basic parts:

- A generic server, wrapped by Elixir libraries to eliminate boilerplate code
- Application-specific code, consisting of an Elixir macro to build state machines, and a video store that uses it
- A dozen or so lines of configuration that we use to glue everything together

We're left with an extremely robust server-side implementation, based on decades of evolution and research. We focus our development efforts on the application-specific code. That's the promise of Erlang with Elixir.

What We Learned in Day 3

In Day 3, we heard from José and his vision for Elixir. We learned about the major influences on the language, and also how Elixir's protocols add some structure and extensibility to Erlang's type system.

Next, we dove into concurrent and distributed code. We learned to spawn concurrent processes, and then we built an amazing amount of functionality with surprisingly little code, extending our macro-driven video store to run under OTP. Then, we used the OTP framework, and saw a beautiful marriage between Elixir and Erlang. The OTP framework is a fantastic abstraction for dealing with concurrent distributed applications, one that has aced every test from an industry famous for chewing up and spitting out distributed programming paradigms and even programming languages.

Both Elixir and Erlang were important to our program. Erlang's libraries handled the tough issues related to monitoring and linking processes, and Elixir simplified the process with excellent tooling and macros that eliminated the need for much of the boilerplate code.

Your Turn

Find...
- The Erlang gen_server behaviors
- The way to code a timeout with an Elixir receive
- Information on Erlang's OTP

Do (Easy):
- How can you crash your server? What happens if you crash it with and without a supervisor?
- Add a timeout to the pitcher or catcher. What happens when you time out?

Do (Medium):
- Write tests for the OTP database. Hint: There are two types of setup in TestUnit.

Do (Hard):

- Build some redundancy into the video store by adding a second process. Writes go to both processes. When one process crashes, make it get the video database from the other OTP server when it starts back up.
- Wrap the state machine in an agent rather than a full OTP application.
- How would you persist the videos into Erlang's DETS database?

Wrapping Up Elixir

We've now put Elixir through its paces. You've seen what José has to say, and used a couple of the more sophisticated language features. In a few short days, you've built a few macros and even ramped up a simple monitored distributed application. Let's look at where Elixir fits in the language spectrum.

Strengths

The hardware landscape, with increased emphasis on better networking, multicore architectures, and modern mobile computing, is increasingly driving modern programming. Our insatiable desire for more mobile applications and more power on the cloud will eventually require programmers to be concurrency experts. Elixir is extraordinarily well positioned to meet the hardware challenges.

In the Elm chapter, we mentioned the rise of reactive programming on the browser. To take best advantage, server-side languages must support streams and web programming models that support them. Though we did not have enough time to robustly cover the whole Stream API, they are there, and they're as rich and powerful as any streaming libraries out there.

The problem with many functional languages is that the syntax is often demanding and even alien. It may be too much to expect programmers to embrace monads (like Haskell), Lisp's notation (like Clojure), or sophisticated type theory (like Scala). Elixir is attempting to provide the right sugar for a whole class of developers making the transition from objects to functions.

At one point, I thought the key to Lisp's macros was a language that was represented in list form, enabling macros. It's not. The key is the uniform syntax tree. With a consistent representation and Lisp-style quote, Elixir pairs rich syntax with beautiful macros. That's hugely important. To achieve a critical mass, a popular general-purpose functional language will need to be able to insulate its users from tedious boilerplate.

The ability to seamlessly access Erlang's rich OTP library is also a game changer. The political challenge is much less severe since Erlang's virtual machine already runs a significant percentage of the world's mobile traffic. That's proven scalability, performance, and reliability.

Finally, the timing for Elixir is very good. Some Ruby developers have had a hard time embracing Clojure or Scala, but they need to go somewhere as the pressure of deploying high-performance distributed applications on multicore hardware increases. They are giving Elixir a serious look. Though the Ruby development community provides an ideal early customer base for Elixir, those developers face a steep learning curve, including learning concurrent programming and functional programming all at once. That's a daunting list, but the most successful languages in the past few decades have tapped existing communities—C++ for Java and JavaScript, and Java for Clojure and Scala. Having this Ruby community helps to quickly establish a critical mass.

Weaknesses

Elixir's weaknesses are the same as most emerging languages. The libraries are changing relatively quickly. If it doesn't settle down soon, an increasing user base will have a tough time keeping up.

Maturity of approach is also uncertain. Some of the concepts are novel. We will need to see how those concepts age over time, though many of the concepts are already aging quite well with the Erlang language. The list of supporters is quite small but growing. It's critical that José and Joe Armstrong, creator of Erlang, continue to work well together.

Finally, many of the features that Elixir developers will need are missing, or not yet well documented. If you want to use a web server, for example, you'll need to pick a very young one, or go with a native Erlang system, of which there are several excellent choices. It will be important for the young community to continue to offer not just growth, but quality growth.

Final Thoughts

Of all the emerging functional languages, Elixir is my favorite. Though it's not as mature, as some of the other alternatives, I think the complete package is well conceived.

People are starting to notice Erlang and its superior distribution model. Elixir, though, can probably go in places that Erlang can't. The rich syntax will make it attractive to Ruby developers who are starting to recognize the true limitations of the language in the face of multicore architectures. Macros will allow it to play a more efficient role as an applications language.

Even within the Erlang programming community, this new language has potential. Erlang developers have gone without some tools that are becoming increasingly important, namely tooling for builds, integration, and scripting. Mix, the rich scripting capabilities, and the DSL tooling will help Elixir establish a role as a scripting language within Erlang's ecosystem.

Will Elixir succeed on a bigger stage? We'll have to wait and see.

CHAPTER 5

Julia

by Jack Moffitt and Bruce Tate

Writing a language is sometimes compared to writing a book. Each language has a voice. Sometimes, if too many people collaborate or if the language is written over too long a period of time, that voice becomes chaotic and disjointed. You can imagine our trepidation when we started working with Julia, which had four primary authors.

So far, the authors of this book have collectively interviewed 14 language creators. Sometimes, as with Haskell, we interviewed more than one, and once, with Prolog, we didn't interview the creator. Each time, the process is different. There's usually a dominant voice on the team. With Clojure, it's unquestionably Rich Hickey, even after his company merged with Relevance, LLC. With Erlang, it's Joe Armstrong. When we approached a Julia mail list with a request to interview the creators, you can imagine our surprise when not one but four of them responded, at once, with a single voice. "We will answer you," the voices said in unison, "within two weeks." And two weeks later, the answer came back, from four voices in unison, with an incredibly thoughtful and well-reasoned interview.

As we dove into the language, we felt ourselves drawn into the community—at once eager and polite. Think "Borg," the Star Trek character of aliens where individuals were drawn into the collective. Julia works in that spirit, like a giant hive-mind, a collective consciousness that subsumes the whole. Working with integers, or rationals made up of integers, or reals or even imaginary numbers? No problem. Julia gets you. Plus is plus. She knows what to do.

What about a multidimensional array? No problem. Plus is still plus, and will add to each element. You can even distribute the plus across the whole.

If you feel yourself drawn toward something bigger, don't fight it. Think of the whole. Let's get to work. Maybe in the end, you too will be assimilated.

Day 1: Resistance Is Futile

Julia is a relatively new language, but the team has been incredibly productive. Even with three days, we won't be able to cover it all.

Day 1 will cover the built-in types and operators. We'll also look at Julia's dictionaries and arrays. The arrays are particularly powerful, with the ability to slice and manipulate them in pieces or in multiple dimensions.

On the second day we'll look at all the major control flow patterns like if, while, and for. We'll look at user-defined types and functions, and discover Julia's multiple dispatch. Concurrency will round out the day, allowing us to do computation in a distributed way.

Our final day, we'll play with Julia's macro system and then build an image codec using everything we've learned.

Before we get to all this code, we'll need to install Julia.

Installing Julia

Prebuilt packages for Julia for Windows, OS X, and Linux can be downloaded from the Julia download site.[1] We'll be using version 0.3.0 in this chapter, which is the current pre-release version.

If you can't find a package for your system, you can install directly from source. The README.md file in the Julia repository contains detailed building instructions. Be warned that because it requires you to build LLVM as well, the build will take quite a while.

Once you have Julia installed, fire up the REPL by running julia, and you should see something like the following:

```
$ julia
```

```
               |  A fresh approach to technical computing
               |  Documentation: http://docs.julialang.org
               |  Type "help()" to list help topics
               |
               |  Version 0.3.0-prerelease+3551 (2014-06-07 20:57 UTC)
               |  Commit 547facf* (12 days old master)
               |  x86_64-apple-darwin12.5.0

julia>
```

---

1. http://julialang.org/downloads/

The language is now at your fingertips. Let's give it a whirl:

```
julia> println("Hello, world!")
Hello, world!

julia>
```

With the world properly greeted, let's explore Julia's syntax a bit.

Built-in Types

Every language has its atoms—its component parts. Most of Julia's atoms should be familiar to you from other languages, but unlike most dynamic languages, Julia has more precise types.

We can explore the atoms and their types at the REPL using the typeof function:

```
julia> typeof(5)
Int64
```

There are floating-point numbers in several sizes: 16, 32, and 64 bits. Integers are even more diverse with both unsigned (Uint8, Uint16, etc.) and signed (Int8, Int16, etc.) variants. Numeric literals are interpreted in the most general way: Int64 and Float64.

```
julia> typeof(5.5)
Float64
```

// is used to make rational number literals.

```
julia> typeof(11//5)
Rational{Int64} (constructor with 1 method)
```

Symbols are convenient when you would otherwise use a string, but they are more efficient and easier to type and read. Julia has borrowed these from Lisp, Erlang, and Ruby.

```
julia> typeof(:foo)
Symbol
julia> typeof(true)
Bool
julia> typeof('a')
Char
julia> typeof("abc")
ASCIIString (constructor with 2 methods)
julia> typeof(typeof)
Function
```

Tuples are fixed-size groups of other types. Their type is a tuple of the types of their components.

```
julia> typeof((5, 5.5, "abc"))
(Int64,Float64,ASCIIString)
```

Arrays look as you'd expect. The extra 1 in the type signature is the array's dimensionality, which we will learn more about later.

```
julia> typeof([1, 2, 3])
Array{Int64,1}
```

Dictionary literals use curly braces and =>, just like older versions of Ruby. The first parameter in the type signature is the type of the key, and the second is the type of the value. Any is Julia's universal type.

```
julia> typeof({:foo => 5})
Dict{Any,Any} (constructor with 3 methods)
```

Now that we've seen what we have available, let's do something with them.

Common Operators

Most of Julia's numeric operators are exactly what you'd expect:

```
julia> 1 + 2
3
```

Numeric operations between different types of numbers auto-promote. Adding two integers gives an integer, but adding a float and an integer gives a float.

```
julia> 1 + 2.2
3.2
```

Division always returns a floating-point number, even when both arguments are integers.

```
julia> 5 / 1
5.0
```

The \ operator is the same as / but with the arguments reversed. Inverse division is primarily useful for linear algebra.

```
julia> 1 \ 5
5.0
```

Truncating integer division can be done with div.

```
julia> div(7, 3)
2
julia> mod(7, 3)
1
```

Julia has bitwise operators, and you can use the bits function to see the binary representation of a value.

```
julia> bits(5)
"0000000000000000000000000000000000000000000000000000000000000101"
julia> bits(6)
"0000000000000000000000000000000000000000000000000000000000000110"
julia> 6 & 5
4
julia> 5 | 6
7
```

Bitwise negation is done with ~, and exclusive or is $.

```
julia> ~0
-1
julia> 5 $ 6
3
```

Boolean operators are the same as in C and Java, as are the operators for comparison.

```
julia> true || false
true
julia> true && false
false
julia> !true
false
julia> !!true
true
julia> mn < x < mx
true
```

You can assign to multiple variables at once using commas—a syntax borrowed from Python. The left and right sides must have the same structure.

```
julia> mn, x, mx = 1, 3, 5
(1,3,5)
```

All of these operators work on the simplest types in the language. Let's look at some of Julia's more complex types.

Dictionaries and Sets

Julia's dictionaries are the same as those in other dynamic languages you might be familiar with, but they can be more explicitly typed. Keys and values in the dictionary must all be of the same type, but that type may be Any.

These two kinds of dictionaries—one dynamic and free and one restricted to specific types—both have their own literal syntax. When you want the typical dynamic behavior, use {...}, but if you want more explicit types, use [...]:

```
julia> implicit = {:a => 1, :b => 2, :c => 3}
Dict{Any,Any} with 3 entries:
  :b => 2
  :c => 3
  :a => 1

julia> explicit = [:a => 1, :b => 2, :c => 3]
Dict{Symbol,Int64} with 3 entries:
  :b => 2, :c => 3, :a => 1
```

(By default Julia lists entries one per line, but we'll take the liberty of condensing its output throughout the chapter.)

Fetching keys and values from the dictionary is easy, as is testing for existence of an entry:

```
julia> explicit[:a]
1
```

get fetches a value by its key, returning the default value if the key isn't found.

```
julia> get(explicit, :d, 4)
4
```

keys returns an iterator of all the keys.

```
julia> numbers = [:one => 1, :two => 2]
julia> the_keys = keys(numbers)
KeyIterator for a Dict{Symbol,Int64} with 2 entries. Keys:
  :two, :one
```

collect constructs an array from the items in an iterator.

```
julia> collect(the_keys)
3-element Array{Symbol,1}:
  :b, :c, :a
```

The in operator can be used to test if an item exists in an array or an iterator.

```
julia> :a in the_keys
true
```

The in function is exactly the same as the operator. It has special syntax support so you can use it either way. Note that for dictionaries, items are represented as a two-tuple of the key and value.

```
julia> in((:a, 1), explicit)
true
```

Julia also has a Set type, which is an unordered set, and functions to manipulate it.

No matter how many times a particular element is given in the constructor, it will appear only once in the set.

```
julia> a_set = Set(1, 2, 3, 1, 2, 3)
Set{Int64}({2, 3, 1})
julia> union(Set(1, 2), Set(2, 3))
Set{Int64}({2, 3, 1})
julia> intersect(Set(1, 2), Set(2, 3))
Set{Int64}({2})
```

Set difference subtracts all the elements of the second set from the first.

```
julia> setdiff(Set(1, 2), Set(2, 3))
Set{Int64}({1})
julia> issubset(Set(1, 2), Set(3, 4, 0, 1, 2))
true
```

These collection types are useful but unsurprising. Arrays in Julia, however, are straight out of the future.

Twenty-Fourth-Century Arrays

Julia's arrays are powerhouses of functionality. You can create arrays of varying dimensions, slice out arbitrary regions (also in multiple dimensions), reshape them, or do complex operations on them. Like dictionaries and sets, they are typed and hold items all of the same type.

First, let's look at how to create arrays.

Arrays constructed with [...] have their type inferred. Note that if a common type cannot be inferred, the root type Any is used. These Any arrays work much like arrays in other dynamic languages.

```
julia> animals = [:lions, :tigers, :bears]
3-element Array{Symbol,1}:
 :lions, :tigers, :bears
julia> [1, 2, :c]
3-element Array{Any,1}:
 1, 2, :c
```

If you want a particular type, you can use Type[...] to construct them. It causes an error if the types aren't convertible to the target type.

```
julia> Float64[1, 2, 3]
3-element Array{Float64,1}
 1.0, 2.0, 3.0
```

There are lots of functions in Julia's standard library for creating arrays. Here are the most common ones:

```
julia> zeros(Int32, 5)
5-element Array{Int32,1}:
 0, 0, 0, 0, 0
julia> ones(Float64, 3)
3-element Array{Float64,1}:
 1.0, 1.0, 1.0
julia> fill(:empty, 5)
5-element Array{Symbol,1}:
 :empty, :empty, :empty, :empty, :empty
```

These functions all take the type of the array (or the value in the case of fill) and the size as arguments.

Indexing and Slicing

Accessing elements of an array can be done with indexing or slicing, both of which use the familiar square bracket notation:

```
julia> animals = [:lions, :tigers, :bears]
3-element Array{Symbol,1}:
 :lions, :tigers, :bears
```

Arrays in Julia are indexed from 1, not 0. This follows the mathematical convention.

```
julia> animals[1]
:lions
```

The end keyword is an alias for the last element of an array. This is similar to Python's -1, but a bit more readable.

```
julia> animals[end]
:bears
```

Using : inside the brackets allows you to return slices of the array. This is a two-element slice, and it can be used just like any other array in Julia. A slice of a single element still returns an array.

```
julia> animals[2:end]
2-element Array{Symbol,1}:
 :tigers, :bears
julia> animals[1:1]
1-element Array{Symbol,1}:
 :lions
```

You can write to slices and indices as well. Indices can be assigned to, which mutates the array.

```
julia> animals[1] = :zebras
:zebras
julia> animals
3-element Array{Symbol,1}:
 :zebras, :tigers, :bears
```

Even slices can be assigned to. If given a single element, it assigns that element to every position of the slice.

```
julia> animals[2:end] = :hippos
:hippos
julia> animals
3-element Array{Symbol,1}:
 :zebras
 :hippos
 :hippos
```

You can also assign arrays to slices.

```
julia> animals[2:end] = [:sharks, :whales]
2-element Array{Symbol,1}:
 :sharks, :whales
julia> animals
3-element Array{Symbol,1}:
 :zebras, :sharks, :whales
```

Slices are really powerful and make it trivial to manipulate arrays in complex ways. Since you can use them just like regular arrays, you can pass them to functions so that those functions operate only on a subset of the data.

Now we'll take arrays into another dimension.

Multidimensional Arrays

Julia is designed as a language for scientific and numerical programming. Those types of tasks typically involve a lot of linear algebra using vectors and matrices. Fortunately, Julia excels with amazing multidimensional arrays.

Let's start by adding just one dimension. We'll create, manipulate, and inspect a small matrix

To write literal arrays with two dimensions, use semicolons between the rows and leave out the commas between elements. Using commas and semicolons both is an error, and using no commas always creates a two-dimensional array, even when there are no semicolons.

```
julia> A = [1 2 3; 4 5 6; 7 8 9]
3x3 Array{Int64,2}:
 1  2  3
 4  5  6
 7  8  9
```

You can retrieve the size and shape of the array using size. It returns a tuple of the length of the array in each dimension. Here our array is 3 by 3.

```
julia> size(A)
(3,3)
```

Use a comma to give multiple indices to an array. Each index is along the respective dimension. Here we ask for the third element of the second row.

```
julia> A[2,3]
6
```

Slicing works in arbitrary dimensions as well. This fetches the second column.

```
julia> A[1:end,2]
3-element Array{Int64,1}:
 2
 5
 8
```

Using a slice with no bounds fetches all elements in that dimension.

```
julia> A[2,:]
1x3 Array{Int64,2}:
 4  5  6
```

Setting a two-dimensional slice also works. This sets everything to zero except the top and left edges.

```
julia> A[2:end,2:end] = 0
0
julia> A
3x3 Array{Int64,2}:
 1  2  3
 4  0  0
 7  0  0
```

All the array constructor functions take the size of the array as the second argument. Before we used an integer, but you can also pass a tuple for multidimensional arrays. rand generates an array with random elements, each between 0 and 1.

```
julia> rand(Float64, (3,3))
3x3 Array{Float64,2}:
 0.12651   0.679185   0.052333
 0.429212  0.0113811  0.886528
 0.639923  0.0794754  0.917688
```

Common operators on matrices and vectors work out of the box. You can add, subtract, and multiply arrays element-wise or with matrix multiplication.

eye constructs the identity matrix. eye(N) makes an N×N matrix, and eye(M, N) creates an M×N matrix.

```
julia> I = eye(3, 3)
3x3 Array{Float64,2}:
 1.0  0.0  0.0
 0.0  1.0  0.0
 0.0  0.0  1.0
```

Multiplying an array by a scalar value is done element-wise.

```
julia> I * 5
3x3 Array{Float64,2}:
 5.0  0.0  0.0
 0.0  5.0  0.0
 0.0  0.0  5.0
```

```
julia> v = [1; 2; 3]
```

Using the dotted version of the * operator does explicit element-wise multiplication. Using * here would have been an error as two 3×1 vectors cannot be matrix multiplied.

```
julia> v .* [0.5; 1.2; 0.1]
3-element Array{Float64,1}:
 0.5
 2.4
 0.3
```

Adding a quote after an array will transpose it; this is shorthand for the transpose function. A 1×3 vector times a 3×1 vector gives the dot product, resulting in a scalar result.

```
julia> v' * v
1-element Array{Int64,1}:
 14
```

A 3×3 matrix multiplied with a 3×1 vector outputs a new 3×1 vector.

```
julia> [1 2 3; 2 3 1; 3 1 2] * v
3-element Array{Int64,1}:
 14
 11
 11
```

Don't worry too much if you aren't familiar with linear algebra. The point is that Julia's arrays and operators are custom made for doing linear algebra. Of course, they are capable of all the normal things arrays are useful for too.

What We Learned in Day 1

This has been a whirlwind tour of Julia's types and operators, and we didn't even cover much of its built-in library functions. Even with this humble beginning, you can imagine just how good of a number cruncher Julia is. It's also built out of familiar pieces from dynamic languages; hopefully you feel right at home.

Julia has a lot of types that you've no doubt seen in other languages: symbols, integers, floats, dictionaries, sets, and arrays. Its operators hold few surprises.

Collection types are multifaceted, since Julia is strongly typed even though it is dynamic. Class dynamic language behavior is achieved through the Any type, but Java-like strongly typed behavior can be used too. Most of the arrays we dealt with were uniform Int64 or Float64. Arrays of only concrete types like this make for very efficient representation and computation.

Julia's arrays are where the language really starts to shine. Not only does it have all the normal things you'd want from an array in Python or Java, but it also has powerful indexing and slices that work even in multiple dimensions. Arrays also support the common linear algebra operations in addition to element-wise operations.

Your Turn

It's your turn to experiment with Julia's types and common operations.

Find...

- The Julia manual
- Information about IJulia
- The Julia language Reddit, which has blog posts and articles related to Julia

Do (Easy):

- Use typeof to find the types of types. Try Symbol or Int64. Can you find the types of operators?
- Create a typed dictionary with keys that are symbols and values that are floats. What happens when you add :thisis => :notanumber to the dictionary?
- Create a 5×5×5 array where each 5×5 block in the first two dimensions is a single number but that number increases for each block. For example, magic[:,:,1] would have all elements equal to 1, and magic[:,:,2] would have all elements equal to 2.

- Run some arrays of various types through functions like sin and round. What happens?

Do (Medium):
- Create a matrix and multiply it by its inverse. Hint: inv computes the inverse of a matrix, but not all matrices are invertable.
- Create two dictionaries and merge them. Hint: Look up merge in the manual.
- sort and sort! both operate on arrays. What is the difference between them?

Do (Hard):
- Brush off your linear algebra knowledge and construct a 90-degree rotation matrix. Try rotating the unit vector [1; 0; 0] by multiplying it by your matrix.

Day 2: Getting Assimilated

Yesterday we looked at Julia's basic types and operators, and we spent quite a lot of time with its arrays. Julia's basic data structures are versatile, but it has even more to offer.

First we'll quickly review control flow, which should feel quite familiar. We'll also hit abstract and user-defined types and learn all about functions and multiple dispatch.

Finally, we'll wrap up the day by playing with Julia's concurrency features, which Julia has assimilated from languages like Erlang.

Control Flow

Julia's if, while, and for are pretty standard. Their syntax feels like a pleasant mix of Ruby and Python. Julia's for loops are able to iterate over a variety of things, which is quite handy.

Let's look at branching with if first:

```
julia> x = 10
10
julia> if x < 10
           println("My chair is too small")
       elseif x > 10
           println("My chair is too big")
       else
           println("My chair is just right")
       end
My chair is just right
```

One notable difference between Julia and languages like C, Python, and JavaScript is that the test expression must evaluate to a Boolean; 0, 1, and empty collections are not coercible to Boolean values. This is Julia's underlying strong typing asserting itself.

while loops are also what you'd expect:

```
julia> x = 8
8
julia> while x < 11
           x = x + 1
           println("More!")
       end
More!
More!
More!
```

Here are some for loops showing several different kinds of iteration.

This example iterates over an array. You can also use in instead of = if you prefer. Also, note that Julia's strings interpolate from the current scope using $. You can reference variable names or entire expressions like $(a + 10).

```
julia> for a = [1, 2, 3]
           println("$a")
       end
1
2
3
```

Here we iterate over a range. 1:10 is all the integers from 1 to 10 inclusive.

```
julia> sum = 0
0
julia> for a = 1:10
           sum += a
       end
julia> sum
55
```

Iterating over other collections like dictionaries is easy too. Here we deconstruct each element, which for a dictionary is a tuple of the key and value.

```
julia> numbers = [:one => 1, :two => 2]
Dict{Symbol,Int64} with 2 entries:
  :two => 2, :one => 1
julia> for (key, value) in numbers
           println("The name of $value is $key")
       end
The name of 2 is two
The name of 1 is one
```

Compared to multidimensional arrays, the control flow of Julia is unambitious. Sometimes simplicity is best, but you'll see control flow shine in more complex examples later.

User-Defined Types and Functions

Julia has some great types, but no language is complete without the ability to make your own. You can define your own types in Julia, and it has a limited form of abstract types and subtyping as well.

After types, we'll talk about user-defined functions, including Julia's powerful multiple dispatch, which is a functional incarnation of polymorphism.

Let's build a simple type to hold movie characters. Types in Julia are like structs in C or classes without methods if you are familiar with Java or Ruby.

Fields in a type definition can be constrained to be of a particular type with the :: operator. If no type constraint is given, the field is of type Any. It has the same kind of behavior as fields in Ruby, Python, or JavaScript.

Constructing a value of type is done with its constructor function, which has the same name as the type and takes an argument for each field.

```
julia> type MovieCharacter
          heart :: Bool
          name
       end
```

```
julia> cowardly_lion = MovieCharacter(false, "Lion")
MovieCharacter(false,"Lion")
```

Accessing fields on a value of a type is done with the . operator, just as in many other languages.

```
julia> cowardly_lion.name
"Lion"
```

Abstract types have no fields, but serve as a way to group multiple types together. Concrete types are then defined as subtypes of the abstract type. This allows for extension and default behavior.

Abstract types cannot be constructed, but they can be used as field type specifiers or in typed array literals.

```
julia> abstract Story
```

```
julia> Story()
ERROR: type cannot be constructed
```

Defining a subtype is done with the <: operator, but looks exactly like a normal type definition otherwise. Multiple subtypes can coexist next to each other.

```
julia> type Book <: Story
           title
           author
       end
julia> type Movie <: Story
           title
           director
       end
```

Like any dynamic language, Julia can use introspection to walk the type hierarchy. You can easily find the supertype as well as all the subtypes.

```
julia> super(Book)
Story
julia> super(Story)
Any
julia> subtypes(Story)
2-element Array{Any,1}:
 Book
 Movie
```

You can't subtype more than one level. This is perhaps unexpected, but avoids many pitfalls of traditional object-oriented languages.

```
julia> type Short <: Movie
           plot
       end
ERROR: invalid subtyping in definition of Short
```

We can now abstract over data, but we still need to abstract over code. Let's see how user-defined functions look in Julia. You'll find they have quite a Python flavor.

Functions return the last expression in their bodies. You can also use return to exit early.

```
julia> function hello(name)
           "Hello, $(name)!"
       end
hello (generic function with 1 method)
julia> hello("world")
"Hello, world!"
```

Default arguments can be provided. If not specified when the function is invoked, the default values will be used.

```
julia> function with_defaults(a, b=10, c=11)
         println("a is $a, b is $b, and c is $c")
       end
with_defaults (generic function with 3 methods)
julia> with_defaults(1, 2)
a is 1, b is 2, and c is 11
julia> with_defaults(1)
a is 1, b is 10, and c is 11
```

Using ... on the final argument will make it a collection of all the remaining arguments if any exist.

```
julia> function it_depends(args...)
         for arg in args
           println(arg)
         end
       end
it_depends (generic function with 1 method)
julia> it_depends(:one, :two)
one
two
```

All of Julia's operators are also functions and can be used in prefix notation too.

```
julia> +(1, 2)
3
julia> numbers = 1:10
1:10
```

When ... appears in a function definition's argument list, it gathers arguments into a collection. When ... appears in a function invocation it expands the collection into arguments. It's a very tidy feature that saves you from what other languages call apply.

```
julia> +(numbers...)
55
```

Functions in Julia really start to shine when you couple them with multiple dispatch. The same function can be defined multiple times for different types.

You might be familiar with overloading from other languages, but multiple dispatch is even more powerful. Instead of picking a function to call based on its first argument (or the object on which it's invoked in object-oriented languages), multiple dispatch actually picks the function based on the types of *all* the arguments.

In Julia, each version of a function is called a method, but unlike object-oriented programming, the methods don't belong to one particular type. This makes a lot of sense given Julia's focus on scientific code; after all, if the dividend and the divisor have different types, which type should the division operator / belong to? In object-oriented languages, it ends up being whichever type is written on the left, which doesn't make a lot of sense, but people have gotten used to it.

Let's see multiple dispatch in action in a simple set of methods to concatenate two values together.

What makes the following a method instead of a function is that the types of the arguments are specified. This method is defined only when both arguments are Int64. This version of concat does a little math to append the numbers together.

```
julia> function concat(a :: Int64, b :: Int64)
          zeros = int(ceil(log10(b+1)))
          a * 10^zeros + b
       end
concat (generic function with 1 method)
julia> concat(117, 5)
1175
```

If we try to call our function on different kinds of arguments, Julia complains that no method was found.

```
julia> concat(117, "5")
ERROR: no method concat(Int64, ASCIIString)
```

Now we'll define a concat method that takes a string as the second argument and returns a string. Now when we call the function, the correct method is selected. Notice that to pick the method, Julia had to look at the types of all the arguments. This is multiple dispatch at work.

```
julia> function concat(a :: Int64, b :: ASCIIString)
          "$a$b"
       end
concat (generic function with 2 methods)
julia> concat(117, "5")
"1175"
```

Multiple dispatch is a rarely seen language feature assimilated directly from Lisps. Clojure is probably the most mainstream language that includes it. Although little known, it is quite powerful and makes for some beautiful code.

It allows for open extension where normal object-oriented methods do not. There's no need to subclass Int64 to add a new type of concat, nor do you need to modify the Int64 object with monkey patching. If your library provides methods for common types, users of the library can extend those methods to their own types without modifying your library at all.

Julia's whole standard library relies heavily on multiple dispatch. The behavior of all the numeric types and operators are built with it. If you're curious, try running methods(+) at the REPL, which will show you all the definitions for addition.

Concurrency

You've now seen all the basics—some familiar, some new. Taken together, it makes for quite a nice dynamic language with strong typing and abstraction. Julia is a language with a prime directive—to make writing numerical code better.

One of the biggest issues with numerical code is that it takes a long time to run, even on supercomputers. To eke out the maximum performance, concurrency and distributed computing are a necessity, and so Julia has it built right in.

Julia concurrency works a lot like Erlang. You communicate with other processes via message passing. Whether those processes are on the same machine or on remote machines makes no difference.

Before we can start using these processes, we must create some. There are two ways to do this. The first is to use addprocs to add local processes. The second is to start Julia with -p N, where N is the number of processes to create.

```
julia> addprocs(2)
2-element Array{Any,1}:
 2, 3
julia> workers()
2-element Array{Int64,1}:
 2, 3
```

addprocs creates new processes and returns their IDs. You might have noticed it starts at 2. Process 1 is the process for the REPL. workers returns the list of processes.

Now that we have some processes, we can send and receive messages from them with remotecall and fetch. Note that these are the low-level primitives the rest of the system is built on, not necessarily things you'd use all the time.

```
julia> r1 = remotecall(2, rand, 10000000)
RemoteRef(2,1,7)
julia> r2 = remotecall(3, rand, 10000000)
RemoteRef(3,1,9)
```

```
julia> println("Not blocking")
Not blocking
julia> rand_list = fetch(r1)
10000000-element Array{Float64,1}:
 0.902002, 0.495766, ...
```

remotecall executes a function on a particular worker. The first argument is the worker's ID. Then comes the name of the function, and the rest of the arguments are passed to the given function. It returns a RemoteRef, which can be used to retrieve the result later.

remotecall returns immediately, as long as the worker ID is not 1—it does not block the shell process. We can still run code even if the processes are busy crunching numbers.

fetch takes a RemoteRef and returns the result of the function the worker was evaluating. If the worker isn't done yet, this will block and wait until the result is available.

Adding processes interactively is a little tedious. It's a bit easier to start a REPL with a bunch of processes already available. Julia takes the -p argument to set the number of processes to start.

```
$ julia -p 8
2014-06-22 10:14:01.021 julia[93233:707] App did finish launching
```

Now we have a REPL with nine processes: one for the shell itself and eight spares to do parallel tasks with. Let's put them to work on something more substantial than generating random arrays.

We're going to write a coin flipping simulator using Julia's higher-level parallel programming features instead of dealing with remotecall and fetch directly. First, we'll start with a nonparallel version.

First, the function flip_coins returns the number of heads after doing all the flips. It uses a simple for loop.

```
julia> function flip_coins(times)
         count = 0
         for i = 1:times
           count += int(randbool())
         end
         count
       end
flip_coins (generic function with 1 method)
julia> flip_coins(20)
9
julia> flip_coins(20)
10
```

The @time macro will evaluate the given expression and print out how much time it took. As the number of flips increases, flip_coins becomes quite slow.

```
julia> @time flip_coins(100000000)
elapsed time: 0.391368303 seconds (96 bytes allocated)
49994306
julia> @time flip_coins(1000000000)
elapsed time: 4.219781844 seconds (96 bytes allocated)
500005355
```

We can speed this code up by flipping coins in parallel with Julia's parallel for loops. Using the @parallel macro we can change a normal for loop into a parallel reducing version. The first argument is the combining operator. Note that the loop's operation must be commutative since the order it runs is arbitrary, as it gets scheduled over the processes.

```
julia> function pflip_coins(times)
          @parallel (+) for i = 1:times
            int(randbool())
          end
        end
flip_coins (generic function with 1 method)
julia> @time pflip_coins(100000000)
elapsed time: 0.293102855 seconds (113932 bytes allocated)
50001665
julia> @time pflip_coins(1000000000)
elapsed time: 2.19619143 seconds (55248 bytes allocated)
499995729
```

The parallel version is even a bit easier to read as the explicit summation is now gone.

If you compare these numbers to the previous nonparallel ones, you'll see the parallel one is 30–50% faster. That's a pretty good result for such a minor syntactic change.

Not all code will be this easy to parallelize, but you'd be surprised at how many things can be expressed as a parallel reduction. Lispers have been expressing things this way for decades, resulting in concise and powerful code, and Clojure has recently added parallel reducers as well.

Before we wrap up the day, let's create a histogram to see the distribution of coin flips across multiple runs. Along the way we'll point out a few more of Julia's many charms.

```julia
julia> function flip_coins_histogram(trials, times)
         bars = zeros(times + 1)
         for i = 1:trials
           bars[pflip_coins(times) + 1] += 1
         end
         hist = pmap((len -> repeat("*", int(len))), bars)
         for line in hist
           println("|$(line)")
         end
       end
flip_coins_histogram (generic function with 1 method)
```

bars[0] tracks the number of simulations that resulted in 0 flips, and so on. There is one more bar than times since the result could range from 0 heads to 10.

In addition to a normal map, Julia provides pmap, which runs the mapping function in parallel across all the processes but preserves the order of the result.

The -> notation is Julia's lightweight anonymous function syntax.

Let's run it:

```
julia> flip_coins_histogram(100, 10)
|*
|
|*****
|*****
|*********************
|****************************
|**********************
|**********
|******
|
|
```

Julia makes short work of data analysis tasks both in terms of the amount of time it takes you to code them and in how fast they run. It's nice to be able to use the whole machine for work without having to juggle processes or mutexes yourself.

Interview with Julia's Founders: Jeff Bezanson, Stefan Karpinski, Viral Shah, Alan Edelman

Now that you've seen some of Julia's main features and put the language through its paces, you have a better appreciation for some of the trade-offs that came into play. Let's check in with all of Julia's founders: Jeff Bezanson, Stefan Karpinski, Viral Shah, and Alan Edelman.

Us: Why did you create Julia?

Julia founders: Our motivation for creating a new language is captured pretty well (if a bit lyrically) in our first blog post about Julia.[2] We wanted a language that combined the best of computer science and scientific computing. Historically, there has been a divide between the practical tools that scientists use to get work done and the systems carefully designed by computer scientists which don't seem to work out in practice for the scientific crowd. There has also been a longstanding tension between productivity and performance. For speed and control, you have to write C or Fortran, but for productivity, people use high-level, dynamic languages like MATLAB, R, or Python. We wanted to have our cake and eat it too: get the performance of C in a language as easy to use as Python; to have all that great programming languages can offer in a form that is usable for hard scientific problems. To a large extent, we feel that Julia has shown that this is possible.

Julia is a bit different from other high-performance dynamic language projects in that the language is designed for performance from the beginning. This means there is more control over memory usage and layout and it's easy to interact with C and Fortran. It also means we didn't need lots of difficult implementation tricks to get speed. Julia's execution model is pretty straightforward and transparent once you get the hang of it.

Us: What do you like most about it?

Julia founders: Once you get used to multiple dispatch it is very hard to go back to single dispatch. It just feels so natural to provide multiple methods of a function that do slightly different things based on what types of values you pass. We're also happy with how clean and uncluttered the language is. The core language is quite minimal, channeling the spirit of Scheme in many ways. Of course, Scheme doesn't have the burden of syntax, which Julia has to deal with. On the other hand, in Julia basic numeric types like Int and Float64 are defined in the standard library instead of being baked into the language spec. Multiple dispatch is absolutely crucial here because mathematical operators like addition and array indexing are by far the most polymorphic things in most languages—in Julia they're just syntax for calling generic functions.

We are most proud of the Julia community. Not only are the people who frequent the Julia mailing lists and GitHub repositories brilliant and knowledgeable, but the standards of politeness, civility, and helpfulness are remarkable. Every time someone new is confused or rude the community response is unfailingly civil and kind.

Us: What kinds of problems does it solve best?

Julia founders: Julia is ideal for really hard technical problems that require a flexible, productive language to explore the problem space efficiently, but also need great performance to get answers in reasonable time. Traditionally, technical computing languages have been quite limited once you stray beyond number crunching. Julia is not like this—it is also a general-purpose language. You can solve hard

---

2.   http://julialang.org/blog/2012/02/why-we-created-julia/

computational problems, but also build a web service in front of that computation, all in the same language.

Us: What's the most surprising place you've seen Julia in production?

Julia founders: We have seen interesting and sometimes quite unexpected applications in aerospace, finance, and real-time audio. We are also starting to see startups deploy Julia in web applications to solve computational problems on demand. There is a surprising amount of interest in using Julia for embedded systems. Our in-progress port to ARM should help accelerate this trend. The ability to compile Julia scripts to executables will also help—you can already do this but it's not as convenient as it should be.

Us: If you were to start from scratch, is there anything you'd do differently?

Julia founders: When we started, there was a trade-off between making new users feel comfortable in Julia vs. clean language design. In hindsight, we were probably more concerned than we should have been with maintaining superficial similarity to other technical computing languages. For example, for our array concatenation syntax, it would have been better to do something more general as long as it was reasonably easy to use. Of course, it's not too late to change some of these choices.

What We Learned in Day 2

We started off today looking into Julia's control flow constructs. Control flow looks similar to many other languages, especially Python and Ruby.

Next we dived into user defined types and functions. There are only two levels of types, abstract types and concrete subtypes, but Julia lets you mix types via the Any type. Functions are built on multiple dispatch, which is a more powerful version of overloading and dynamic dispatch that you might be familiar with from object-oriented languages.

Finally we dove into Julia's concurrency, starting from the primitives and then working up to the high level with parallel for loops and pmap. With just a few tweaks we made a coin flipping function twice as fast.

Your Turn

Now that you have nearly the whole language in your grasp, you can work on some more interesting problems.

Find...

- The parallel computing part of the Julia manual. Specifically, read up on @spawn and @everywhere.
- The Wikipedia page on multiple dispatch.

Do (Easy):

- Write a for loop that counts backward using Julia's range notation.
- Write an iteration over a multidimensional array like [1 2 3; 4 5 6; 7 8 9]. In what order does it get printed out?
- Use pmap to take an array of trial counts and produce the number of heads found for each element.

Do (Medium):

- Write a factorial function as a parallel for loop.
- Add a method for concat that can concatenate an integer with a matrix. concat(5, [1 2; 3 4]) should produce [5 5 1 2; 5 5 3 4].
- You can extend built-in functions with new methods too. Add a new method for + to make "jul" + "ia" work.

Do (Hard):

- Parallel for loops dispatch loop bodies to other processes. Depending on the size of the loop body, this can have noticeable overhead. See if you can beat Julia's parallel for loop version of pflip_coins by writing something using the lower-level primitives like @spawn or remotecall.

Day 3: Become One with Julia

On our final day with Julia, it's time to look at a larger example of what the language can do. After a brief tour of Julia's macro system, we'll explore image processing algorithms and see how easy it is to manipulate data using all the tools you've seen on previous days.

Macros are familiar to most people from their incarnation in C as simple string substitution systems, but Julia's macros come from Lisp. Julia's macros take code as input and output a transformed version. They don't operate on strings but on the parsed tree structure of the language.

Julia, though young, has a rich set of functions for doing scientific computing. Statistics, linear algebra, and finite element methods all have ample tooling due to Julia's inclusion and integration with well known mathematical libraries. We'll use some of these to build a toy version of an image encoder and decoder that works similarly to JPEG and takes advantage of many of Julia's features.

That's a lot to do in one day, so let's get started.

Transforming Code Instead of Data

Programs transform and manipulate data structures like lists and trees. In Julia, your code is just another data structure, and it can be manipulated by your program. This property of the code and its internal data structure being the same is called *homoiconicity*. It's a powerful feature familiar to any Lisp hacker.

Normally when you enter code into the REPL, or when Julia sees code in a source file, the code is evaluated. However, you can prevent evaluation of code by quoting it with the : operator. You've actually already seen this in a limited form with symbols.

```
julia> x = 1
1
julia> x # Julia evaluates a variable by default, and returns its value
1
```

By quoting the variable with :, Julia returns a Symbol, which is the representation of a variable in the code's tree structure.

```
julia> :x
:x
julia> println("Hello!")
Hello!
```

Similarly, if you quote a function invocation, you get the data structure for the code instead of Julia printing out the greeting. The extra parentheses are sometimes needed to help out the parser.

```
julia> :(println("Hello!"))
:(println("Hello!"))
```

The printed representation of the code looks exactly like the original syntax. You can see its component parts by inspecting the data:

```
julia> e = :(println("Hello!"))
:(println("Hello!"))
julia> typeof(e)
Expr
julia> names(e)
3-element Array{Symbol,1}:
 :head
 :args
 :typ
julia> (e.head, e.args)
(:call,{:println,"Hello!"})
julia> e = :(x = 5)
julia> (e.head, e.args)
(:(=),{:x,5})
```

The type of a Julia expression is Expr.

The names function tells us the properties of a data type. Each Expr has a head, args, and typ field. The first two contain everything we need. The last is used by Julia for type inference.

For println("Hello!") the head of the expression is :call, which represents a function call. The first argument is the function's name, and the rest are the arguments for the called function.

An assignment has a head of :(=). Notice that the variable got turned into a symbol.

Exprs can be constructed just like other types. You can also explicitly evaluate them:

```
julia> e = Expr(:call, +, 1, 2, 3)
:(+(1,2,3))
julia> eval(e)
6
```

The interpolation you saw with $ in strings also works here, except that it evaluates the thing and replaces itself with the result. This works like the unquote operator in Lisp or Clojure.

```
julia> s = "A string"
"A string"
julia> :(println($s))
:(println("A string"))
```

This ability to quote and unquote at will makes it very easy to write macros, although it can be tough to get your head around them at first. You have to keep track of the two types of evaluation. Quoted things will be evaluated when the expression is evaluated at runtime. Interpolated things will be evaluated immediately when the expression is constructed.

Building Exprs by hand is a little tedious, so Julia includes a little code templating feature with quote:

```
julia> quote
           println($s)
       end
:(begin  # none, line 2:
       println("A string")
    end)
```

This allows you to write large blocks of expressions easily and still supports the interpolation with $.

We now have all the pieces to write our own macros. Macros in Julia are defined like functions but take expressions as input. The macro returns a modified expression, which is then evaluated.

This will probably make more sense once you see an example:

```
julia> macro unless(t, b)
         quote
           if !$t
             $b
           end
         end
       end
```

This macro defines a new control structure for Julia that works like Ruby's unless. It takes a test expression and a branch expression and builds the equivalent negated if expression.

The neat thing about this is that a normal function cannot do this, as normal function arguments get evaluated immediately before the function is invoked. We certainly don't want the branch expression executed unless the test is false, and macros allow us to control when code is executed.

```
julia> a = [1, 2, 3]
3-element Array{Int64,1}:
 1, 2, 3
julia> @unless isempty(a) println("a has elements")
a has elements
julia> @unless in(a, 4) begin
         println("a does not have 4")
       end
a does not have 4
```

Invoking macros is done with @ followed by as many expressions as the macro takes as arguments.

You can use begin and end to create a block expression making multiline unless clauses. There are some restrictions on the syntax you can use, but it's a small price to pay for being able to easily extend the language.

Hopefully now you can start to see how things like @parallel and @time work behind the scenes. Macros excel at removing boilerplate code, and Julia's quoting and interpolation makes them pretty easy to create.

Slicing and Dicing Images

We've seen Julia's multidimensional arrays, its support for parallel programming, and its laser focus on scientific computing. For the rest of the day we'll combine these tools to build a toy image codec. The code we'll write is not going to rival JPEG any time soon, but the example should demonstrate how easy it is to get practical work done in this new language.

Image Coding

Before we get started, it's useful to review how image codecs work so that the techniques will make sense. Don't worry, though; we don't need any complex mathematics—Julia will do all the mathematical lifting.

Compression techniques work by finding a more compact representation for data. For example, run length encoding replaces sequences of characters with a single character and a count. Long runs of the same value are dramatically shortened with no loss of information.

Just as audio samples can be transformed into their constituent frequencies, images can also be transformed into frequencies in two dimensions. In this frequency representation, the energy of an image is very compact.

To be more concrete, imagine a picture and try to pick out which pixels are the most important. It's pretty difficult. Change any one pixel, even by a large amount, and the image is hardly different. However, after transforming an image to frequencies, the important values tend to be at the lowest frequencies. This means that in the frequency domain, it's easy to identify the important values.

Compression is then just a matter of getting rid of the unimportant information or finding easier-to-represent approximations of it. Decompression is the reverse process. We take the approximated and important frequencies and transform them back to pixels. We won't get exactly the same image—some information has been lost—but by being very clever we can get back something that a human won't perceive as different.

This will be obvious with an example, but first, we need to get some images into Julia to play with.

Working with Images

Out of the box, Julia does not contain a library for loading images from arbitrary formats. What it does have is an amazing package manager that we can use to download and install an image library.

The Pkg module contains functions to query and manipulate the package database. You can see the list of available packages at Julia's package site.[3] For our image work, we'll need the Images, TestImages, and ImageView packages:

```
julia> Pkg.add("Images")
INFO: Initializing package repository /home/jack/.julia/v0.3
INFO: Cloning METADATA from git://github.com/JuliaLang/METADATA.jl
...
INFO: Cloning cache of Images from git://github.com/timholy/Images.jl.git
...
INFO: Installing Images v0.2.45
...
INFO: Building Images
INFO: Package database updated

julia> Pkg.add("TestImages")
...
julia> Pkg.add("ImageView")
...
```

The Images package contains libraries for loading and saving images in various formats. TestImages contains sample images we can play with. ImageView is a simple tool to draw images on the screen. You might also need to install Gtk and make sure the GTK libraries are available on your system. See the Gtk package page[4] for details.

When you're using Pkg.add for the first time, it will initialize the package database in ~/.julia and then download and build the package you requested along with any dependencies it needs. As soon as it's finished, the package is ready to use; you don't even have to restart the REPL.

```
julia> using TestImages, ImageView
julia> img = testimage("cameraman")
Gray Image with:
  data: 512x512 Array{Uint8,2}
  properties:
    colorspace: Gray
    spatialorder:  x y
    limits: (0x00,0xff)
julia> view(img)
(ImageCanvas,ImageSlice2d:
    zoom = BoundingBox(0.0,512.0,0.0,512.0))
```

If everything is working, you should now see an image of a cameraman on your screen.

---

3.   http://pkg.julialang.org/

4.   https://github.com/JuliaLang/Gtk.jl

Now that we can load and view images, let's take a closer look at their data.

From Pixels to Frequencies

The data field of an image contains the pixel values. Here you can see the top 8×8 corner of pixels for the cameraman image. (We must convert the pixel values to a floating-point type since the library functions we need aren't implemented for integer types.)

```
julia> pixels = im.data[1:8,1:8]
julia> pixels = convert(Array{Float32}, pixels)
8x8 Array{Float32,2}:
 156.0  156.0  158.0  160.0  158.0  156.0  158.0  160.0
 157.0  157.0  157.0  157.0  157.0  157.0  157.0  157.0
 160.0  159.0  156.0  154.0  156.0  159.0  156.0  154.0
 159.0  158.0  156.0  154.0  156.0  159.0  156.0  154.0
 158.0  158.0  157.0  156.0  157.0  159.0  157.0  156.0
 156.0  156.0  157.0  157.0  156.0  156.0  156.0  157.0
 155.0  155.0  157.0  158.0  155.0  154.0  155.0  158.0
 156.0  156.0  157.0  157.0  155.0  155.0  155.0  157.0
```

Other than the values being similar, are you able to tell which pixels are important?

Let's use Julia's library routine dct to transform these pixels to frequencies. The dct function uses the discrete cosine transform to change pixels into frequencies. This transform is related to the Fourier transform,[5] which you may have heard of before.

```
julia> freqs = dct(pixels)
julia> round(freqs)
8x8 Array{Float32,2}:
 1254.0   2.0   1.0   0.0  -0.0  -0.0   1.0  -1.0
    4.0  -0.0   0.0   3.0  -1.0  -0.0  -1.0   0.0
   -0.0  -3.0  -1.0  -6.0   4.0   1.0  -1.0   0.0
    2.0  -3.0  -2.0  -4.0   2.0   1.0  -1.0   0.0
    1.0  -0.0  -0.0   0.0  -0.0  -0.0   0.0  -0.0
   -1.0   0.0   0.0  -1.0   1.0   0.0   0.0  -0.0
    0.0   1.0   0.0   1.0  -0.0  -0.0   0.0  -0.0
    1.0   0.0   0.0   0.0  -0.0  -0.0  -0.0  -0.0
```

After the DCT we can see clearly which values are important. In order to make the point more obvious, the values are rounded. The very first frequency is three orders of magnitude bigger than all the others, which are all close to zero. The first coefficient represents the average color of the pixels. The original pixels were basically all the same except for a little bit of noise.

---

5.   http://en.wikipedia.org/wiki/Fourier_transform

Hopefully now you have some intuition about how the transformation results in a more compact representation.

We can also go from frequencies to pixels with idct, which runs the inverse transform:

```
julia> pixels2 = convert(Array{Uint8}, idct(freqs))
8x8 Array{Uint8,2}:
 0x9c  0x9c  0x9e  0xa0  0x9e  0x9c  0x9e  0xa0
...
julia> pixels == pixels2
true
```

Because we didn't change any frequency information, we got back the same pixels we started with. Both the pixels and the frequencies are just two different views of the same underlying data.

Lossy Compression

Thanks to the frequency representation of the data, we can now easily determine the most important pieces of the data. If you start looking at lots of image frequencies, you'll notice a common pattern. Most of the large values are in the low frequencies—the frequencies toward the top left. If we throw out the unimportant frequencies, we can shrink the data while preserving its basic characteristics.

We're going to start by throwing away almost 90% of the data.

The last thing you need to know before we look at the code to do this is that we'll be working on 8×8 tiles of pixels and frequencies at a time. This is how JPEG works as well. The main reason to work on small tiles has to do with limiting unwanted artifacts. In the pixel domain, changing a single value changes only one pixel, but in the frequency domain, changing a single frequency affects many pixels. By using small groups of pixels, we ensure that the extent of unwanted pixel changes is minimized.

We're going to use a module to organize the code since this example is a little longer:

```
julia/Codec.jl
module Codec

using Images

❶ function blockdct6(img)
    pixels = convert(Array{Float32}, img.data)

    y, x = size(pixels)
```

```
❷      outx = ifloor(x/8)
       outy = ifloor(y/8)

❸      bx = 1:8:outx*8
       by = 1:8:outy*8

❹      mask = zeros(8,8)
       mask[1:3,1:3] = [1 1 1; 1 1 0; 1 0 0]

❺      freqs = Array(Float32, (outy*8,outx*8))

❻      for i = bx, j = by
           freqs[j:j+7,i:i+7] = dct(pixels[j:j+7,i:i+7])
           freqs[j:j+7,i:i+7] .*= mask
       end

       freqs
    end

    function blockidct(freqs)
        y, x = size(freqs)
        bx = 1:8:x
        by = 1:8:y

        pixels = Array(Float32, size(freqs))
❼      for i = bx, j = by
           pixels[j:j+7,i:i+7] = idct(freqs[j:j+7,i:i+7]) ./ 255.0
        end
❽      grayim(pixels)
    end

 end
```

❶ blockdct6 transforms an image to frequencies by 8×8 blocks. In addition, it deletes all frequencies except the most important six.

❷ To keep the example simple, we crop the image to a multiple of 8 in each dimension.

❸ bx and by are block indices in the image.

❹ The mask is 1 for the coefficients we want to keep and 0 everywhere else.

❺ We create an empty freqs array of the right size to hold the result.

❻ Iterating over each 8×8 block, we run the DCT and store it in the corresponding 8×8 block in freqs. Then, we multiply it element-wise by the mask to delete the unimportant data. Since the mask keeps only 6 out of the 64 coefficients, this is almost 90% less data.

❼ Transforming from frequencies back to pixels is even easier and follows the same pattern. Note that we must scale the value appropriately because graying expects pixel values between 0 and 1 instead of 0 and 255.

❽ grayim makes an Image out of a 2D array.

We can test this by running the REPL in the same directory as Codec.jl:

```
julia> using Codec
julia> freqs = Codec.blockdct6(img)
512x512 Array{Float32,2}:
...
julia> img2 = Codec.blockidct(freqs)
Gray Image with:
  data: 512x512 Array{Float32,2}
  properties:
    colorspace: Gray
    spatialorder:  x y
julia> view(img2)
(ImageCanvas,ImageSlice2d: zoom = BoundingBox(0.0,512.0,0.0,512.0))
```

The output should look similar to the following:

You can see there is a small loss of fine detail, but overall the version missing 90% of the data looks pretty good. Not bad for a few dozen lines of code.

What We Learned in Day 3

Today you saw how to manipulate code like data with Julia's macro system. We used it to write @unless, which added a new control flow structure to the language. Between quoting and interpolation, Julia makes writing code that writes code so easy you'll actually do it.

We wrapped up the day with a bigger example focused on writing a toy image codec. We used lots of new tools to accomplish the task—packages, modules, and math functions from Julia's standard library. Our codec won't replace

JPEG any time soon, but it is amazing how easy slicing and dicing data is with Julia.

Your Turn

The problems are a bit tougher today, but you should find Julia more than capable of helping you make quick work of them.

Find…

- Julia's documentation on modules and packages.
- A description of how JPEG works. What parts were left out of our example?

Do (Easy):

- Write a macro that runs a block of code backward.
- Experiment with modifying frequencies and observing the effect on an image. What happens when you set some high frequencies to large values? What happens if you add lots of noise? (Hint: Try adding scale * rand(size(freqs)).)

Do (Medium):

- Modify the code to allow masking arbitrarily many coefficients, but always the N most important ones. Instead of calling blockdct6(img) you would call blockdct(img, 6).
- Our codec outputs a frequency array as big as its input, even though most frequencies are zero. Instead, output only the six nonzero frequencies for each block so that the output is smaller than the input. Modify the decoder to use this smaller input as well.
- Experiment with different block sizes to see how block size affects the appearance of coding artifacts. Try a large block size on an image containing lots of text and see what happens.

Do (Hard):

- The code currently only works on grayscale images, but the same technique works on color too. Modify the code to work on color images like testimage("mandrill").
- JPEG does prediction of the first coefficient, called the DC offset. The previous block's DC value is subtracted from the current block's DC value. This encodes an offset instead of a number with full range, saving valuable bits. Try implementing this in the codec.

Wrapping Up Julia

We had a lot of fun working in Julia. It is young, but its unique assimilation of the best features of its competitors is not an amalgamation of parts but a coherent and designed assembly. It is fast and dynamic, yet it has strong types and macros.

To us, it feels like the focus on a particular domain—scientific computing—while taking inspiration from many sources has produced a tool that is well thought out and executed. Julia has pushed the frontier of what is possible to achieve when trading off dynamic language ease of use and static language performance, and it may get previously esoteric features like multiple dispatch and real macros in front of everyday programmers.

Julia is, above all else, extremely practical, but unlike other more practical languages, it doesn't feel that anything we would have wanted was sacrificed to get the job done. If you've ever worked with MATLAB or R, using Julia is like moving from Perl to Python or Ruby.

Strengths

Julia excels at number crunching as we've seen, but features that scientists need are useful in many domains. Having a solid concurrency story is going to give Julia staying power in the current crop of languages and a leg up against older languages.

Julia's home page doesn't have one mention of the word "functional," yet Julia has clearly been put together by people with a deep respect for functional programming. The line will continuously shift as languages like Julia push functional programming concepts into the mainstream.

Julia's package system is built right in, and there are already a number of packages for doing many tasks. Previously this level of interactivity—being able to install packages and then continue working—was reserved for people who use Emacs for everything.

Weaknesses

Julia has two downsides, both of which will correct themselves over time. The first is its youth, and the second is the lack of available packages.

Julia is new and still growing, possibly not even out of the awkward teenage years. The syntax may still change. Some things don't quite work yet. This affects Julia more than the other languages in this book because Julia's competitors include Fortran, and the libraries people depend on are decades old and rock solid.

R and MATLAB have enormous libraries of packages that have been built up over their lifetimes. Because Julia is new, its package library is pretty small. Julia's ecosystem is surely going to grow like wildfire due to having packaging built in from the start. The lack of packages is a feature that Julia shares with all new languages.

Final Thoughts

We love and use a lot of languages, but the list of languages we look to first to solve problems is fairly short. Previously we have used Fortran, Python (with NumPy), and MATLAB for scientific computing, but we are now believers in Julia.

If you are more comfortable with functional languages than object-oriented ones, you'll feel right at home in Julia. If you've wanted access to powerful features from Lisp but lacked a language capable of being grokked by the rest of your team, give Julia a try.

As Graydon Hoare, creator of the Rust language, puts it, Julia is a "Goldilocks language."[6] It's just right.

---

6. http://graydon2.dreamwidth.org/189377.html

miniKanren

by Jack Moffitt

I've spent decades telling the computer how to do things. Logic programming offers a reprieve from this drudgery. While programming with logic, you describe the relations and constraints of your problem, and the computer figures out the solutions required.

I remember the first time I realized just how different logic programming is. At a conference, Dan Friedman and William Byrd were demoing a small language interpreter written in miniKanren. They first showed how it could evaluate simple numerical programs and get the correct answer. Then in an act of wizardry, they ran the same interpreter backward to produce programs that generated the answer 6.

Logic programming is the closest we may ever come to real magic. I feel a bit like Harry Potter when programming with logic. I don't need to worry about every little detail of implementation; I just say "Lumos!" and there is light.

There are many implementations of miniKanren.[1] In this chapter we will explore core.logic, an embedded miniKanren for programming in Clojure. Similar ideas extend all the way back to Prolog. The focus on rules and constraints can feel liberating for some problems, but for others it can be frustrating. Core.logic helps bridge the gap between the realms of mystical logic and our day-to-day work. The result is a paradigm that will delight yet remain practical.

---

1. http://minikanren.org/

Day 1: Unified Theories of Code

Three days is all we have to get you using logic productively, but because core.logic is embedded in Clojure, the more familiar functional programming is always nearby to help.

On the first day we'll learn about unification and the basic logic operations. We'll build a database of facts and see how core.logic can reason about them. Finally we'll take a peek at conditionals in logic.

Day 2 will add some pattern matching and other macro sugar to the previous day's topics. We'll see how to unify and work with maps as well.

Finally, on the last day we'll wrap up by learning about finite domains. By then you'll be ready for some more complex examples too.

We'll move fast, but by the end you should be able to explore on your own and start using logic in your own work.

Installing core.logic

To install core.logic you'll need a Java Virtual Machine (JVM) and the Leiningen build tool. Leiningen will do all the hard work of fetching libraries for your project and managing Java's library paths.

You can find a JVM for your platform in your system's package manager or at Oracle's Java download page.[2] Leiningen and instructions to install it on most platforms can be found on its home page.[3]

Once these are working, you can create a project with lein new:

```
$ lein new logical
Generating a project called logical based on the 'default' template.
To see other templates (app, lein plugin, etc), try `lein help new`.
```

This will create a project skeleton in the logical directory. In order to use core.logic in this project, you'll need to add a few dependencies to the project's project.clj file. Edit logical/project.clj to look like this:

minikanren/logical/project.clj
```
(defproject logical "0.1.0-SNAPSHOT"
  :dependencies [[org.clojure/clojure "1.5.1"]
                 [org.clojure/core.logic "0.8.5"]])
```

---

2. http://www.oracle.com/technetwork/java/javase/downloads/index.html

3. http://leiningen.org/

Now inside the project's directory, you should be able to fire up the Clojure REPL and load core.logic:

```
$ lein repl
nREPL server started on port 48235 on host 127.0.0.1
REPL-y 0.3.0
Clojure 1.5.1
    Docs: (doc function-name-here)
          (find-doc "part-of-name-here")
  Source: (source function-name-here)
 Javadoc: (javadoc java-object-or-class-here)
    Exit: Control+D or (exit) or (quit)
 Results: Stored in vars *1, *2, *3, an exception in *e

user=> (use 'clojure.core.logic)
WARNING: == already refers to: #'clojure.core/== in namespace: user, being
  replaced by: #'clojure.core.logic/==
nil
user=>
```

Logic is now at your fingertips. Note that the warning is benign and just lets you know that one of core.logic's symbols has replaced one of the default ones.

Your Goal Is to Succeed

Logic programs are like puzzles where only some information is given and the solution to the puzzle is to find the rest of the information. Imagine a Sudoku square where at the start of the puzzle only the rules and a few numbers are known. Or think of a jigsaw puzzle, where only pieces of the picture and shapes are visible.

Programming with logic means providing some starting data and the rules of the puzzle. Core.logic does the actual work of solving the puzzle and provides the resulting solutions.

Let's jump right in and look at some simple logic programs. We'll be working at the REPL, which makes exploration easy. Try the following:

```
user=> (run* [q] (== q 1))
(1)
```

This may look like a simple program, but a lot is going on.

run* runs a logic program and returns the set of solutions. q is a logic variable. When logic variables are created, they are unbound or free. They have no value and could represent anything at all. The set of solutions will be the values of q that solve our puzzle. q seems to be the name most often used for the main logic variable, perhaps standing for "query."

Every square in Sudoku would be a logic variable. Some of the squares are empty (*free*, *unbound*), and some are filled in (*bound*).

This logic program contains a single expression, (== q 1), which is not the equality test you are used to. == in core.logic is the *unification* function, and this expression attempts to unify the logic variable q with the number 1.

Unification is similar to pattern matching. You're asking the language to try to make the left and right sides the same, assuming that's possible. The left and right sides are compared as in normal equality tests, and any unbound logic variables are bound to values that would make the two sides match. In this example, q is bound to 1, which is a solution because there are no other rules. It may seem a bit strange, but we'll see some more examples shortly that should give you an intuitive feel for what's going on.

The expressions in a logic program are goals. They don't return true or false but succeed or fail. It's possible that success is achieved multiple times in different ways or not at all. This brings us to the last bit of our example: the result.

Our example returned (1). run* returns the values of q that result in success. In our example, unifying q with 1 binds q to the number 1 and succeeds. Our result is the list containing the single binding for q.

Let's look at a failed goal:

```
user=> (run* [q] (== q 1) (== q 2))
()
```

This program has two expressions, each a goal. A program with multiple goals will succeed only if all of the goals succeed, similar to && or and operators in other languages. Here, the first unification will bind q to the number 1 just as before and succeed. The second unification will fail, since q is bound to 1 and 1 does not unify with 2. Because no binding of q can cause both goals to succeed, the resulting list is empty.

Getting Relational

It's time for a look at logical functions:

```
user=> (run* [q] (membero q [1 2 3]))
(1 2 3)
```

membero is a *relation*. membero says that its first argument is a member of the collection given in the second argument. It is a goal, so it will either succeed or fail, and in doing so will bind q to values for which the goal succeeds. The result of our example shows that values of 1, 2, or 3 result in success. Note that we've not told core.logic how to solve a puzzle, only the rules.

run* will return all the possible bindings for q that result in success, so this is a complete list. It's easy to look at this small program and convince yourself that the answer is correct. This is kind of an amazing trick.

You can use run to get a set number (or fewer) answers:

```
user=> (run 2 [q] (membero q [1 2 3]))
(1 2)
```

This is handy to know about because there might be an infinite number of ways to satisfy a goal.

Logic programming has even more magic up its sleeve. Let's see what happens when we reverse the order of the arguments to membero:

```
user=> (run 5 [q] (membero [1 2 3] q))
(([1 2 3] . _0) (_0 [1 2 3] . _1) (_0 _1 [1 2 3] . _2) (_0 _1 _2 [1 2 3] . _3)
  (_0 _1 _2 _3 [1 2 3] . _4))
```

You may find this result surprising, so let's dig into it. Our original goal formulation, (membero q [1 2 3]), asked what the possible members of the collection are. The new formulation, (membero [1 2 3] q) asks what collections contain [1 2 3] as a member. There are an infinite number of possible collections that could contain [1 2 3]; thankfully we only asked for five answers.

The first answer is ([1 2 3] . _0). The . is the list construction operator. To the left of the . is the first element of the list (the head), and to the right of the . is the rest of the list (the tail). The weird _0 is the notation for an unbound logic variable. In this case it means the tail of the list could be anything. In other words, the first answer is that any list where [1 2 3] is the first element would satisfy the goal.

Now you can probably understand the other answers, too. The next answer is that any list with [1 2 3] as the second element would satisfy the goal, no matter what the first element and the rest of the list are.

This is like taking a fully solved Sudoku and asking for the possible starting states. I think it's pretty cool, and I've never seen other languages able to run programs backward.

> ## What's with the "o" suffix?
>
> In *The Reasoned Schemer [FBK05]*, a superscript "o" is used to denote relations, and this tradition has been followed by the miniKanren and core.logic communities.
>
> It's just a small visual hint that something is different about a particular function, which comes in handy when you start mixing regular Clojure code into your logic programs. It may seem weird at first, but you'll get used to it, and as a side benefit, it makes explaining your programs to others much more amusing.

Programming with Facts

We've played a little with the basics of core.logic and seen that it finds bindings for q that satisfy the program's goals. We also examined membero, a built-in relation that relates a member with a collection. Now we'll try to write some relations of our own.

Core.logic includes a database, pldb, that allows us to construct simple relations built up with lists of facts. This is similar to a table in traditional database systems. For example, we can build two relations called mano and womano. We do this using db-rel. The first argument is the name of the relation, and the remaining arguments are placeholders.

```
user=> (use 'clojure.core.logic.pldb)
nil
user=> (db-rel mano x)
#'user/mano
user=> (db-rel womano x)
#'user/womano
```

Here we've created the two relations, which both take a single argument and will succeed if that argument is a man or a woman respectively.

We populate the relation by giving a list of facts to the db function and binding it to the variable facts. Each fact is a vector containing the relation and its arguments.

```
user=> (def facts
  #_=>    (db
  #_=>      [mano :alan-turing]
  #_=>      [womano :grace-hopper]
  #_=>      [mano :leslie-lamport]
  #_=>      [mano :alonzo-church]
  #_=>      [womano :ada-lovelace]
  #_=>      [womano :barbara-liskov]
  #_=>      [womano :frances-allen]
  #_=>      [mano :john-mccarthy]]))
#'user/facts
```

Querying our database is easy. Let's find all the women:

```
user=> (with-db facts
  #_=>   (run* [q] (womano q)))
(:grace-hopper :ada-lovelace :barbara-liskov :frances-allen)
```

The with-db function sets the data source for the database relations. It allows multiple databases to be used together or separately. Our logic program succeeds when q is one of the women, and so the answer is the list of women.

Let's add some more relations, vitalo and turingo, which will relate men and women to their vital status and whether they've received the Turing Award:

```
user=> (db-rel vitalo p s)
#'user/vitalo

user=> (db-rel turingo p y)
#'user/turingo

user=> (def facts
  #_=>   (-> facts
  #_=>      (db-fact vitalo :alan-turing :dead)
  #_=>      (db-fact vitalo :grace-hopper :dead)
  #_=>      (db-fact vitalo :leslie-lamport :alive)
  #_=>      (db-fact vitalo :alonzo-church :dead)
  #_=>      (db-fact vitalo :ada-lovelace :dead)
  #_=>      (db-fact vitalo :barbara-liskov :alive)
  #_=>      (db-fact vitalo :frances-allen :alive)
  #_=>      (db-fact vitalo :john-mccarthy :dead)
  #_=>      (db-fact turingo :leslie-lamport :2013)
  #_=>      (db-fact turingo :barbara-liskov :2008)
  #_=>      (db-fact turingo :frances-allen :2006)
  #_=>      (db-fact turingo :john-mccarthy :1971)))
#'user/facts
```

We have enough facts to ask some interesting questions:

```
user=> (with-db facts
  #_=>   (run* [q]
  #_=>      (womano q)
  #_=>      (vitalo q :alive)))
(:barbara-liskov :frances-allen)
```

The goal succeeds for living women. Note that when a successful goal causes the logic variable q to be bound, that binding must hold in further relations.

To express more complicated programs, we often need more logic variables. The fresh function can create new, unbound logic variables:

```
user=> (with-db facts
  #_=>    (run* [q]
  #_=>      (fresh [p y]
  #_=>        (vitalo p :dead)
  #_=>        (turingo p y)
  #_=>        (== q [p y])))))
([:john-mccarthy :1971])
```

❶ We use fresh to create two new logic variables that are unbound.

❷ Passing p to vitalo will cause it to be bound to a deceased person.

❸ With p bound to something, we can now use turingo to bind to the year the person won the Turing Award. Note that only people who've won the Turing Award will satisfy the relation.

❹ Finally, we bind q to a vector containing the person and the year.

The previous example can be summarized as "Which deceased people won the Turing Award?" One interesting property of logic programs is that the order of the goals is not important. In the previous example, it may appear that first we bind p, then y, and finally q, but these are declarative goals, not procedural steps—they can be satisfied regardless of their ordering:

```
user=> (with-db facts
  #_=>    (run* [q]
  #_=>      (fresh [p y]
  #_=>        (turingo p y)
  #_=>        (== q [p y])
  #_=>        (vitalo p :dead))))
([:john-mccarthy :1971])
```

Now we've shuffled the order of the goals. Specifically, q is unified before the goal that binds p. Core.logic will fill in the unbound placeholders when those variables are eventually bound. Or, as we saw previously, they may never get bound and will show up as _0, _1, and so on.

Parallel Universes

One macro remains for us to have all the logical ingredients for our programs: conde. You've seen that run, run*, and fresh all succeed only when all their goals succeed. This is similar to and and && in other languages. conde is a bit like or and ||.

Like or, conde succeeds if any of its goals succeed. However, unlike or, conde succeeds for every goal that succeeds independently. It's a bit like running your program in parallel universes, where each branch of a conde runs in a new universe and you can detect all the possible successes.

Let's see it in action:

```
user=> (run* [q]
  #_=>    (conde
  #_=>      [(== q 1)]
  #_=>      [(== q 2) (== q 3)]
  #_=>      [(== q :abc)]]))
(1 :abc)
```

Each branch of the conde is a list of goals. The branch succeeds if all its goals succeed, but the conde succeeds once for every branch that succeeds. The first branch succeeds and binds q to 1. In another universe, the second branch fails. In yet another universe, the third branch succeeds, binding q to :abc. The result is the list of successful bindings for q across all universes.

Dissecting a Spell

Earlier today you saw membero, which relates members to their collections. You're almost ready to construct such a relation yourself, but first you need to learn about conso.

cons is the list construction function in Lisp, and unsurprisingly, conso is its relational cousin. conso relates the head and tail of a list to the whole list. Because it is a relation, it takes three arguments instead of two— Passing a logic variable as the last argument results in list construction very similar to cons.

```
user=> (run* [q] (conso :a [:b :c] q))
((:a :b :c))
```

We can pull out just the tail of the list as well.

```
user=> (run* [q] (conso :a q [:a :b :c]))
((:b :c))
```

Running conso backward destructures the list into its head and its tail. Here we create two new logic variables to hold these, and then we bind q to a vector of the results.

```
user=> (run* [q] (fresh [h t] (conso h t [:a :b :c]) (== q [h t])))
([:a (:b :c)])
```

Now that you know how to pull apart and put together lists relationally and how to manipulate space-time with conde, we can build powerful recursive relations.

Let's build insideo, which is equivalent to the built-in membero:

```
user=> (defn insideo [e l]
  #_=>   (conde
  #_=>     [(fresh [h t]
  #_=>       (conso h t l)
❶ #_=>       (== h e))]
  #_=>     [(fresh [h t]
  #_=>       (conso h t l)
❷ #_=>       (insideo e t))]]))
#'user/insideo
```

❶ The first branch deconstructs the collection with conso and succeeds if the head is the same as the element that was passed in.

❷ The second branch recursively calls insideo, looking for the element in the tail.

We can check that insideo works as we expect:

```
user=> (run* [q] (insideo q [:a :b :c]))
(:a :b :c)
user=> (run 3 [q] (insideo :a q))
((:a . _0) (_0 :a . _1) (_0 _1 :a . _2))
user=> (run* [q] (insideo :d [:a :b :c q]))
(:d)
```

insideo works forward and backward, and in the last example, it can even figure out what element is required for it to succeed.

What We Learned in Day 1

If you've made it this far, you're well on your way to mastering logic as well as space and time. You must formulate problems and constraints, but you needn't worry about step-by-step solutions.

Today we covered a lot of logical ground. We learned how to write logic programs using run* and run. We also learned how logic variables and unification work. It's a bit like having the computer solve a puzzle for you given some data and the rules. Using these, we were able to see the first bits of logic programming's unique style by running the membero relation both forward and backward. If only functions in every language were so flexible!

Databases of facts can help build up bases of knowledge for your logic programs to reason over. You can use them to make inferences and queries. Databases can be combined and extended with new relations.

conde gives you power over multiple universes where all possibilities are calculated and observed. It's the logical equivalent of branching like if and cond in other languages. Unlike traditional branching, all the branches get taken, but only the successful paths contribute to the answer.

Finally we learned how to create our own relations, even recursive ones. It may not seem like a lot of parts, but with just these pieces you can build a great many things.

Your Turn

Now's your chance to practice solo with core.logic. Don't worry, though, it starts off easy.

Find...

- The core.logic home page
- One of the many wonderful talks on core.logic or miniKanren by David Nolen or Dan Friedman and William Byrd
- A core.logic tutorial
- What other projects are doing with core.logic

Do (Easy):

- Try running a logic program that has two membero goals, both with q as the first argument. What happens when the same element exists in both collections?
- appendo is a core.logic built-in that will append two lists. Write some logic programs similar to the membero examples to get a feel for how it works. Be sure to use q in each of the three argument positions to see what happens.
- Create languageo and systemo database relations and add the relevant facts based on which category best classifies the person's work.

Do (Medium):

- Use conde to create scientisto, which succeeds for any of the men or women.
- Construct a logic program that finds all scientists who've won Turing Awards.

Do (Hard):

- Create a genealogy system using a family tree database and relations like childo and spouseo. Then write relations that can traverse the tree like ancestoro, descendanto, and cousino.
- Write a relation called extendo, which works like the built-in appendo, mentioned in the easy problems.

Day 2: Mixing the Logical and Functional

The implementation of miniKanren appears in an amazing book called *The Reasoned Schemer [FBK05]* and is only two printed pages. That's impressively concise considering what it is capable of. Core.logic's implementation is larger due to its focus on high performance and additional features that help leverage its host language, Clojure.

Those extra pages of core.logic's code are not wasted. Today we'll dig into the ways in which mixing Clojure and logic programming are mutually beneficial. You may feel like a muggle instead of a wizard still, but stick with it and soon you'll be mixing your own amazing potions.

Patterns, Patterns Everywhere

A common feature of functional programming languages is pattern matching, and while Clojure has a limited form of this feature in its destructuring syntax, there are libraries that provide powerful pattern matching macros. David Nolen, who wrote core.logic, also wrote core.match, one of the best of these pattern matching macros, and it should come as no surprise that core.logic has pattern matching built in.

Let's look again at the insideo example from yesterday, which used conde to test different cases:

```
(defn insideo [e l]
  (conde
    [(fresh [h t]
       (conso h t l)
       (== h e))]
    [(fresh [h t]
       (conso h t l)
       (insideo e t))]))
```

The first thing each branch of conde does is to deconstruct the head and the tail of the list. You can imagine that many other functions will need to do this same operation.

Matching with match

match is a pattern matching version of conde that makes this kind of code much more clear and concise. Here's the same function rewritten with matche:

```
(defn insideo [e l]
  (matche [l]
    ([[e . _]])
    ([[_ . t]] (insideo e t))))
```

The first argument to matche is a list of variables that we'll be matching. Each clause is its own list, the first item of which is the pattern it will try to match. Note that this pattern contains brackets just like the argument list.

The first pattern it tries to match for l is [e . _]. The dot is the list construction symbol; the left side of the dot will match the first element, and the right side will match all the rest of the elements. The _ is treated as a dummy value. It unifies with anything, just like a fresh variable, but its value is ignored and never used. The pattern match will succeed when the target element e is the first element of l.

The second pattern contains a variable that hasn't been introduced. matche will automatically create fresh logic variables for any unknown symbols it sees in a pattern. This keeps the code concise. When the pattern matches, t will be unified with the tail of the list, and we can invoke the recursive rule to keep searching.

These patterns are very simple, but patterns can be arbitrarily complex, unifying fresh variables to deeply nested items. This proves extremely useful in practice; instead of massaging inputs to get at the data you want, you can use patterns to deconstruct the input directly into the form you need.

Function Patterns

When you begin using patterns, you may notice that most of your functions end up containing a big matche block. This is such a common occurrence that core.logic has another pattern macro, defne, built in to further reduce this boilerplate.

defne defines a function that uses patterns on its input arguments. This will be clearer if we look at an example macro expansion:

```
(defne exampleo [a b c]
  ([:a _ _])
  ([_ :b x] (membero x [:x :y :z])))

;; expands to:

(defn exampleo [a b c]
  (matche [a b c]
    ([:a _ _])
    ([_ :b x] (membero x [:x :y :z]))))
```

Notice that the argument list is repeated verbatim in the matche form. This syntax starts to feel a bit like Erlang or Haskell, which both have pattern matching built into regular function definitions.

Let's rewrite insideo one last time with defne. I think you'll have a hard time writing a shorter version!

```
(defne insideo [e l]
  ([_ [e . _]])
  ([_ [_ . t]] (insideo e t)))
```

Since we don't care about the first argument in the different clauses, we use _ to ignore it. The one downside of defne is that you must always match on all the function's arguments, not just the ones you care about. In most cases, this a great trade-off.

Go back and look at where we started with insideo and compare that to this defne version. Pattern matching has reduced the function to its essence.

Working with Maps

Maps, hash tables, dictionaries—no matter what your favorite language calls them, they are among the most often used and important data structures. One of the ways Clojure innovates on its Lisp heritage is first-class support for maps. By this point it should be no surprise that core.logic supports maps too.

Maps in core.logic work mostly as they do in Clojure. You can even use maps with pattern matching:

```
user=> (run* [q]
  #_=>    (fresh [m]
  #_=>      (== m {:a 1 :b 2})
  #_=>      (matche [m]
  #_=>        ([{:a 1}] (== q :found-a))
  #_=>        ([{:b 2}] (== q :found-b))
  #_=>        ([{:a 1 :b 2}] (== q :found-a-and-b)))))
(:found-a-and-b)
```

This code shows both how easy it is to work with maps and that all is not quite as you'd expect. First it unifies m with a simple map. Then matche is used to test various patterns. If you're familiar with Clojure, you'd probably expect all three patterns' goals to succeed. Why does only the last goal succeed?

The answer is that unlike Clojure, which doesn't require you to destructure every key, core.logic map patterns must match exactly. It's still useful to match on many kinds of maps where you know how many key-value pairs there will be, but if you're just looking for specific pieces, you'll have to try something else.

What we need is a function that will constrain a logical variable to a map containing at least some specific fields. In core.logic this is called featurec. Let's see it in action:

```
user=> (run* [q]
  #_=>   (featurec q {:a 1}))
((_0 :- (clojure.core.logic/featurec _0 {:a 1}))))
```

We have constrained q to be a map that has a key :a with a value 1 and then asked for all possible values of q. The answer takes a little practice reading. The :- symbol can be read as "such that." Basically any map such that it has the feature {:a 1} is a solution. This is how core.logic expresses constraints on solutions.

Let's reimplement the previous map pattern using conde and featurec:

```
user=> (run* [q]
  #_=>   (fresh [m a b]
  #_=>     (== m {:a 1 :b 2})
  #_=>     (conde
❶  #_=>       [(featurec m {:a a}) (== q [:found-a a])]
❷  #_=>       [(featurec m {:b b}) (== q [:found-b b])]
  #_=>       [(featurec m {:a a :b b}) (== q [:found-a-and-b a b])])))
❸ ([:found-a 1] [:found-b 2] [:found-a-and-b 1 2])
```

❶ This branch succeeds if the map contains the :a key, but any value will do. This will also unify the fresh a variable to the key's value.

❷ The same thing applies here, but for maps with a :b key.

❸ The set of solutions contains all three branches, unlike our previous example. Notice that we've also extracted the values of the keys.

featurec is a very useful tool, as we'll see. Bringing maps and partial maps into logic programming makes expressing many kinds of problems much clearer.

You might ask why featurec is not featureo. The simple answer is that it's not a relation. The second argument must be a map, even if some of its values are logic variables. This means you can't run it backward, asking for all possible feature constraints for a given map:

```
user=> (run* [q]
  #_=>   (featurec {:a 1 :b 2 :c 3} q))
```

```
ClassCastException clojure.core.logic.LVar cannot be cast to
clojure.lang.IPersistentMap
clojure.core.logic/eval3753/map->PMap--3764 (logic.clj:2443)
```

This small limitation won't prevent us doing great things with partial maps.

Other Kinds of Cond

The languages you are probably familiar with have a single kind of conditional. Tests are run in order and whichever test passes, the code for the corresponding branch is run. It may surprise you to learn that core.logic has multiple types of conditionals. You saw the first of these, conde, yesterday, but now we'll learn about two more, conda and condu.

If you think about core.logic evaluating your branches in parallel universes, the different kinds of cond control which universes and how many solutions contribute to the final solution.

A Single Universe

The easiest way to understand conda is with an example. Let's create a relation, whicho, that will tell us which of two lists an element appears in. It takes an element, two lists, and a result. The result can be either :one, :two, or :both depending on whether the element is in the first, second, or both sets. Let's try using regular old conde first:

```
user=> (defn whicho [x s1 s2 r]
  #_=>     (conde
  #_=>       [(membero x s1)
  #_=>        (== r :one)]
  #_=>       [(membero x s2)
  #_=>        (== r :two)]
  #_=>       [(membero x s1)
  #_=>        (membero x s2)
  #_=>        (== r :both)]]))
#'user/whicho
user=> (run* [q] (whicho :a [:a :b :c] [:d :e :c] q))
(:one)
user=> (run* [q] (whicho :d [:a :b :c] [:d :e :c] q))
(:two)
user=> (run* [q] (whicho :c [:a :b :c] [:d :e :c] q))
(:one :two :both)
```

This all seems very straightforward until we get to the last solution, which has too many answers.

Consider why this happens. Core.logic evaluates every branch in its own universe, then collects all the successful goals and presents them. In the case of :c, all three branches are successful, so we have three answers in our solution set.

Sometimes this is just what you want, but in this case, you probably expected to see only :both. Let's try again but using conda.

```
user=> (defn whicho [x s1 s2 r]
  #_=>   (conda
  #_=>     [(all
  #_=>       (membero x s1)
  #_=>       (membero x s2)
  #_=>       (== r :both))]
  #_=>     [(all
  #_=>       (membero x s1)
  #_=>       (== r :one))]
  #_=>     [(all
  #_=>       (membero x s2)
  #_=>       (== r :two))]))
#'user/whicho
user=> (run* [q] (whicho :a [:a :b :c] [:d :e :c] q))
(:one)
user=> (run* [q] (whicho :d [:a :b :c] [:d :e :c] q))
(:two)
user=> (run* [q] (whicho :c [:a :b :c] [:d :e :c] q))
(:both)
```

Now we've got the results we wanted. What is conda doing?

conda only looks for solutions in the first branch that has a successful first goal. In our many universes metaphor, conda throws away all the other universes and their solutions except for one.

In this version of whicho, conda first tries the first goal of the first branch. If that succeeds, it's as if none of the other goals ever existed. If it fails, it will try the next one. Once it has found a successful goal, all the other branches, regardless of whether or not they would be successful, are eliminated.

You may note that we've both reordered the branches in this version and enclosed all the goals in all. The reordering is necessary because conda is order dependent, unlike conde. If the :both branch is not first, then it will always get eliminated when one of the other branches succeeds. all is needed since whether to choose an exclusive branch depends on the success of the branch's first goal, not the success of the whole branch. If we didn't use all, then (membero x s1) succeeding in the first branch would eliminate the others, even if the (membero x s2) would fail. This would cause (whicho :b [:a :b c:] [:d :e :c] q) to have no solutions, instead of :one.

conda is much more like conditionals you are used to, although it is not as common in logic programming as conde.

A Single Solution

condu works similarly to conda, except that instead of limiting solutions to a single branch, it stops completely after a single solution is found.

Before we see condu in action, let's run insideo backward again:

```
user=> (run* [q] (insideo q [:a :b :c :d]))
(:a :b :c :d)
```

insideo, which is a reimplementation of membero if you recall, returns all the elements inside its second argument. Let's replace conde in its implementation with condu:

```
user=> (defn insideo [e l]
  #_=>    (condu
  #_=>      [(fresh [h t]
  #_=>         (conso h t l)
  #_=>         (== h e))]
  #_=>      [(fresh [h t]
  #_=>         (conso h t l)
  #_=>         (insideo e t))]))
#'user/insideo
user=> (run* [q] (insideo q [:a :b :c :d]))
(:a)
```

This time, insideo stops at the first solution, even though with run* we asked for all solutions. condu is also called the *committed choice* macro, since once it has made any successful choice, that is the only choice it will make.

The Three Conds

Which kind of conditional you choose depends on what you're trying to do. If you're not sure which to use, start with conde. If the solutions you get aren't quite right, you can try conda if you have too many branches succeeding or condu if you need only a single solution. Tomorrow we'll see an example where conde won't cut it and we'll have to use conda.

Each version of cond has a corresponding match and defn form. For conde, we already saw matche and defne, which do pattern matching and pattern function definition, respectively. Core.logic provides conda versions of these, matcha and defna, and condu versions, matchu and defnu.

Multiple kinds of conditionals is a lot to absorb. While it soaks in, let's take a break and talk to core.logic's creator.

An Interview with David Nolen

The implementation of miniKanren we've been using is core.logic, written by David Nolen. David is the author of many great Clojure and JavaScript libraries and shares our fascination for logic programming.

Us: *How did you get interested in logic programming, and what motivated you to create core.logic?*

David: *I encountered logic programming for the first time in 2009. I had recently read a blog post by Jim Duey about logic programming—he had created a simple Clojure port of miniKanren and demonstrated that he could solve a classic logic puzzle (the Zebra/Einstein puzzle) in a declarative manner. I found this both surprising and intriguing and so I emailed him asking how it worked. He pointed to me to The Reasoned Schemer and I picked up a copy for travel reading on the way to the very first Clojure conference. For fun I decided to do a simple implementation myself. The Reasoned Schemer was short on implementation details and I went hunting for more information. Eventually I found William Byrd's dissertation, which clarified quite a few points and guided my first working miniKanren implementation. Shortly thereafter Clojure introduced deftype, defrecord, and protocols and I suspected that a reasonably efficient implementation of miniKanren could be written. After four or five months of development I had an implementation of miniKanren that could solve the Zebra/Einstein puzzle nearly as quickly as SWI-Prolog. This was encouraging, and I immersed myself in logic and constraint logic programming literature and ported interesting ideas as I encountered them into what eventually became core.logic.*

Us: *What kind of problems do you find logic programming best for solving?*

David: *Any problem that benefits from a declarative solution where performance is not the utmost concern.*

Us: *What can you do in core.logic that you can't do in a language like Prolog?*

David: *Modern Prologs are extremely powerful, flexible, and customizable. I think the main advantage of miniKanren over Prolog is the shallow embedding in a functional programming language. That is, miniKanren allows you to easily leverage the best paradigm for the problem at hand.*

Us: *What other features would you like to have in core.logic?*

David: *I would like integration with Clojure data structures to be greatly improved. I would also like to port all the finite domain functionality to ClojureScript, but this awaits a better official cross compilation story. There's also a huge pile of performance enhancement ideas that I need to find time to assess and implement.*

What We Learned in Day 2

Declarative programming is powerful and concise, but by mixing the relations of miniKanren with the functional workhorse Clojure, we can make new syntax with macros and work with data structures like maps.

We learned how to do pattern matching with matche, which turned conde expressions into beautiful deconstructions. Between matche and its friend defne, Clojure macros have made the logic programmer's job that much easier.

Next, we tried matching maps and found that core.logic supports partial maps with constraints. We used featurec to constrain maps and to pick out values for keys in a map.

Finally, we explored the three conditionals: conde, conda, and condu.

Your Turn

Tomorrow, we'll put all these things together to build something practical, so practice the new skills you learned today to get ready.

Find...
- Examples of code using featurec
- The source code for core.logic's membero

Do (Easy):
- Rewrite extendo from Day 1's problems using matche or defne.
- Create a goal not-rooto which takes a map with a :username key and succeeds only if the value is not "root".
- Run whicho in reverse, asking for elements in one or both of the sets.
- Add a :none branch to whicho. What happens when you use the :none branch in the whicho version built on conde?

Do (Medium):
- Using the database from yesterday, create unsungo, which takes a list of computer scientists and succeeds if none of them have won Turing Awards. conda may prove useful.

Do (Hard):
- Play with (insideo :a [:a :b :a]). How many times does it succeed? Make it succeed only once but have (insideo q [:a :b :a]) return all distinct elements. Hint: Try using the != constraint.

Day 3: Writing Stories with Logic

Over the last two days, you've seen a lot of what core.logic has to offer. Now it's time to put that knowledge to use in a larger and more practical example.

There are many problems that involve route planning. For example, how do you fly to a distant city? Sometimes there are direct flights, but sometimes the path involves multiple connections, different planes, and even several airlines. Alternatively, think of a truck making deliveries. After enumerating possible paths, you must then optimize for the shortest or the quickest.

If you think about it, generating a story is similar but more fun. Instead of connection cities, you have plot points. Routes through the plot make up the entire story, and as an author, you'll want to optimize to achieve the desired effect. Should the story be short? Should everyone die at the end?

We're going to build a story generator using the logic tools you've acquired so far. Although the end result may seem frivolous on the surface, the techniques we use are the same for the more mundane problems.

Before we get to the story generator, there's one last feature of core.logic that merits attention: finite domains.

Programming with Finite Domains

Logic programming is implemented behind the scenes with directed search algorithms. You specify constraints and the language searches for solutions that satisfy the criteria.

So far, we've been working with elements, lists, and maps in our logic programs. These structures may be infinite in size, but they are composed of a finite set of concrete elements. To search for solutions to (membero q [1 2 3]), core.logic only needs to look through all the elements.

What happens when we want to work with numbers? Imagine searching for integer solutions to (<= q 1). There is an infinite number of answers. Even worse, there is an infinite number of possibilities to try, and depending on where you start and how you search, you may never find a solution.

The problem is tractable if we constrain q to the positive integers or any finite set of numbers. In core.logic we can make such constraints with finite domains. Finite domains add knowledge about the set of valid states in the search problem. Let's use our example (<= q 1), but within a finite domain:

```
user=> (require '[clojure.core.logic.fd :as fd])
nil
user=> (run* [q]
  #_=>    (fd/in q (fd/interval 0 10))
  #_=>    (fd/<= q 1))
(0 1)
```

❶ This constraint establishes that q is in a given interval of numbers.

❷ The solution set is finite and found quickly because of the constrained domain.

Finite domains over numeric intervals also allow you to start doing mathematic operations on logic variables. We can ask core.logic to solve for every triple of distinct numbers whose sum is 100:

```
user=> (run* [q]
  #_=>   (fresh [x y z a]
  #_=>     (== q [x y z])
  #_=>     (fd/in x y z a (fd/interval 1 100))
  #_=>     (fd/distinct [x y z])
  #_=>     (fd/< x y)
  #_=>     (fd/< y z)
  #_=>     (fd/+ x y a)
  #_=>     (fd/+ a z 100)))
([1 2 97] [2 3 95] [1 3 96] [1 4 95] [3 4 93] [2 4 94] ...)
```

❶ x, y, and z are the three numbers we're solving for. a is just a temporary helper.

❷ All the logic variables are constrained to the finite range of 1 to 100.

❸ fd/distinct sets the constraint that none of the variables can be equal to another. This prevents solutions such as [1 1 98].

❹ We constrain x to be less than y, and y less than z. If we failed to order the variables, then we'd have duplicate solutions such as [6 28 66] and [66 28 6].

❺ There are 784 solutions. My machine found the entire set of solutions in 5 milliseconds. Core.logic is no slouch.

The code as written works quite well, although having to do arithmetic operations two numbers at a time with a temporary logic variable feels rather clumsy. Fortunately, core.logic provides some macro sugar to sprinkle on its math. fd/eq allows us to write normal expressions for our equations and transforms those expressions into code that creates the appropriate temporary logic vars and calls the appropriate finite domain functions.

```
user=> (run* [q]
  #_=>   (fresh [x y z]
  #_=>     (== q [x y z])
  #_=>     (fd/in x y z (fd/interval 1 100))
  #_=>     (fd/distinct [x y z])
  #_=>     (fd/< x y)
  #_=>     (fd/< y z)
  #_=>     (fd/eq
  #_=>       (= (+ x y z) 100))))
([1 2 97] [2 3 95] ...)
```

The last line is much simpler, and the resulting program is easier to read.

Take a minute to think about what's going on here. Macros are turning logic into normal syntax, finite domains are constraining the search problem to a small space, and the program isn't just finding a single solution but all possible solutions. Best of all, it's declarative and reads like a problem statement instead of a solution method.

Magical Stories

So far, the examples have been tailored to help you understand individual concepts in core.logic, and now we'll put what you've learned into practice with a more realistic and comprehensive example. In the end, even Harry Potter uses his spells for opening locks and other common tasks.

Our task will be one of path finding, subject to some constraints. Whether finding transit routes or scheduling deliveries, path planning problems abound, and logic programming excels at solving them.

Instead of finding a route for a delivery truck or solving for how to reach one city from another via available transit options, we'll be generating stories. From a database of plot elements, we can search for a story that reaches a certain end state. Following the path through the plot elements becomes a little narrative, controlled by logic and the destination you provide.

Getting Inspired

This example was inspired by a wonderful talk I saw at Strange Loop 2013. It's called "Linear Logic Programming" by Chris Martens.[a] She also co-wrote a paper on the same topic: "Linear Logic Programming for Narrative Generation."[b] Chris explains linear logic programming and then uses it to generate and explore narrative using Madame Bovary as a reference. I highly recommend investigating her work.

---

a.   http://www.infoq.com/presentations/linear-logic-programming
b.   https://www.cs.cmu.edu/~cmartens/lpnmr13.pdf

Core.logic will generate many possible stories for us, but it is up to us to pick out the ones that might be interesting. We'll use Clojure to postprocess possible stories to select ones that fit our criteria. For example, we may filter small stories out to get at more interesting, longer narratives.

Problem Details

Before we begin, we should define the problem a little better.

First, we need a collection of story elements and a method for moving from one element to another. We can easily store facts in a database about various plot points, but we'll need to create them. I'll let Hollywood do the hard work here and use the plot of the cult comedy movie *Clue*, a murder mystery loosely based on the board game where six guests, a butler, a maid, a cook, and the master of the house are in for a potentially deadly ride.

Here's a snippet of the story from the movie:

(1) Wadsworth opens the door to find a stranded motorist whose car broke down nearby. The motorist asks to use the phone, and Wadsworth escorts him to the lounge. The group locks the motorist in the lounge while they search for the killer in the rest of the house. (2) After some time, a policeman notices the abandoned car and starts to investigate. (3) Meanwhile, someone kills the motorist with the wrench.

We can simulate and manage moving from one plot point, (1), to another, (2), by the use of linear logic. Linear logic is an extension of the logic you're probably familiar with, which allows for the use and manipulation of resources. For example, a logical proposition may require and consume a particular resource. Instead of "A implies B," we say that "A consumes Z and produces B," where Z is some particular resource. In the previous snippet, (3) takes the motorist as input and produces a dead motorist. Similarly, (2) takes the motorist as input and produces a policeman.

We can craft a simple linear logic in core.logic. Each plot element will have some resource that it needs and some resource that it produces. We'll represent this as a two-element vector of the needed and produced resource. For example, [:motorist :policeman] means that for this story element to happen, we must have a :motorist available and it will create a :policeman. In the movie, a stranded motorist rings the doorbell for help, and later a policeman who discovers his car comes looking for him. Without the motorist, the policeman will never show up.

We'll have a starting state, which is a set of initial, available resources. A relation will govern selecting a legal story element given the state and moving to a new state. We'll control where the story goes by putting requirements on the final state. For example, the story will finish when a particular character is caught or dies.

The final touch will be to print out the resulting stories in a readable form.

Story Elements

Our story elements need to contain the resource being consumed and the resource being produced. Additionally, we'll put in a string describing the element in prose that we'll make use of when printing out the narrative.

We'll need a large list of elements to make interesting stories, but the plot of *Clue* gives us plenty to work with. You might notice that several people can be murdered in multiple ways; *Clue* had three different endings, which are all represented.

Here are the first few elements of story-elements in story.clj:

minikanren/logical/src/logical/story.clj
```
(def story-elements
  [[:maybe-telegram-girl :telegram-girl
    "A singing telegram girl arrives."]
   [:maybe-motorist :motorist
    "A stranded motorist comes asking for help."]
   [:motorist :policeman
    "Investigating an abandoned car, a policeman appears."]
   [:motorist :dead-motorist
    "The motorist is found dead in the lounge, killed by a wrench."]
   [:telegram-girl :dead-telegram-girl
    "The telegram girl is murdered in the hall with a revolver."]
   [:policeman :dead-policeman
    "The policeman is killed in the library with a lead pipe."]
   [:dead-motorist :guilty-mustard
    "Colonel Mustard killed the motorist, his old driver during the war."]
   [:dead-motorist :guilty-scarlet
    "Miss Scarlet killed the motorist to keep her secrets safe."]
   ;; ...])
```

The structure is a vector of vectors. The inner vectors have three elements: the two resources and the string description. There are 27 elements in full story-elements, which is enough to get some interesting results.

We'll need to postprocess this to turn it into our story database in core.logic.

Building the Database and Initial State

Our goal is to turn the story-elements vector into a database of facts that core.logic can use. We'll use a simple relation, ploto, which will relate the input resource to the output. The end result we want would be equivalent to this:

```
(db-rel ploto a b)

(def story-db
  (db
    [ploto :maybe-telegram-girl :telegram-girl]
    [ploto :wadsworth :dead-wadsworth]
    ;; ...)))
```

We'll use Clojure's reduce function to effect the transformation:

```
minikanren/logical/src/logical/story.clj
(db-rel ploto a b)

(def story-db
❶  (reduce (fn [dbase elems]
              (apply db-fact dbase ploto (take 2 elems)))
❷          (db)
❸          story-elements))
```

❶ Reducing functions take two arguments. The first is the accumulator that holds the initial, intermediate, or final result of the reduction. The second is the current element to reduce. Here we extend the database passed as the first argument with a new fact using the ploto relation and the first two elements of the story element vector.

❷ Our initial state is just a blank database.

❸ Running the reduction over all the story elements will turn our vector of vectors into a core.logic database of facts.

Now that we have our story elements, we need an initial state. This contains all the people who may appear and all the people who are already in the house who might later be killed. Note that only resources that are used in the story elements need to be listed.

```
minikanren/logical/src/logical/story.clj
(def start-state
  [:maybe-telegram-girl :maybe-motorist
   :wadsworth :mr-boddy :cook :yvette])
```

The story elements database and the initial state define all the data for our story. As you'll see shortly, the data used is much larger than the code we need to generate stories.

Plotting Along

The next task is to create a transition relation to move the story from one state to the next by selecting an appropriate story element. This is the workhorse of our generator:

```
minikanren/logical/src/logical/story.clj
(defn actiono [state new-state action]
  (fresh [in out temp]
❶    (membero in state)
❷    (ploto in out)
❸    (rembero in state temp)
❹    (conso out temp new-state)
     (== action [in out])))
```

❶ The in resource must be something from the current state. We can't use any of the story resources unless they are available.

❷ Once we have an in resource, ploto picks a corresponding resource to create in out.

❸ The resource is consumed as part of the story action, so we remove it from the state.

❹ The newly created resource is added to the state to produce the new state.

We can load logical.story in a REPL and experiment with actiono:

```
user=> (require '[logical.story :as story])
user=> (with-db story/story-db
  #_=>    (run* [q]
  #_=>      (fresh [action state]
  #_=>        (== q [action state])
  #_=>        (story/actiono [:motorist] state action))))
([[:motorist :policeman] (:policeman)]
 [[:motorist :dead-motorist] (:dead-motorist)])
```

This query uses a starting state of [:motorist] and asks for all the actions and their corresponding new states that are possible. Either a policeman can come looking for the stranded motorist, or the motorist can be murdered.

For generating our stories, we want to run the transitions backward. Starting from some goal conditions—resources we want to exist in the final state—we want to find a sequence of actions that will achieve the goals from the starting state.

```
minikanren/logical/src/logical/story.clj
(declare story*)

(defn storyo [end-elems actions]
❶  (storyo* (shuffle start-state) end-elems actions))

(defn storyo* [start-state end-elems actions]
  (fresh [action new-state new-actions]
❷    (actiono start-state new-state action)
❸    (conso action new-actions actions)
    (conda
❹     [(everyg #(membero % new-state) end-elems)
        (== new-actions [])]
❺     [(storyo* new-state end-elems new-actions)]))))
```

❶ storyo simply calls storyo* so that the user doesn't have to pass in the initial state themselves. Shuffling the initial state will produce a randomized solution sequence.

❷ We transition to a new state by taking some action.

❸ We prepend the action we took onto the list of actions.

❹ everyg succeeds if the goal function provided as the first argument succeeds for every element of the collection in the second argument. If all our goal resources in end-elems are in new-state, our story is done. We set new-actions to the empty vector at the end since there won't be any more taken.

❺ If not all our goals have succeeded, we recursively call storyo* to keep going.

Let's play with storyo at the REPL to generate some simple stories:

```
user=> (with-db story/story-db
  #_=>   (run 5 [q]
  #_=>     (story/storyo [:dead-wadsworth] q)))
(([:wadsworth :dead-wadsworth])
 ([:maybe-motorist :motorist] [:wadsworth :dead-wadsworth])
 ([:maybe-telegram-girl :telegram-girl] [:wadsworth :dead-wadsworth])
 ([:maybe-motorist :motorist] [:motorist :policeman]
  [:wadsworth :dead-wadsworth])
 ([:maybe-motorist :motorist] [:motorist :dead-motorist]
  [:dead-motorist :guilty-mustard] [:wadsworth :dead-wadsworth]))
```

Core.logic has used our story database to generate five stories where Wadsworth ends up dead. Each solution is a list of actions, and if you squint at it and remember the story elements, you can figure out what is happening. For example, the last story in the list has a stranded motorist appearing, who is then murdered by Colonel Mustard, and then Wadsworth is killed in the hallway with the revolver.

We still have some work to do. The stories need to be human readable instead of the simple list of actions, and we'll need to filter stories to get more interesting results.

Readable Stories

Creating more readable stories is just a matter of reusing our description strings from story-elements in the output. We'll transform story-elements into a map from actions to the strings, and then generate a human-readable plot summary from the result.

minikanren/logical/src/logical/story.clj
```
(def story-map
❶  (reduce (fn [m elems]
            (assoc m (vec (take 2 elems)) (nth elems 2)))
          {}
          story-elements))
```

```
(defn print-story [actions]
  (println "PLOT SUMMARY:")
  (doseq [a actions]
    (println (story-map a)))))
```

❶ For each element, our reduction associates a new key and value to the map. The key is a two-element vector of the input and output resources, which is the same format as our actions. The value is the last item in the story element, the description.

❷ print-story just looks up the description in the map and prints the result for each action in the sequence.

Let's test it out on a story:

```
user=> (def stories
  # =>    (with-db story/story-db
  # =>      (run* [q]
  # =>        (story/storyo [:guilty-scarlet] q))))
#'user/stories
user=> (story/print-story (first (drop 10 stories)))
PLOT SUMMARY:
A stranded motorist comes asking for help.
The motorist is found dead in the lounge, killed by a wrench.
Colonel Mustard killed the motorist, his old driver during the war.
The cook is found stabbed in the kitchen.
Miss Scarlet killed the cook to silence her.
nil
```

❶ run* will produce a stream of all the solutions. This is lazily computed, so it will return immediately and then do the work to give us solutions when we ask for them. Lazy streams are one of the more powerful features of Clojure.

❷ We can drop a few of the initial stories to get some more interesting and longer ones. Here we've dropped the first 10 and picked the first one in the remaining stream.

Now we're getting somewhere. The stories are fun to read now, but a little too short. We can postprocess the story stream with Clojure's powerful stream manipulation tools.

Mining Stories

Clojure has an enormous number of tools for dissecting, filtering, and manipulating data of all kinds. You saw in the previous example how core.logic solutions are a lazy stream and just how easy it is to pick that stream apart.

We can put these tools to work for us and try to find more interesting stories from the random story stream that run* and storyo generate. Using the goal states in combination with postprocessing, we direct the generation and select the most interesting results:

```
user=> (defn story-stream [& goals]
  #_=>   (with-db story/story-db
  #_=>     (run* [q]
  #_=>       (story/storyo (vec goals) q))))
#'user/story-stream

user=> (story/print-story
  #_=>   (first
  #_=>     (filter #(> (count %) 10)
  #_=>             (story-stream :guilty-peacock :dead-yvette))))
PLOT SUMMARY:
A stranded motorist comes asking for help.
Investigating an abandoned car, a policeman appears.
The policeman is killed in the library with a lead pipe.
Mrs. Peacock killed the policeman.
Mr. Boddy's body is found in the hall beaten to death with a candlestick.
Wadsworth is found shot dead in the hall.
Mr. Green, an undercover FBI agent, shot Wadsworth.
A singing telegram girl arrives.
The telegram girl is murdered in the hall with a revolver.
Miss Scarlet killed the telegram girl so she wouldn't talk.
Yvette, the maid, is found strangled with the rope in the billiard room.
nil
```

Asking for stories with more than 10 elements in which Yvette dies and Mrs. Peacock is a murderer produces something particularly grim.

Keep playing with it and see what interesting narratives you can create. You'll be extending the system in today's exercises.

What We Learned in Day 3

Today you saw a more practical view of core.logic. Logic programming isn't just about puzzles. Many real-world problems benefit from a logical approach.

We started by looking at finite domains, which are extremely useful in constraint-solving problems. For example, Mac OS X's layout engine is a constraint solver. Not only does core.logic make these types of problems easy to express, but the solutions are obtained extremely quickly.

We used logic to generate paths, but instead of finding routes connecting cities, we discovered narratives through various plot elements. Combining simple linear logic, recursive functions, and Clojure's data manipulation tools, we were able to craft a story generator in just a few lines of code.

Your Turn

If you've yet to play with any code in this chapter, now is your chance to get your hands dirty with the new tools introduced today.

Find...

- Examples of other people using core.logic's finite domains.
- Commercial products that are powered by logic engines. Hint: Include Prolog in your search.

Do (Easy):

- Code some other mathematical equations and have core.logic fill in the answers.
- Generate stories where the motorist never appears and there are at least two murderers.

Do (Medium):

- It's more suspenseful if we learn who the killers are at the end of the story. Use Clojure's data manipulation tools to push those story events to the end.
- If the policeman arrives, the motorist can no longer be killed. This is a limitation of our linear logic because inputs are always consumed. Extend the generator such that story elements can have multiple outputs and use this to enable stories where the policeman and the motorist are both murdered.

Do (Hard):

- Try to write a Sudoku solver using finite domains. Hint: You'll need to create unnamed logic variables with (lvar) at empty places in the grid. Build multiple views on the same grid by row, column, and square.
- Create a new set of story elements and initial state using your own imagination or inspiration from a favorite book. Use the narrative generator to find the most interesting version.

Wrapping Up miniKanren

Logic programming is a strange thing. Where else can you run programs backward or create programs that achieve your goals without having any concrete steps? It takes some time getting used to, but for some kinds of problems, you'll have a tough time writing a better or shorter program with any other tool.

Embedding a powerful logic system inside a practical programming language like Clojure provides an environment where logic can be used seamlessly alongside your regular code, making it easy to use the right tool for the job.

Strengths

The primary strength of miniKanren is the use of declarative programming to achieve almost magical ends. Goals can be reordered and programs run backward. This makes it easy to express problems such as constraint solving, scheduling, and path finding.

Core.logic adds to this mix the integration with a practical, everyday programming language, Clojure, along with the entire Java ecosystem. Your logic programs can make use of existing SQL databases and the myriad of other existing libraries.

To give you an idea of the leverage core.logic is giving you, imagine implementing the narrative generator in Java or Ruby. Would it still be as concise and easy to extend?

Weaknesses

Logic programming is mind-bending. When it goes wrong, it is hard to tell why as the search going on behind the scenes can derail in subtle ways. For example, while writing this chapter I spent many hours debugging an example that in the end I was unable to get fully working.

Although this is true of every new language you attempt to learn, logic programming makes it even more difficult since there are no familiar landmarks to help you out.

Final Thoughts

More than a library, miniKanren is a new language with a new programming paradigm. It's also one of the most fun programming languages I've ever played with. Running programs backward will always put a smile on my face.

Problems that fit its domain are so easily and concisely expressed that it's a wonder to me that every language doesn't have an embedded logic system like miniKanren. Core.logic does a particularly fine job of integrating with Clojure and using the strengths of Clojure to make logic programming practical. It will be amazing to watch as core.logic and miniKanren keep getting better and are used in more places.

CHAPTER 7

Idris

by Ian Dees and Bruce Tate

No one likes a debate like a passionate programmer. Developers argue endlessly but sometimes productively about tools, techniques, and approaches to programming. Type models in particular have been a source of constant tension throughout the history of programming languages.

When type zealots collide, the fireworks can be fascinating. Want to be safe and secure? Tired of being burned by things like SQL injection errors? You're probably a static-typing kind of character. You've likely seen compile-time checks pay for the extra weight in code, or for the extra time it takes to pacify the compiler.

If on the other hand you're in the dynamic camp, you probably like working with sharp tools without safety features—even if there's a little more risk of being cut. You've seen static type systems with way too much ceremony (remember public static void main?). You're willing to do the extra testing and put up with the possibility of some instability to keep your code simple and clean. You like being able to change your program's fundamental design while it's still running, like changing tires on a car in mid-drive.

As this theoretical battle marches on, we've seen the pendulum swing between static and dynamic type systems. In language research, tremendous advances are happening. One interesting development in type theory is the family of *dependently typed languages* that are expanding the limits of what static types can do for us. Think of dependent types as types that depend on values, such as a list that's always in the correct order—guaranteed by the compiler. Enter Idris.

With richer information in dependent types, Idris can do things other languages can't:

- Find more errors at compile time
- Prove, or disprove, that certain elements of your program are correct—including input parameter checking
- Provide powerful editing, with much more sophisticated completion than you can get in traditional languages

Think Sherlock Holmes. With his nearly supernatural observation skills, he has information to put together insights that most people don't. He demands excruciating detail when he questions witnesses or colleagues. But these extra demands pay off when he solves the case.

Even if you're from the Church of the Dynamic Type, Idris will at least show you what the fuss is all about. You'll have to do more up-front thinking about your types, and express them in more detail than you're used to. But when you've done so, those same types will boost your productivity in ways you've never experienced before.

For this story's mystery, we'll seek the answer to one simple question. Is all of the effort of expressing these rich types worth the effort? There's no time to lose. Let's jump on this case.

Day 1: The Basics

Like Elm, Idris has roots firmly planted in Haskell. You already know that it can be challenging to learn much about a language in one short week. For languages in the Haskell family, the task is doubly daunting. We're not going to try to give you a full review of Idris. Instead, we'll focus on what dependent types bring to the table.

Here's what's in store. In Day 1, we'll introduce the basic building blocks of the language and build a foundation for dependent types. For Day 2, we'll actually write some dependent types and see Idris dazzle us with its understanding of our programs. In Day 3, we'll use dependent types to accomplish great feats: advanced editor completion, proofs, and improving real-world programs.

Grab your deerstalker cap and magnifying glass. The game's afoot!

Installing Idris

Idris has roots firmly planted in the Haskell ecosystem. Install it from the excellent installation directions on the Idris site.[1] When you are done, you should be able to crack open the shell, like this:

---

1. http://www.idris-lang.org/download/

```
→ idris
```

```
Version 0.9.12
http://www.idris-lang.org/
Type :? for help
```

```
Idris>
```

You can exit the REPL by typing :q; go ahead and do that now.

To make sure things are working, let's build a quick program. Add the following to a text file called hello.idr:

```
module Main
main : IO ()
main = putStrLn "Elementary, dear Idris."
```

Then, you can compile and run the program like this:

```
> idris hello.idr -o hello
> ./hello
Elementary, dear Idris.
```

If things are working as they should, you're ready to code!

Understanding the Basics

If you have some Haskell experience, the first part of Day 1 is going to be quite familiar to you. Though we can't as easily declare functions in the console, we can still do quite a bit of work here. Let's start to put it through its paces.

Primitive Types and Expressions

We'll start with a few primitive data types:

```
Idris> True
True : Bool
Idris> 4
4 : Integer
Idris> 4.567
4.567 : Float
Idris> 'c'
'c' : Char
Idris> "Watson"
"Watson" : String
```

Fair enough. Boolean, Integer, Float, String, and Char are primitive types that do about what you'd expect them to.

You can also type it to get the value of the last expression:

```
Idris> it
"Watson" : String
```

Let's do some simple expressions next:

```
Idris> 4 + 5
9 : Integer
Idris> True || False
True : Bool
Idris> True && False
False : Bool
Idris> not True
False : Bool
Idris> "a" ++ " clue"
"a clue" : String
Idris> it ++ ", " ++ it
"a clue, a clue" : String
```

There are no real surprises here. Let's try to combine types:

```
Idris> 5 + 6 / 2
8.0 : Float
Idris> 4.567 > 4
True : Bool
Idris> 8 == 8.0
True : Bool
```

Still no surprises. When types are compatible, Idris will coerce them. Let's try a little harder to break type safety:

```
Idris> 1 + "one"
Can't resolve type class Num String
Idris> 'a' + "bc"
Can't resolve type class Num Char
```

Integer and String are incompatible for this operator, as are Char and String. The second is mildly surprising, because Char seems to be derived from Num. Jot this fact down in your detective's notebook for later consideration, before we move on to functions.

Functions

The syntax for declaring functions in the REPL is cumbersome. Instead, let's put a few simple ones into a file, then dissect them in the console. We'll start with functions that return primitive types. Type the following into a file called functions.idr:

idris/day1/functions.idr
```
module Functions

intFunction : Int
intFunction = 1887

stringFunction : String
stringFunction = "A Study in Scarlet"
```

Load it into the console with :l like this:

```
> :l functions
```

Now, try calling the functions you wrote:

```
*functions> stringFunction
"A Study in Scarlet" : String
*functions> intFunction
1887 : Int
```

They seem to work fine. Now, let's ask Idris about the type of each function. You do this with the :t command:

```
*function> :t stringFunction
Functions.stringFunction : String
*function> :t intFunction
Functions.intFunction : Int
```

The REPL parrots back our type definitions, qualified by our module name.

We can also build anonymous functions, and pass them into other functions. Let's try this with the map function. You've probably seen this in other languages; it calls a function on every item in a collection and returns a collection containing the results.

In pseudocode, map takes the following types:

```
map: function_from_a_to_b -> list_of_a -> list_of_b
```

Idris comes with a map implementation; let's see what it's made of.

```
*functions> :t map
Prelude.Functor.map : Functor f => (a -> b) -> (f a) -> f b
```

As we expect, map takes a function from one type a to another type b. Prelude is the library that Idris, and many versions of Haskell, include by default, and a Functor is something you can map over. We don't see the words List a or Vector a anywhere, because this concept is more general than any specific collection type.

Now, let's look at the type of an anonymous function. Here's one that multiplies its input x by 0.5:

```
*functions> :t (\x => x * 0.5)
\ x => x * 0.5 : Float -> Float
```

Idris has inferred the type of x to be a function taking a Float and returning another Float.

Now, let's try to map our anonymous function onto the series of numbers [3.14, 2.72]:

```
*functions> map (\x => x * 0.5) [3.14, 2.72]
Can't disambiguate name: Prelude.List.::, Prelude.Stream.::, Prelude.Vect.::
```

The Prelude includes a few similar functions named map in different namespaces: one for lists, one for vectors, and so on. In a full program, we'd write the types explicitly—there'd be no ambiguity.

The REPL, however, does not have enough information to infer the type of [3.14, 2.78]. It could be a list, a stream, or a vector. Let's give Idris more specific information:

```
*functions> map (\x => x * 0.5) (the (List Float) [3.14, 2.78])
[1.57,1.3900000000000001] : List Float
```

That's better. For those cases where Idris can't infer the type, we can supply it ourselves.

In another language, you'd need a special notation to add type information. In Idris, you can use an ordinary function, because functions can take types as parameters. The standard library supplies the un-Google-able the for this purpose.[2]

Let's take a look at this function's type:

```
*functions> :t the
Prelude.Basics.the : (a : Type) -> a -> a
```

The the function takes two parameters:

1. A *type*; in our example, the pair (List Float)
2. A *value*, the list [3.14, 2.72]

map now happily applies our anonymous function to each element in the list.

We could get lost in the basic Idris language features without ever touching the type system. If you know a little Haskell, you'll find Idris pretty similar.

---

2. https://github.com/idris-lang/Idris-dev/blob/master/libs/prelude/Prelude/Basics.idr#L13

If not, pick up a resource, like perhaps the original *Seven Languages in Seven Weeks [Tat10]*. When you're ready, let's pick up by defining some data types.

Defining Data Types

Let's create some data types to get a handle on how the base Idris type system works.

Getting to Know Numbers Again

We'll start with a naïve number system. Type the following into a file called data_types.idr:

idris/day1/data_types.idr
```
data DumbNumber = Naught | One | Two | Three
```

Now, fire up your console, or load the file, and try it out:

```
*data_types> :l data_types.idr
Type checking ./data_types.idr
*data_types> Naught
Naught : DumbNumber
*data_types> Two
Two : DumbNumber
```

We can use the new number type we created, but we can't do too much with it. The numbers have no relationship with one another. Let's take a shot at a slightly more sophisticated number system: natural numbers.

Natural Numbers

Way back in elementary arithmetic, we learned that natural numbers are the integers from zero upward. Every natural number is either zero, or the number after some other natural number. This recursive definition is easy to express in Idris. Tack this type onto the end of your data_types.idr file:

idris/day1/data_types.idr
```
data Natural = Zero | After Natural
```

Now, load your code up into the console and take a look:

```
*data_types> :l data_types.idr
Type checking ./data_types.idr
*data_types> Zero
Zero : Natural
*data_types> After Zero
After Zero : Natural
*data_types> After (After Zero)
After (After Zero) : Natural
```

In fact, Idris has its own natural numbers defined like these, but with Nat, Z, and S that stand for Natural, Zero, and Successor, respectively. Take a look:

```
*data_types> :t Z
Prelude.Nat.Z : Nat
*data_types> S Z
1 : Nat
*data_types> :t S Z
1 : Nat
*data_types> S (S Z)
2 : Nat
```

Idris shortens the integers for display, showing us 2, for example, instead of S (S Z).

This type definition maintains the relationship between one number and the next. That's important because later, we're going to use these natural numbers *in the definition of other types.*

Now, let's take a look at a slightly more sophisticated type.

Parameterized Types

idris/day1/data_types.idr
```
data MyList a = Blank | (::) a (MyList a)
```

This type is the definition of a list of, well, something. a is a *parameterized type.* That means you can use any type in place of a. This system allows many similar types to be treated in the same way—that is, types are *polymorphic.*

The list, called MyList, can hold anything of type a. Breaking it down, our type has two cases: an empty list, called Blank, and a list with one more item. The (::) operator adds an item to a list, and a represents a type. So, (::) a (MyList a) represents something of type a added to MyList a—that is, a list of items of type a.

The parentheses around (::), by the way, mean that :: can also be used as an infix operator without the parens. The following two function calls are the same:

```
*data_types> (::) "Watson" Blank
"Watson" :: Blank : MyList String
*data_types> "Watson" :: Blank
"Watson" :: Blank : MyList String
```

Let's look at one more parameterized type before we close the door on Day 1.

The Billion-Dollar Mistake

If you've spent most of your time in dynamically typed languages or even languages like Java and C with very limited type systems, you might have noticed that nil or null values represent a significant percentage of all bugs. These bugs are so prevalent that Tony Hoare referred to null references as a billion-dollar mistake.[3]

In Idris, as in Haskell, you can save yourself a billion dollars by defining a type that might or might not have a value. The following definition ships with Idris:[4]

```
data Maybe a = Nothing | Just a
```

A value of type Maybe a can neatly represent either Nothing or a value of type a. For example, let's say you're writing a function that returns the first element of a list. Your function might have a type like this:

```
idris/day1/data_types.idr
first : MyList a -> Maybe a
first Blank = Nothing
first (x :: xs) = Just x
```

In this definition, first takes a list of type a and returns a Maybe of type a. If the list is empty, first returns Nothing. Otherwise, the list returns Just x, meaning the value of x.

Go ahead and take first out for a spin:

```
*data_types> first ("Elementary" :: Blank)
Just "Elementary" : Maybe String
*data_types> first (the (MyList String) Blank)
Nothing : Maybe String
```

As you can see, it's impossible for a null value to sneak out of this function. Idris forces callers to handle the case where the list was empty.

A Little Deeper

So far, this type system is expressive and powerful. The types have other features that we're not going to talk about in depth, but you should know a little bit about them.

Type classes allow the representation of increasingly specialized types. Think of the universe of numbers, called Num. You've already seen Nat, Integer, and Float, which are all instances of Num. By organizing types in this way, we allow

---

3. http://www.infoq.com/presentations/Null-References-The-Billion-Dollar-Mistake-Tony-Hoare
4. https://github.com/idris-lang/Idris-dev/blob/master/libs/prelude/Prelude/Maybe.idr

any function to use all compatible types. This feature is called *type polymorphism*. That's why you'll see Idris functions use a generic type, like a, instead of a more specific one.

> ### What About Lazy Evaluation?
>
> If you're coming from a Haskell background, where values aren't computed until they're needed, you may be wondering: what's Idris's stance on lazy evaluation?
>
> Though Idris is not a lazy-by-default language like Haskell, it does support primitive lazy type definitions.[a] For example, if/then statements use lazy types to execute logic conditionally, only when it's needed. Since it's sometimes difficult to reason about the performance of lazy programs, and since Idris exists to make reasoning about programs easier, we'll steer away from lazy semantics.
>
> ---
> a.   http://www.idris-lang.org/documentation/faq

Idris contains many other sleuthing techniques we can apply to our code. Alas, in the short time we have together, we won't be able to cover them all. We hope to instead give you a flavor of dependent types and how they might help you. We'll focus Day 2 exclusively on dependent types.

What We Learned in Day 1

In Day 1, we covered Idris as a cousin of Haskell and learned that it is a pure functional language based on Haskell. We walked you through some primitive values and operators. We looked at primitive types and coded some basic functions, all while staying primarily in Prelude, the library in Idris that is included by default.

We also started to explore the type system. We focused mainly on types that you could define in other languages like Haskell. We built a simple natural number and saw the type definition of a list. We also saw the way static type systems might protect us from errors like possible null values. These are the highlights:

- The language is strongly typed.
- Type classes allow parameterized polymorphism.
- We laid the foundation for exploring dependent types in Day 2.

Next, you'll put many of these features to use.

Your Turn

These exercises will focus on using Idris as a general-purpose programming language. If you don't find ones you like here, search for some Haskell problems that look appealing. You'll see a few problems to get you used to writing general programs in Idris, and a few more that will focus on building basic types.

Find...

The Idris language is new, and though the name is unique, a Google search on the name will find more people than lambdas. For better detective work, mix the word "lang" or "language" into your search.

- The official Idris language home page
- Editor plugins or syntax highlighting for your editor of choice
- Talks about Idris from the creator, Edwin Brady
- Idris mailing lists, where you can ask questions
- The definition of List that ships with Idris

Do (Easy):

- Find the numbers in a list that are greater than a given number.
- Find every other member of a list, starting with the first member.
- Build a data type representing a playing card from a standard poker deck.
- Build a data type representing a deck of cards.

Do (Medium):

- Create data types representing even and odd numbers such that:
  - The successor to an even number is an odd number, and
  - The successor to an odd number is an even number.

- Build a parameterized data type representing a binary tree.

Do (Hard):

- Reverse the elements of a list. (Hint: You may need some helper functions.)

Day 2: Getting Started With Dependent Types

Day 1 was about the basics, laying the foundation for today. Today, we're going to take some of the mystery out of whether or not a program works. We'll start with our type model.

Understanding Dependent Types

In most languages, types and values are independent. List, String, and Integer are types that describe the values [], "Hello", and 6. Said another way, *types describe values*.

In dependently typed languages like Idris, types still describe values, but *types may also depend on values*. This allows us to use more of the language to define our types.

For example, Idris has a vector family of types: Vect n a represents lists of length n and element type a. With most traditional type systems, you could define a function that takes a list, but you couldn't specifically say it takes, for instance, a list of exactly five items.

In Idris, though, you can express these sorts of constraints. Imagine the possibilities for your API:

- chessRow can return a list of length 8.
- sort can take a list *and return a list of the same length*.
- zip x, y, z can take n lists of the same length, and return a list of that length.
- transpose x can enforce the relationship between matrix x and the result.

Today, we'll learn to write exactly these sorts of types. Keep in mind that all of this expressiveness comes at a cost: type declarations that can be significantly more complicated and difficult to understand. The benefits, though, are substantial. Each time you give the compiler more information, bugs must creep further away to avoid detection. All compilers do basic syntax checking. Haskell has rich type compatibility information. Idris begins to invite the *meaning of your programs* into that bug-free zone.

Dependent typing is for more than safety, though. Editors designed for the language can do more sophisticated code completion. We can even use a built-in proof engine to prove or disprove assertions, based on the type model.

Excited? Great! Let's build some dependent types.

Creating Vector Types

A spouse's traditional first anniversary gift is paper, and a programmer's traditional first program is Hello, world. If you're going to fit in among the coffee shop geeks who use dependent typing, your first dependent type should be a vector. Don't ask why; just roll with it.

Our type declaration will require a natural number and a type. Here's the definition for Vect that you would find in Prelude:

```
data Vect : Nat -> Type -> Type where
  Nil : Vect Z a
  (::) : a -> Vect k a -> Vect (S k) a
```

That's a data type definition with just three lines, but they are pretty dense. Let's start at the top. We are building a type family called Vect that takes a Nat and a Type and returns a Type.

Using more precise terminology, we'd say Vect is indexed by Nat and parameterized by Type. *Indexed by* means that the numeric parameter changes across a data structure. *Parameterized by* means that the element type stays the same over the entire data structure.

The where clause further qualifies the definition. For elements of this type, one of the two definitions must be true. In this clause, we're going to define certain types of Vect elements, and an operator.

Whitespace is significant. Each line of the where clause must be indented more than the where line. In each line of the clause, a is a Type, and k is a Nat.

Let's think about what we need to do in order to represent the whole universe of vectors. We need to:

- Define vectors of length zero
- Define the types of all other vectors that are one element larger than the previous vector

Let's look at the lines of the where clause now.

The second line defines Nil as a vector of size zero, or Z.

The last line defines the (::) operator for adding elements. The first argument is an element of type a, and the next is a vector of type Vect k a. The resulting type is a vector that's one larger than k, or S k. Thus the type is Vect (S k) a.

So... we're saying that Vect k a is a type where one of the following is true:

- Either k is Z (an element we will call Nil), or
- The vector of size k + 1 is a concatenation of an element of type a onto a vector of size k.

Whew. If you're not used to reasoning about types in this way, that code might seem intense. That dense code opens up a whole universe. We shouldn't gloss too quickly over what we've done here, so once more: In our definition, a is a *type* and k is a *value*.

On Day 1, we used arithmetic operators in plain old expressions—for example, 4 + 5. In the next section, we're going to use them in our *function declarations*.

Deriving Dependent Types

Let's think about functions that might operate on our vectors. Concatenating two vectors of known size is not too difficult. We can declare such a function like this:

```
(++) : Vect 3 Integer -> Vect 2 Integer -> Vect 5 Integer
```

That's cute, but not too interesting. When we have two vectors of arbitrary size, some magic happens. We can use the same functions and operators that manipulate natural numbers within our function declaration. Here's the actual definition of the concatenate operator in Prelude:

```
(++) : Vect n a -> Vect m a -> Vect (n + m) a
(++) Nil ys = ys
(++) (x :: xs) ys = x :: xs ++ ys
```

That + operator in the first line is a big deal. It presents the promise of dependent types. Instead of limiting type declarations and programs to different universes, we can use much more of the expressive power of the Idris language within our type definitions. This type definition actually maintains the relationship of two vectors of fixed size.

The recursive code is straightforward. Adding a vector to a Nil vector gives you the original vector, and adding a list to vector ys concatenates the head of that vector to the concatenation of the tail with ys.

Sure, the types make it more complex, but you get something for the exchange. Try to find the bug in this program, a *logic* error, not a *syntax* error:

```
idris/day2/bad_vector.idr
add : Vect n a -> Vect m a -> Vect (n + m) a
add Nil ys = ys
add (x :: xs) ys = x :: add xs xs
```

Did you spot it? We've added xs to xs instead of ys. Idris can catch the error. Compile the file, and you'll get this:

```
bad_vector.idr:3:5:When elaborating right hand side of add:
Can't unify
        Vect n a
with
        Vect m a

Specifically:
        Can't unify
                n
        with
                m
```

Now, you can start to imagine the possibilities. Idris spots the problem that dynamically typed languages could not because the type system has more information and reports the bug. Fix the problem, and the code compiles and works just fine.

From Vectors to Matrices

Let's use similar function type declarations to look at some other functions. Rather than focus on implementation, let's focus strictly on the type definitions.

Say we have a matrix with dimensions x and y, of type a. We'd express a 4×5 matrix of integers with Matrix 4 5 Integer. It's easy to express matrix arithmetic between arbitrary matrices, like this:

```
(+) : Matrix x y a -> Matrix x y a -> Matrix x y a
...
```

We're not limited to operators that have identical data types. Let's say we want to implement transpose. For example, we might want to transpose the matrix to a 5×4 matrix of integers. The type definition is strikingly simple:

```
transpose : Matrix x y a -> Matrix y x a
```

Since we are using parameterized natural numbers and referring to them by name, we can use those definitions elsewhere in the type definition.

Restricting Values in a Leap Year

Let's get a bit more complex. We can also build invariants to ensure that a dynamic check has occurred. Put another way, we can use the compiler to prevent the programmer from forgetting to deal with bad data.

Look at this data type, from Prelude:

```
data so : Bool -> Type where
  oh : so True
```

Doesn't look like much, does it? But let's go over what we know about this type:

- so is a dependent data type taking a Bool (we say it's *indexed* over Bool).
- There is one inhabitant called oh, so that the Bool must be True

If we combine this type with a data structure, callers will only be able to get at the contents that go with so True. That property is exactly what we want when we're trying to restrict the dates to something valid.

Using Our Dependent Type

Date math is particularly troubling because it has so many exceptions. Leap years are especially tedious because of the rules governing them. Leap years happen every four years, unless the year is divisible by 100 but not 400. Let's build a couple of functions to see whether the components of a leap year are correct.

We can start by creating a few functions. These functions will help us determine whether a year is a leap year and whether the values of year, month, and day are all valid:

idris/day2/leap_year.idr
```
isLeap : Integer -> Bool
isLeap year = (mod year 400 == 0) ||
              ((mod year 4 == 0) && not (mod year 100 == 0))

numberOfDays : Integer -> Integer -> Integer
numberOfDays year 2 = if isLeap year then 29 else 28
numberOfDays _   9 = 30
numberOfDays _   4 = 30
numberOfDays _   6 = 30
numberOfDays _  11 = 30
numberOfDays _   _ = 31

validDate : Integer -> Integer -> Integer -> Bool
validDate year month day = (day >= 1) &&
                           (day <= numberOfDays year month) &&
                           (month >= 1) &&
                           (month <= 12)
```

The helper functions are pretty straightforward. isLeap determines whether or not a given year is a leap year, numberOfDays tells us how many days are in a month for a given year, and validDate tells us whether the year, month, and day combination is valid.

How might we implement a Date type in a language without dependent types? We'd probably throw together a data structure containing three arbitrary integers: year, month, and day. Maybe we'd get fancy and create separate types for each of those.

In Idris, we can go one step further and say that not just any integers will do. The year, month, and day have to satisfy an *invariant* that's part of the data type:

idris/day2/leap_year.idr
```
data Date : Integer -> Integer -> Integer -> Type where
    makeDate : (y:Integer) -> (m:Integer) -> (d:Integer) -> so (validDate y m d)
            -> Date y m d
```

A Date has Integer components for days, months, and years, as we expected. The magic happens in the constructor we build for the type. makeDate enforces an invariant using so. That means when we create a date, we'll get the following result:

```
*leap_year> makeDate 1964 2 29
makeDate 1964 2 29 : (so True) -> Date 1964 2 29
*leap_year> makeDate 1965 2 29
makeDate 1965 2 29 : (so False) -> Date 1965 2 29
```

Invalid dates have a completely different type than valid dates! This means we can write programs where it's impossible for our fellow programmers (or us) to forget to check a date. The compiler won't let them forget.

What would such a check look like? One approach would be to use the choose function:

```
Idris> :t choose
Prelude.Either.choose : (b : Bool) -> Either (so b) (so (not b))
```

Either can represent one of two outcomes, dubbed Left and Right. So, choose (validDate y m d) will return either Left (so True) or Right (so False), depending on the numbers.

So, someone calling our makeDate function might use it as follows with potentially unsafe data:

idris/day2/leap_year.idr
```
dateFromUnsafeInput : (y:Integer) -> (m:Integer) -> (d:Integer)
                   -> Maybe (Date y m d)
dateFromUnsafeInput y m d = case choose (validDate y m d) of
                                 Left valid => Just (makeDate y m d valid)
                                 Right _    => Nothing
```

The case construct pattern-matches the result of choose with either the Left (valid date) or Right (invalid date) path. Only if we have valid input can we extract the Date out of makeDate.

Before we wrap up for the day, let's hear from Edwin Brady, creator of Idris.

Us: *Why did you write Idris?*

Brady: *The first implementation of Idris arose around 2000 from some experiments I had been doing with a couple of Haskell libraries. One was a theorem proving library called Ivor, and the other a simple functional language intended as a compiler target called Epic. After a little bit of glue and some surface syntax, it became Idris. So, to some extent, it was an accident!*

I studied type theory and dependent types as a graduate student at the University of Durham, in the north of England, under James McKinna and Conor McBride. I decided it would be nice to have my own system in which I could experiment with syntax, runtime systems, optimizations, high-level language features, and so on, without having to be constrained by any design choices made by existing systems. For example, Idris is more liberal about termination checking than Coq or Agda.

By mid-2011 Idris had become a very useful tool to support my own research, but it wasn't really usable by anyone else except a few brave early adopters. So I decided to throw it all away and start again from scratch, now that I had a better understanding of the kind of language I wanted. Furthermore, I had an idea about how to implement it in a modular way such that it would be much easier to experiment with new features.

Us: What is your favorite language feature?

Brady: Generally my favorite features of any language are the ones which allow me to translate my ideas into a running programming with as little typing as possible! So my favorite Idris feature is not so much a language feature, but the support in the REPL for interactive editing. This has allowed us to build interactive editor modes for Emacs and Vim fairly quickly, supporting case splitting, proof search, and other useful features for program generation.

Us: If you could go back and start over, what's the one feature you'd most love to change?

Brady: Strictly speaking, I did go back and start over! That would be a lot harder now, however. Idris is built on a small core language with very few features, and as a result we have found that we can make fairly large changes or extensions to the surface language without breaking existing code. A recent example of such a change is the change to explicitly typed laziness, which required no changes to the core and only minor changes to code generation.

Having said that, there are other choices we could have made for the core language itself. I now think it would have been a good idea to build on OTT (Observational Type Theory). OTT is, essentially, a type system which is friendly for programmers but has better support for mathematical reasoning. I think we could still do this without changing the high-level language, but that is a project for the future!

Us: What's the most interesting problem you've seen solved with Idris?

Brady: Researchers at the Potsdam Institute for Climate Impact Research have been using Idris to model and verify solutions to dynamic programming problems. This is an interesting project in its own right, but has been particularly useful to the Idris project as a whole because, as one of the largest pieces of Idris code around, it has really helped uncover a lot of tricky bugs in the language implementation! The code is not (yet) publicly available, but a part of the work is documented in a paper published at PLMMS 2013, available from http://eb.host.cs.st-andrews.ac.uk/writings/plmms13.pdf.

Really, though, the most interesting problems for me are the ones which haven't been solved yet! In particular, there are currently quite a few efforts to implement and verify aspects of secure communicating systems, the protocols, and cryptograph-

ic primitives. The effects library is a big part of this, in particular because it tracks resource state (for example, whether a file is open or what the next action in a protocol must be) in the type. Since actions must be executed in the right order (for example, open a file for reading, read the file, close) and the protocol must be run to completion, errors such as the notorious "goto fail" can be caught by the type checker! There is some way to go before this is a reality, but I think it is an exciting prospect, and an important problem.

What We Learned in Day 2

In Day 2, we left behind our Haskell roots and eased our way into dependent types. We built a couple of simple vector and matrix types, and then jumped into leap year calculations. Here are the highlights:

- Types can depend on values, such as a list having a fixed integer size.
- We can do arithmetic (or other operations) on types at compile time.
- We can embed sophisticated invariants into the type system.

Now, it's your turn to try out dependent types.

Your Turn

These problems will focus on dependent types. In your solution, try to use the most restrictive type you can, such as Vect instead of List.

Find...

- Other languages that use dependent types

Do (Easy):

- Write a type for an m×n matrix.
- Write a function to mirror a matrix horizontally.

Do (Medium):

- Write a data type to hold the pixels in a display, taking into account color and size.
- Write a function to transpose the matrix so that element m, n in the argument is element n, m in the result.

Do (Hard):

- Write a function using so that does not allow colors or dimensions that are out of bounds.

Day 3: Dependent Types in Action

In Day 2, you built some dependent data types, including vectors and a leap year. You may have noticed that these types took more up-front work than before. What features could possibly make all that extra effort worthwhile? Settle in. We're on the case.

First, we'll look at the spectacular ways the type system can help you write programs. With more information, Idris can take code completion places you've likely never been before. Then, we'll look at using the type system to reason about the way our programs behave by constructing a proof. Finally, we'll see how reasoning in Idris can help us improve our programs in other languages. It's a busy day, so let's get started.

Smarter Completion

In this section, we're going to use the Vim editor with an Idris plugin called idris-vim to get a powerful development environment with autocompletion. This tool doesn't come with the main Idris package, but you can install it easily using the instructions on the project page.[5]

The plugin works by communicating with a running Idris shell. Launch Idris with a nonexistent file, proof.idr, and then edit the file in Vim by typing :e from within Idris:

```
> idris proof.idr
*proof> :e
```

Now, add the following code to the file in Vim:

idris/day3/proof.idr
```
module Proof

data Natural = Zero | Suc Natural

plus : Natural -> Natural -> Natural
```

At this point, you've done the heavy lifting: you've defined a data type to represent natural numbers. Now, you're going to write a function to add two natural numbers—but with the help of Idris.

Since Idris knows what your type looks like, it can help with the structure of the program. With the cursor at the end of the last line, type \d, the default key to ask idris-vim for a template definition. The skeleton of your function will appear:

---

5.   https://github.com/idris-hackers/idris-vim

```
plus : Natural -> Natural -> Natural
plus x x1 = ?plus_rhs
```

Idris has generated a function body from our signature and left a hole, ?plus_rhs, for us to fill (we'll see how later). This is something any IDE could do. But now, we're going to go a step further.

Take a peek at the type definition again. We have two cases to cover: Zero and Suc. Idris can use that information to provide a better function definition. Put the cursor over x and hit \c. The body of the function will expand to two cases:

```
plus : Natural -> Natural -> Natural
plus Zero x1 = ?plus_rhs_1
plus (Suc x) x1 = ?plus_rhs_2
```

Look at that. Idris read your type definition and correctly produced the pattern match on the second argument. Let's see how far the tool can take us. Place your cursor over the first hole, ?plus_rhs_1, and type \o (for *obvious*):

```
plus Zero x1 = x1
plus (Suc x) x1 = ?plus_rhs_2
```

This is indeed the correct behavior for adding Zero to any value x. And we didn't even have to write the code! The only part we have to provide on our own is the body of the second hole:

```
plus : Natural -> Natural -> Natural
plus Zero x1 = x1
plus (Suc x) x1 = Suc (plus x x1)
```

You could switch over to a console to run the program, but there's a faster way to run a quick test. In idris-vim, you can type \e followed by an expression you want to evaluate:

```
Expression: plus (Suc Zero) (Suc Zero)
```

Idris will run the code and show you the result:

```
 = Suc (Suc Zero) : Natural
```

```
Press ENTER or type command to continue
```

1 + 1 never looked so sweet.

As your type definitions get more sophisticated, the tool will be able to write more of your program for you. In the exercises, you'll get the chance to practice this technique. If you'd like to try it now, have a look at the first medium-difficulty assignment in *Your Turn*, on page 273 before we move on.

QED, Dear Watson

Idris can do more than just check types and write parts of programs. It can also prove theorems. There is a deep and beautiful relationship between checking types and proving theorems.[6] In the limited time we have today, we'll just be cracking the door into this world.

Idris has an arsenal of different proof strategies. Today, we're going to combine a few of the simpler tactics to write a *proof by induction*, a staple of mathematics and computer science.[7]

What are we going to prove? Let's show that the plus function we just wrote is *commutative*—in other words, that plus x y is equal to plus y x for all natural numbers x and y.

A proof by induction has two parts:

- The *base case*, where we show the property (commutativity) is true for zero
- The *inductive step*, where we show that, if the property is true for y, then it's also true for y + 1

For our plus function, that means we need to prove the following two statements:

- plus Zero y = plus y Zero
- If plus x y = plus y x, then plus (Suc x) y = plus y (Suc x)

Where will these proofs go? With Idris, you can embed proofs in your source code files, or you can build them interactively in the REPL. We're going to hop back and forth between these techniques today.

Anatomy of a Proof

Let's start by putting the outline of our proof in the source code, and then we'll fill in the gaps at the console. Add the following line to the end of your proof.idr file:

```
idris/day3/proof.idr
plusCommutes : (x : Natural) -> (y : Natural) -> plus x y = plus y x
```

Our proof has a signature, just like any other function. Now, it needs a body. Let's put in the base case first, leaving a hole that we'll fill in later:

---

6.   https://en.wikipedia.org/wiki/Curry-Howard
7.   https://en.wikipedia.org/wiki/Mathematical_induction

```
idris/day3/proof.idr
plusCommutes Zero y = ?plusCommutes_0_y
```

The final piece of the outline is the inductive step.

```
idris/day3/proof.idr
plusCommutes (Suc x) y = let hypothesis = plusCommutes x y in
                             ?plusCommutes_Sx_y
```

On the right side, you can see how we've assumed that plusCommutes x y. It's up to us to get from there to plusCommutes (Suc x) y, using tiny steps that nudge the proof forward one expression at a time.

The outline of our proof is ready for us to fill in. But we're going to need some *axioms*, which are a bit like helper functions. They're properties of addition that we're going to use in our proof. Add the following two axioms just before your proof outline:

```
idris/day3/proof.idr
plusZero : (x : Natural) -> plus x Zero = x
plusSuc  : (x : Natural) -> (y : Natural) -> Suc (plus x y) = plus x (Suc y)
```

plusZero says that any number plus zero is itself. plusSuc deals with adding numbers and then taking the successor. Both of these will come in handy for our proof.

Isn't it cheating just to assume these two properties are true? Shouldn't we prove them first, before we're allowed to use them in another proof? Don't worry; you're going to get the chance to do exactly that in the exercises.

Interactive Proof

For now, though, let's press on. Launch the REPL and load your proof.idr file:

```
Idris> :l proof.idr
Type checking ./proof.idr
```

Now, ask Idris which parts of our proof are missing, using the :m command:

```
*proof> :m
Global metavariables:
        [Proof.plusCommutes_Sx_y,Proof.plusCommutes_0_y]
```

We see the two holes we left in our outline. Let's prove the base case first. The :p command starts a proof:

```
*proof> :p plusCommutes_0_y
----------                    Goal:                  ----------
{ hole 0 }:
  (y : Natural) -> y = Proof.plus y Zero
```

Idris is telling us what we have to do to satisfy the conditions of the proof. We have to show that, given y is a natural number, y = plus y Zero.

The first simplfication we can make is to assume that y is indeed a natural number. We do so with the intros proof tactic, which essentially means, "Yes, assume we have the arguments to our function."

```
-Proof.plusCommutes_0_y> intros
----------              Other goals:              ----------
{ hole 0 }
----------              Assumptions:              ----------
 y : Natural
----------              Goal:                     ----------
{ hole 1 }:
 y = Proof.plus y Zero
```

Idris has filled in our assumption (that y is a natural number), and has given us a new and simpler goal. There's a bunch of bookkeeping in the middle: holes we haven't filled yet and assumptions we've made so far. From now on, we'll skip over that stuff in the output.

Look at the bottom line: y = plus y Zero. That's our new goal. We need to transform the left side of the equals sign until it matches the right.

Do we have any axioms that say we're allowed to transform y into plus y Zero? Indeed, the plusZero axiom spells out exactly this property. We'll use Idris's rewrite proof tactic to rewrite y using plusZero:

```
-Proof.plusCommutes_0_y> rewrite (plusZero y)
...
----------              Goal:                     ----------
{ hole 2 }:
 Proof.plus y Zero = Proof.plus y Zero
```

Now, all we have left to prove is that plus y Zero matches plus y Zero. But these already match! The trivial proof tactic exists for this situation:

```
-Proof.plusCommutes_0_y> trivial
plusCommutes_0_y: No more goals.
```

No more goals; that means we're done with the base case. Use the qed command to finish the proof:

```
-Proof.plusCommutes_0_y> qed
Proof completed!
Proof.plusCommutes_0_y = proof
  intros
  rewrite (plusZero y)
  trivial
```

Idris has helpfully summarized our proof steps for us. You can now paste those three lines into proof.idr like so:

```
idris/day3/proof.idr
plusCommutes_0_y = proof {
  intros
  rewrite (plusZero y)
  trivial
}
```

And that's it for the base case.

The Next Step

Back in the REPL, we can ask Idris which holes still need filling:

```
*proof> :m
Global metavariables:
        [Proof.plusCommutes_Sx_y]
```

Ah, yes, the inductive step. Let's start the proof for it:

```
*proof> :p plusCommutes_Sx_y
----------                    Goal:               ----------
{ hole 0 }:
 (x : Natural) ->
 (y : Natural) ->
 (Proof.plus x y = Proof.plus y x) -> Suc (Proof.plus x y) = Proof.plus y (Suc x)
```

As before, we use the intros tactic to assume we have natural numbers for arguments:

```
-Proof.plusCommutes_Sx_y> intros
...
----------                    Goal:               ----------
{ hole 3 }:
 Suc (Proof.plus x y) = Proof.plus y (Suc x)
```

Now, we need to transform the left side of the equals sign to match the right side. We need to change Suc (plus x y) into plus y (Suc x). Our plusSuc axiom will make this transformation for us. Let's apply it, using the rewrite tactic again:

```
-Proof.plusCommutes_Sx_y> rewrite (plusSuc y x)
...
----------                    Goal:               ----------
{ hole 4 }:
 Suc (Proof.plus x y) = Suc (Proof.plus y x)
```

So close! The only change left to make is to transform plus x y into plus y x. Do we have anything in our toolbox to fit this situation? Indeed, we do.

Recall that we're in the inductive step of our proof. We're showing that, if commutativity holds for x, then it also holds for x + 1. In other words, we're allowed to assume that plus x y = plus y x. In our proof skeleton, we defined this as the hypothesis variable:

idris/day3/proof.idr
```
plusCommutes (Suc x) y = let hypothesis = plusCommutes x y in
                            ?plusCommutes_Sx_y
```

Once again, we use the rewrite tactic to change the expression on the left:

```
-Proof.plusCommutes_Sx_y> rewrite hypothesis
----------               Goal:               ----------
{ hole 5 }:
 Suc (Proof.plus x y) = Suc (Proof.plus x y)
```

We're left with a matching left and right side that we can dispatch trivially:

```
-Proof.plusCommutes_Sx_y> trivial
plusCommutes_Sx_y: No more goals.
-Proof.plusCommutes_Sx_y> qed
Proof completed!
Proof.plusCommutes_Sx_y = proof
  intros
  rewrite (plusSuc y x)
  rewrite hypothesis
  trivial
```

Go ahead and paste the proof steps into your source file:

```
plusCommutes_Sx_y = proof {
  intros
  rewrite (plusSuc y x)
  rewrite hypothesis
  trivial
}
```

Whew! Let's take a step back and look at what we've accomplished.

What Proofs Do for Us

Imagine how you might make sure plus is commutative in another programming language. You'd probably write a few test cases: zero, equal numbers, large numbers, and so on. Every time you changed your function, you'd rerun your tests.

With Idris, you don't have to worry about thinking up enough test cases to gain confidence. Your proof shows that plus is commutative for *all* natural numbers, not just a few arbitrary test values. And it runs every time you compile your source code!

Now, let's look at a slightly different definition of plus. Can you spot the error?

```
idris/day3/badProof.idr
plus : Natural -> Natural -> Natural
plus Zero x1    = x1
➤ plus (Suc x) x1 = Suc (Suc (plus x x1))
```

When we try to load the program in Idris, we can see the result:

```
Idris> :l proof.idr
Type checking ./proof.idr
proof.idr:72:19:When elaborating right hand side of Proof.plusCommutes_Sx_y:
Can't unify
        Suc (Proof.plus x y) = Suc (Proof.plus x y)
with
        Suc (Suc (Proof.plus x y)) = Suc (Proof.plus x y)

Specifically:
        Can't unify
                Proof.plus x y
        with
                Suc (Proof.plus x y)
```

Indeed, x + y does not equal x + y + 1.

Commutativity is a pretty simple property. But Idris allows you to construct longer and more useful proofs about your functions *and their types*. On a typical day, you might try a few different strategies in interactive mode, and then combine them into a programmatic proof.

You can't prove that every line of your program is correct, of course. But you can check a lot more than you might think. You can show that a function's behavior is defined for all inputs, or that you're encrypting your critical data correctly. Once you've been down this road, you might be shocked at how little we protect our important programs today.

Does all this talk of theorems and proofs sound a bit lofty? Do dependent types seem like an academic idea that's difficult to apply in the real world? If so, read on. In the next section, we're going to see how to use Idris to understand and improve programs written in more mainstream languages.

The Real World

Ideas move faster than codebases can. Most of us will find ourselves working on an older programming language sometimes, or even most of the time. Old programming languages usually fall out of favor because they can no longer express ideas as concisely or powerfully as new ones.

Surely we have to leave the beauty of Idris behind when we go back to our day-to-day programming tasks. Or do we?

Old languages will shape the way you think as surely as newer ones will. As we'll see, the lessons Idris teaches us apply perfectly well in the real world. In this section, we're going to use the clean mathematical notation of Idris to design the types for a C++ program.

Part of the joy of defining types in this way is that the implementations are obvious. Accordingly, we're just going to focus on the types today. If you'd like to implement and compile them, you can do so with the tools we used in *Outfitting for Adventure*, on page 33.

A C++ Mess

Let's say we're building a GPS application for a bike computer. We will need to track our bike as it moves from location to location. If you've read or written much C++ code, you've probably seen some classes that look like this:

```
idris/day3/gps.h
#include <string>
#include <vector>

class Trip
{
public:
    class Point
    {
    public:
        Point(double lat, double lon, double time);

        double lat()  const;
        double lon()  const;
        double time() const;

        // ...
    };

    void addPoint(double lat, double lon, double time);

    void setName(const std::string& name);
    std::string name() const;

    size_t count() const;
    const Point& getPoint(size_t index) const;

    // ...
};
```

A Ride is a list of Points, each of which consists of a latitude, longitude, and time. Each time we get an updated location from the GPS unit, we add a new item to the list.

Our API also allows us to find out how many locations we've collected and to get the properties for any particular location.

This design may not get us on the pages of The Daily WTF, but it is definitely a little chaotic. The API doesn't really capture the intent of what we're doing, and it's going to be difficult to answer critical questions:

- Where was the vehicle at a given point in time?
- When was a vehicle closest to a given location?

We can get this information out of the API indirectly, by grabbing the individual points and then doing a bunch of math. As we write more and more code, you're going to see more and more duplication of effort, and you'll have to work harder and harder to express the intention behind the design. We need to take a step back.

Denotational Design

We'll use Idris as a virtual whiteboard for exploring the shape of our program. This technique is called *denotational design*. Despite the intimidating name, the concept is quite simple. Conal Elliott describes it eloquently in his 2009 term paper *Denotational design with type class morphisms*.[8]

Elliott says that programmers should follow two steps to design their types:

1. Describe in mathematical notation what each type should do, without worrying about implementation details.

2. Implement the type using whatever languages, performance hacks, and trade-offs you need.

Idris gives us a nice mathematical notation to describe each type, including the operations we want to perform with it. We're not just talking about basic function signatures here; we can specify what these operations *do*. For instance, we could describe a collection's clear method, and then assert that the collection is empty after clear is called.

Back to the Roots

Let's boil our GPS example down to its essentials. What is a bike trip? More generally, what is a trip?

---

8.   http://conal.net/papers/type-class-morphisms/

Switching to Idris for a second, we want to say that a trip is a sequence of locations over time. We can already hear you jumping ahead to implementation: internal arrays of data points, sampling frequency, and so on. Hold those thoughts and just think about what we need from this type.

What is a location? *It doesn't matter.* Maybe it's a pair of degree coordinates. Maybe it's a three-dimensional point. Maybe it's a named waypoint. Any of these concepts would work, and it's too early to nail down this implementation detail.

At its most basic level, a trip just gives us *a location at a point in time.* With Idris, we don't actually have to say what the location type is yet. Thanks to parameterized types, we can write a function that's valid no matter what the details are.

Here's how we might express this idea in Idris:

```
idris/day3/gps.idr
Trip : (Location : Type ** (Float -> Location))
```

That is, a Trip is a pair of two items: a Location type (whatever that might eventually be) and a function that gives us the location at a particular time (represented by a Float).

Dependent Pairs

You may have noticed a new syntax here for defining pairs: (first ** second) instead of (first, second). The ** notation means that the type of the second item may depend on the type of the first. For instance, here's a pair containing a length and a vector of that length:

```
idris/day3/evens.idr
firstThreeEvens : (n ** Vect n Int)
firstThreeEvens = (3 ** [2, 4, 6])
```

The number and the length of the vector have to match; otherwise, you'll see a type error.

An Improvement

Now that we've spilled some hard-earned ink on our virtual whiteboard, let's shift back to C++. How do we express a pair, where one element is a data type and the other is a function?

In C++, we can't pass data types into ordinary functions. We *can*, however, pass them into templates, C++'s closest equivalent to dependent types:

```
idris/day3/gps.h
template <typename Location>
class Trip
{
public:
    Location operator()(double);

    // ...
};
```

This template takes as input a Location type and generates—what, exactly? Not quite a function, like we did in Idris. Instead, we generate the next best thing: a class that we can call like a function; that's what the operator() method does.

As we did with Idris, we're using floating-point numbers to represent time.

So, what is a Location? It depends on the application. For this GPS device, it may be something simple like a latitude/longitude pair:

```
idris/day3/gps.h
typedef std::pair<double, double> BikeLocation;
typedef Trip<BikeLocation> BikeTrip;
```

For the aerospace simulator we're writing tomorrow, it'll be three-dimensional Cartesian coordinates.

Because we started by sketching in Idris, we have a much better conceptual start for our GPS tool. We've captured the core idea of our type: providing the location at any given time.

In the first version of the C++ code, we were thinly wrapping a collection type from the standard library. Callers had to worry about individual data points, indices, and counts. But now, we're exposing only what the user needs. And we're doing a better job of answering the questions the user cares about.

Even though this is a toy example, you can see the benefit of building a conceptual type in a stronger language and then moving it to C++. As your problem domains get more complex, this benefit grows even stronger.

With a powerful and rich language like Idris, we can only just begin scratch the surface in one short chapter of a book.

It's time to wrap things up so that you can go make your own discoveries.

Your Turn

Find...

- The mathematical definitions of *total function* and *partial function*

- Video and slides for David Sankel's C++Now 2013 talk, "The Intellectual Ascent to Agda"

- The source code to the Prelude library's Nat module, which contains several example proofs

- A list of proof tactics available in Idris

Do (Easy):
- Write the signature of a function, typeNamed, that will take the name of a type and return that type. For example, typeNamed "Int" would return the type Int.

- Implement your typeNamed function for a few different types.

Do (Medium):
- Use the techniques in *Smarter Completion*, on page 262 to write a Vector data type and a vectorAdd function to add two vectors together.

- Add the keyword total to the beginning of your typeNamed function signature from the Easy section—that is, total typeNamed : .... Reload your file, and see that your function is not total (defined for all inputs). Make your function total by giving it behavior for bad inputs such as "ThisIsNotAType".

Do (Hard):
- Prove the plusZero and plusSuc axioms from *Anatomy of a Proof*, on page 264.

- The bike GPS example currently uses plain floating-point numbers to represent time. Change the type definition to allow a custom Time type to be passed in.

Wrapping Up Idris

If you're used to dynamically typed languages, Idris represents a tremendously steep technical challenge. If, on the other hand, you're already comfortable with dependent types and category theory, you'll likely appreciate the many advances that Edwin Brady has made to bring this language closer to the mainstream. Let's break down the strengths and weaknesses.

Strengths

With Idris, types *know* more, so they can *do* more. In this chapter, we looked at four practical improvements due to dependent types:

1. With more type information, compilers can catch more complex bugs, including logic errors, at compile time.
2. When types can express structure, automatic code completion can go far beyond basic syntax—to a degree that's potentially revolutionary.
3. The same information about types allows better proofs about your code. In certain fields, like protocols and cryptography, mistakes are much harder to find and more expensive when they slip through. In Idris, you can prove certain properties about your code (rather than just spot-checking with unit tests).
4. Idris allows a good virtual whiteboard to reason about program structure and types. This capability is useful to students and working programmers alike.

Building more information into types leads to smarter tools and compilers. It can lead to better programs, even ones we know are correct.

Weaknesses

There's a downside to that extra information in dependent types: you have to take the time to express them. The learning curve is steep, even more so than for Haskell, and the code can be quite dense. Idris is not for everyone.

One other drawback to Idris, and one we're hoping to remedy in part by introducing it here, is that there aren't many examples of its use floating around. The tutorials will get you to Hello, world!, but then the trail ends abruptly at an edifice of types.

Final Thoughts

Very few languages change the way that you fundamentally approach programming. Idris certainly had that effect on us. It improved our habits and gave us a clear way to think through our types—and yet, it did so without imposing a lot of overhead and ceremony. This mental revolution will serve us well on all our projects, no matter what the type system looks like.

The tooling, particularly theorem proving and code completion, is much more powerful and advanced than we've seen in other languages—and we didn't even need an expensive IDE to get the benefit.

Idris may not be a commercially popular language, but that will not lessen its contribution. Idris will increasingly make its mark in places where behavior is complex and mistakes are expensive. It may also be the language that finally brings programming rigor to the masses.

CHAPTER 8

Wrapping Up

by Bruce Tate

Hopefully, you've made it through another seven languages in seven weeks. In the foreword, José Valim compared walking through these seven languages to the beginning of your own journey. This particular trip has taken you through diverse programming models, including Factor's concatenative style, Elm's reactive programming, Lua's prototypes, miniKanren's combination of logic and functional techniques, and various takes on functional programming.

Some will try to tell you that this journey is worthless, that you can't truly learn a language in seven days any more than you can learn Italian by eating at the Olive Garden once a week. If you've worked through these exercises, *you know different*. Traveling for the sake of traveling is *not* worthless. True, on your brief trip you've not yet accumulated the fluency of a permanent resident, but you have *been there*. The books in this series are designed to give you quick immersions in the community that will leave more than a passing, shallow impression. You've done things, from building a game to telling a story with code. As José says, the lessons will be different for each reader.

As a programmer, you'll never be more than the sum of your experiences. Any journey will leave lingering impressions of the steps along the path. Let's take a few moments to reinforce those images so they become a more permanent part of our mental toolbox. For now, I'd like to think about that journey as a passage through time.

The Origins

True, none of the languages in this book go all of the way back to the origins of computing. Still, we can look at where we want to go and consider the languages that will help us form a better mental image of how to get there.

Of the languages in this book, Lua and Factor have the oldest foundations. The other five are much newer. Lua has been around in some form for over 20 years and was formally released some 15 years ago. Factor was created in 2003. After working through those chapters, you can probably appreciate why they're in this book.

The Power of Prototypes

Though JavaScript programming has exploded, few people understand what prototype programming is all about. JavaScript, in some ways, muddies the waters around programming models. If you're not a JavaScript expert, it helps to step back and take in another prototype language, one that's more pure.

Lua is putting its mark on everyday programming as a language for embedded systems and scripting because the language is compact, pure, adaptable, and clean. The prototype model, at its simplest, is a marvelously malleable paradigm for organization.

I'll go one step further. The prototype programming model does a fantastic job as an embedded foundation for programming languages on the browser. You even used Lua to build an object model. Understanding tricks like these, you can see why so many are enthusiastically embracing JavaScript as a compilation target for a wide variety of browser technologies like Elm, and that's why the language is in the book. It's not just Lua that's interesting.

Reinforcing Functional Composition

As our industry creeps closer to a broad adoption of functional languages, all developers will need to learn the widest possible variety of techniques for composing with functions. After you've worked through both Factor and Elixir, you can appreciate the similarities between composing with pipes and stacks.

One of the best things about working with Factor as an object-oriented programmer for me was that I could start to deprogram the way that I've been structuring the world without giving up rich libraries. I also thought the development environment reflected the strengths of the language very well.

Initial Stepping-Stones

We chose the functional programming model for the preponderance of the languages in this book and the original *Seven Languages in Seven Weeks* *[Tat10]* because we believe that is where this industry is going. Languages like Lua and Factor are clearly steps toward us getting there; they helped us experiment with code organization and with the way projects and libraries hung together, and they helped to increase our idioms—our vocabulary for dealing with the world in code.

Like any expedition, ours had to step beyond those initial stepping-stones. Let's talk about the next three languages—those practical languages that formed the well-marked pathways through the heart of our journey.

The Central Expressway

The next few languages in the book are deeply anchored in critical problems plaguing our industry today. Julia is addressing performance and organizational problems in the R language; Elixir is José's answer to the same sorts of problems he found as a central Ruby developer; and Elm is a deeply practical language stretching the limits of reactive programming in a functional language with a better type model.

In these few chapters, you saw some of the major thrusts in language development today. Let's review the major messages.

Functional Programming Meets Practical and Reactive

There was a day when the term *functional programming* conjured up images of heavily bearded wizards in the dank halls of academia that brought monads down to the masses...well, at least the masses who wanted to write programs without any side effects, like input or output. Elm's goal is to bring some of that same purity and power to the browser. The whole language oozes practicality, and the end result is as pleasing and surprising as any new language I've experienced.

It's my strong belief that as clients get more powerful, we're going to see more and more code run there. Since the languages embedded in a browser are not likely to change, any change in programming language is going to need to compile to JavaScript as a target. Elm does so, and it allows the user to solve the most difficult problems without having to redefine problems in terms of callbacks. When you don't have to cripple your mental model to express a program, great things can happen, as you saw as you built the game with fewer than 200 lines of code. After some exploration in the browser, we shifted squarely to the server side.

Macros, Beautiful Syntax, and Concurrency

As we picked up speed, we found ourself in the land of Elixir. This community has an excitement unmatched by any other language in the book right now. I'm not sure if it's a magic potion, but something is in the communal water supply. The base language was growing almost faster than I could write. It's my belief that macros allow that speed. Good developers using macros can just move more quickly, especially when creating basic building blocks that require new syntax.

The language itself has marvelously good taste. With Ruby as a model, the Elixir syntax feels friendly and mixes in powerful concepts like pattern matching. Elixir allows plenty of rich options for dealing with all aspects of functions. The ecosystem, though it is young, is already rich and robust; it offers great build tools, a package manager, and smooth distributed debugging tools.

It's not just the core language that's so exciting. José is not building in a vacuum. He's building on top of perhaps the most robust distribution framework in the world: Erlang's OTP. The most critical element of that system is the way that you can use the language to manage failure. When processes die, the overall system can deal with those problems in practical ways.

Technical Computing Gets an Overhaul

The next stop was Julia. Truth be told, the Julia language was one of the last we added to this lineup. We didn't think there was enough to say about yet another technical language, and if we did decide to do one, MATLAB or R seemed to be more prominent choices. When we saw what the language creators were trying to do, we gave it a look. Jack met the language creators in St. Louis for the Strange Loop conference, and he was solidly convinced.

After spending some time with the language, we could see what all of the buzz was about. Where other technical languages offer optimizations and C interfaces, Julia seeks to achieve strong performance right out of the box with compiler features and excellence of language design. The language is well positioned for the future, with good support for parallel computing and the functional features that a new developer community will increasingly demand.

Now, it's all about building the libraries. When you look at a new language with an eye for adoption, it's important to understand the growth of the community, as well as the pace of growth of the libraries and core language. Both of these metrics look great for Julia. It's my firm belief that Julia, or something like it, will absolutely emerge as an important player in the technical community.

Happening Spots

Each of the languages in this section represents a strong attempt to build a general-purpose language that's squarely aimed at a specific problem domain. These languages were not built for learning; they were built for use. You can see the decisions that the designers made and see the impacts of those decisions.

These languages represent where we *are*. Though none of them has yet accumulated a full and practical community, they are each starting to pick up some traction. You'll get to see in real time whether those solutions capture the imagination of enough programmers to accumulate that incredibly difficult early majority.

For now, though, let's move on, way out to the edge.

The Frontier

In the last two languages in the book, we traverse the frontiers of programming theory. We look at a new programming model that combines macros, logic, and functional programming with a general-purpose language in miniKanren. We also look at the concepts related to a powerful typing theory in Idris.

Logic, Meet World

Prolog and I have a love-hate relationship. I love the way I can focus on the problem and leave the solution to the computer. My primary problems with Prolog have mostly been related to making those ideas more practical. It's those areas around the edges, where I'm filtering, presenting, trimming, or otherwise manipulating a stream of solutions that come up short. I also have problems extending Prolog when I move into a new problem domain.

Enter miniKanren. The ability to take a logic engine and drop it into the middle of a powerful general-purpose programming language changes everything. The result, though, is entirely new. When you combine macros with functions, rules, and logic, you get something that is entirely new. It's a new programming model that doesn't act like anything else out there. I could imagine miniKanren as a flash in the pan, a model that's just too difficult or alien for typical programmers to understand. I can also see it as a game changer, becoming a critical component of general-purpose languages. Right now, there's just not enough experience. You can decide if you can make it work for you.

Are You My Type?

I have often thought that the language for expressing types and languages could be more unified. A vector is interesting—a vector of size n more so. Seeing dependent types in front of me really floored me. I do confess, sometimes, it felt like too much. I do think these ideas have promise. Languages like Idris and Agda will help us explore these critical ideals.

The real Idris eye-opener was not just the way my code changed, but how my attention shifted in the programming process. In one of the many phone conversations among the authors over the course of writing this book, Ian and I both expressed the same idea. As we wrote code in Idris, we spent more time thinking about *types* than *behavior*. As the code completion gets more sophisticated and tools get better, this change would only get more pronounced.

Idris represents a reinforcement of a critical value for me: let the computer do the work. With Idris, editors can do more comprehensive code completion. Compilers can do more sophisticated enforcement, such as making sure you can only write to open files. Provers can do more of the jobs dedicated to handwritten tests today. At some point, the work required to express and think about those types could be offset by gains on these other frontiers. I guess you could say that I'm captivated by the promise of what Idris can become.

The Dirty Map

I've taken many vacations with my family, and whenever we go somewhere special, we always sit the kids down and pull out the map, with all of its coffee stains and fragile fold lines. The goal is to start a conversation so that each voyager can generalize the lessons learned. Eventually, we want our kids to answer for themselves one question: "What does this trip tell you about the world that you didn't know before?" For this journey, your lessons may be different from mine, but these are some of the trends that I notice.

The Type Pendulum Swings Again

When I started working with Ruby, many developers were rebelling against the type system in Java. I was a hard-core proponent of dynamic typing. My stance has softened over time, and I'm not the only one. You can see Idris and Elm are both doing excellent work on types. After reviewing my chapter, Evan Czaplicki asked me to review a paper he wrote. He wanted to introduce

Monads to Elm users but using much more practical terminology, exposing only the details that are useful to get practical work done.

Edwin Bray with Idris is working on the jagged frontiers of type theory, and we're starting to see what magic is possible with tooling and proof engines if only our compilers have more information to work with. The same things are generally true across the broader spectrum of language design. It's early, but my guess is that we'll see a new family of strongly typed languages soon, and we'll see many more languages with a strong Haskell emphasis.

Concurrency Pushes Hard

Y2K, the date problem that ominously arrived at the turn of the millennium, came with dire warnings from every corner of the globe but went out with barely a whimper. A silent killer is coming that will have much more business impact. Hardware is moving aggressively toward multicore without the software to support it. Most existing languages will be too slow, too buggy, and too complicated. A few extra locks and threads won't solve the problem. The overhaul must be much more foundational. Most of the languages in this book have a good story for concurrency. For Julia and Elixir, simple parallel programming is one of the fundamental problems each language solves. Programmers and companies must start moving toward languages that support new hardware today to have any chance of competing in the next few years to come.

The Browser Needs Help

I overheard a language expert as he and a colleague were trying to name all of the languages that compiled to JavaScript. They were able to name over 20. When they looked online to see if they had gotten them all, there were 128! Innovation doesn't just happen because new technologies are cool. It happens when there's a market need. In this case, the market is keenly feeling the need for better control, cleaner programs, and better reliability, which can only come from a better language, one that treats types in a cleaner way. Since JavaScript isn't going to slip away any time soon, that new language is going to have to support JavaScript compilation.

Functional Languages Evolve

In 2010, *Seven Languages in Seven Weeks [Tat10]* described a new wave of functional languages. Those languages focused primarily on basic functional concepts. The next generation, languages like Elixir, Julia, and Elm, is more practical and easier to understand, and generally has cleaner foundations.

Each of these languages does something very well and significantly raises the bar of their counterparts. Elixir's macros are allowing the language to evolve much more quickly than the Erlang counterpart. Elm's signals allow a more beautiful implementation, especially where callbacks are concerned. Julia's compiler technology allows more intuitive code through constructs that the typical technical programmer understands and achieves optimizations through better libraries and just-in-time compilation rather than forcing use of obscure libraries or writing significant chunks in C. Across the board, we're seeing excellent support for things like macros, with an eye for developing good libraries quickly.

The World Shrinks

For rapid adoption, languages depend on a large and active community, perhaps more so than any other technology. When Erlang was developed in the late 1980s, just about all of the team was from Stockholm, Sweden. Fast-forward to 2014. José Valim, who created the language, is from Brazil and lives in Poland. Eric Meadows Johnson, the other core team member, lives in Sweden, as does Joe Armstrong, one of the original creators of Erlang and key advisor. Dave Thomas, who wrote the first book on Elixir, is from Dallas, and Elixir committers span five continents.

The language team is not the only part of the global equation. Today, Elixir workshops have been held in more than ten countries, and hundreds enjoyed the first dedicated Elixir conference in Austin, Texas this year.

The world is smaller than it used to be. Once again, we're seeing small teams use programming languages for a competitive advantage, and teams once again correctly fear failure more than they do lack of language adoption. It's just much easier to do business with a smaller ecosystem, as long as that community is active and effective.

A Final Challenge

From the bottom of our hearts, thanks for sharing this journey with us. Rather than preach at you for a couple more minutes, I'm going to let José's foreword do the talking. Take what you've learned in this book and use it. Maybe you can use the languages in this book to implement your own language as José did. Or maybe you'll take one of the five languages that are still very much in the formative developmental stages and dive in. You won't have to look too far to find your own wide open road. Open up the throttle and see where it takes you.

Bibliography

[Arm07]   Joe Armstrong. *Programming Erlang: Software for a Concurrent World*. The Pragmatic Bookshelf, Raleigh, NC and Dallas, TX, 2007.

[Cyl07]   Topher Cyll. *Practical Ruby Projects*. Addison-Wesley, Reading, MA, 2007.

[FBK05]   Daniel P. Friedman, William E. Byrd, and Oleg Kiselyov. *The Reasoned Schemer*. MIT Press, Cambridge, MA, 2005.

[MD14]   Jack Moffitt and Fred Daoud. *Seven Web Frameworks in Seven Weeks: Adventures in Better Web Apps*. The Pragmatic Bookshelf, Raleigh, NC and Dallas, TX, 2014.

[RW12]   Eric Redmond and Jim R. Wilson. *Seven Databases in Seven Weeks: A Guide to Modern Databases and the NoSQL Movement*. The Pragmatic Bookshelf, Raleigh, NC and Dallas, TX, 2012.

[Tat10]   Bruce A. Tate. *Seven Languages in Seven Weeks: A Pragmatic Guide to Learning Programming Languages*. The Pragmatic Bookshelf, Raleigh, NC and Dallas, TX, 2010.

Index

Seven in Seven

From Web Frameworks to Concurrency Models, see what the rest of the world is doing with this introduction to seven different approaches.

Seven Web Frameworks in Seven Weeks

Whether you need a new tool or just inspiration, *Seven Web Frameworks in Seven Weeks* explores modern options, giving you a taste of each with ideas that will help you create better apps. You'll see frameworks that leverage modern programming languages, employ unique architectures, live client-side instead of server-side, or embrace type systems. You'll see everything from familiar Ruby and JavaScript to the more exotic Erlang, Haskell, and Clojure.

Jack Moffitt, Fred Daoud
(302 pages) ISBN: 9781937785635. $38
http://pragprog.com/book/7web

Seven Concurrency Models in Seven Weeks

Your software needs to leverage multiple cores, handle thousands of users and terabytes of data, and continue working in the face of both hardware and software failure. Concurrency and parallelism are the keys, and *Seven Concurrency Models in Seven Weeks* equips you for this new world. See how emerging technologies such as actors and functional programming address issues with traditional threads and locks development. Learn how to exploit the parallelism in your computer's GPU and leverage clusters of machines with MapReduce and Stream Processing. And do it all with the confidence that comes from using tools that help you write crystal clear, high-quality code.

Paul Butcher
(296 pages) ISBN: 9781937785659. $38
http://pragprog.com/book/pb7con

More Seven in Seven

There's so much new to learn with the latest crop of NoSQL databases. And instead of learning a language a year, how about seven?

Seven Databases in Seven Weeks

Data is getting bigger and more complex by the day, and so are your choices in handling it. From traditional RDBMS to newer NoSQL approaches, *Seven Databases in Seven Weeks* takes you on a tour of some of the hottest open source databases today. In the tradition of Bruce A. Tate's *Seven Languages in Seven Weeks*, this book goes beyond your basic tutorial to explore the essential concepts at the core of each technology.

Eric Redmond and Jim R. Wilson
(354 pages) ISBN: 9781934356920. $35
http://pragprog.com/book/rwdata

Seven Languages in Seven Weeks

You should learn a programming language every year, as recommended by *The Pragmatic Programmer*. But if one per year is good, how about *Seven Languages in Seven Weeks*? In this book you'll get a hands-on tour of Clojure, Haskell, Io, Prolog, Scala, Erlang, and Ruby. Whether or not your favorite language is on that list, you'll broaden your perspective of programming by examining these languages side-by-side. You'll learn something new from each, and best of all, you'll learn how to learn a language quickly.

Bruce A. Tate
(330 pages) ISBN: 9781934356593. $34.95
http://pragprog.com/book/btlang

Put the "Fun" in Functional

Elixir puts the "fun" back into functional programming, on top of the robust, battle-tested, industrial-strength environment of Erlang.

Programming Elixir

You want to explore functional programming, but are put off by the academic feel (tell me about monads just one more time). You know you need concurrent applications, but also know these are almost impossible to get right. Meet Elixir, a functional, concurrent language built on the rock-solid Erlang VM. Elixir's pragmatic syntax and built-in support for metaprogramming will make you productive and keep you interested for the long haul. This book is *the* introduction to Elixir for experienced programmers.

Maybe you need something that's closer to Ruby, but with a battle-proven environment that's unrivaled for massive scalability, concurrency, distribution, and fault tolerance. Maybe the time is right for the Next Big Thing. Maybe it's *Elixir*.

Dave Thomas
(340 pages) ISBN: 9781937785581. $36
http://pragprog.com/book/elixir

Programming Erlang (2nd edition)

A multi-user game, web site, cloud application, or networked database can have thousands of users all interacting at the same time. You need a powerful, industrial-strength tool to handle the really hard problems inherent in parallel, concurrent environments. You need Erlang. In this second edition of the best-selling *Programming Erlang*, you'll learn how to write parallel programs that scale effortlessly on multicore systems.

Joe Armstrong
(548 pages) ISBN: 9781937785536. $42
http://pragprog.com/book/jaerlang2

Roll Your Own Languages

From domain-specific languages to your own full-blown parsers, let Terence Parr show you how.

Language Implementation Patterns

Learn to build configuration file readers, data readers, model-driven code generators, source-to-source translators, source analyzers, and interpreters. You don't need a background in computer science—ANTLR creator Terence Parr demystifies language implementation by breaking it down into the most common design patterns. Pattern by pattern, you'll learn the key skills you need to implement your own computer languages.

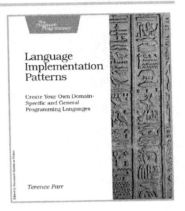

Terence Parr
(350 pages) ISBN: 9781934356456. $34.95
http://pragprog.com/book/tpdsl

The Definitive ANTLR 4 Reference

Programmers run into parsing problems all the time. Whether it's a data format like JSON, a network protocol like SMTP, a server configuration file for Apache, a PostScript/PDF file, or a simple spreadsheet macro language—ANTLR v4 and this book will demystify the process. ANTLR v4 has been rewritten from scratch to make it easier than ever to build parsers and the language applications built on top. This completely rewritten new edition of the bestselling *Definitive ANTLR Reference* shows you how to take advantage of these new features.

Terence Parr
(328 pages) ISBN: 9781934356999. $37
http://pragprog.com/book/tpantlr2

The Pragmatic Bookshelf

The Pragmatic Bookshelf features books written by developers for developers. The titles continue the well-known Pragmatic Programmer style and continue to garner awards and rave reviews. As development gets more and more difficult, the Pragmatic Programmers will be there with more titles and products to help you stay on top of your game.

Visit Us Online

This Book's Home Page
http://pragprog.com/book/7lang
Source code from this book, errata, and other resources. Come give us feedback, too!

Register for Updates
http://pragprog.com/updates
Be notified when updates and new books become available.

Join the Community
http://pragprog.com/community
Read our weblogs, join our online discussions, participate in our mailing list, interact with our wiki, and benefit from the experience of other Pragmatic Programmers.

New and Noteworthy
http://pragprog.com/news
Check out the latest pragmatic developments, new titles and other offerings.

Save on the eBook

Save on the eBook versions of this title. Owning the paper version of this book entitles you to purchase the electronic versions at a terrific discount.*

PDFs are great for carrying around on your laptop—they are hyperlinked, have color, and are fully searchable. Most titles are also available for the iPhone and iPod touch, Amazon Kindle, and other popular e-book readers.

Buy now at *http://pragprog.com/coupon*

Contact Us

Online Orders:	*http://pragprog.com/catalog*
Customer Service:	*support@pragprog.com*
International Rights:	*translations@pragprog.com*
Academic Use:	*academic@pragprog.com*
Write for Us:	*http://write-for-us.pragprog.com*
Or Call:	+1 800-699-7764